Reorienting Retirement Risk Management

Reorienting Retirement Risk Management

EDITED BY

Robert L. Clark
and Olivia S. Mitchell

OXFORD
UNIVERSITY PRESS

OXFORD

UNIVERSITY PRESS

Great Clarendon Street, Oxford OX2 6DP

Oxford University Press is a department of the University of Oxford.
It furthers the University's objective of excellence in research, scholarship,
and education by publishing worldwide in

Oxford New York

Auckland Cape Town Dar es Salaam Hong Kong Karachi
Kuala Lumpur Madrid Melbourne Mexico City Nairobi
New Delhi Shanghai Taipei Toronto

With offices in

Argentina Austria Brazil Chile Czech Republic France Greece
Guatemala Hungary Italy Japan Poland Portugal Singapore
South Korea Switzerland Thailand Turkey Ukraine Vietnam

Oxford is a registered trade mark of Oxford University Press
in the UK and in certain other countries

Published in the United States
by Oxford University Press Inc., New York

British Library Cataloguing in Publication Data
Data available

Library of Congress Cataloging in Publication Data
Data available

Typeset by SPI Publisher Services, Pondicherry, India
Printed in Great Britain
on acid-free paper by
MPG Books Group, Bodmin and King's Lynn

ISBN 978–0–19–959260–9

1 3 5 7 9 10 8 6 4 2

Preface

How can we find new ways to identify and then successfully manage the risks associated with retirement saving and dissaving? In the aftermath of the global financial crisis, it is becoming ever clearer that more must be done to enhance financial knowledge and financial education. Employers, employees, and other institutions – including governments – must play a more proactive role in this process. At the same time, new financial products will be required to help retirement plans innovate in the financing arena. This volume identifies ways to enhance retirement risk management so as to offset some of the uncertainty surrounding retirement saving, build more assets for retirement, better fund retirement plans, and help manage assets during the payout phase.

In the process of preparing this book, several key people and institutions played essential roles. Excellent editorial help was provided by my coeditor Robert Clark, a capable partner and colleague in research and development. On behalf of the Council, I thank him along with all the contributors to the book, the many reviewers who helped bring this work to fruition, and the PRC Advisory Board on whom we rely for guidance. We are also grateful for the intellectual and financial sustenance provided by our Senior Partners and the Institutional Members of the Pension Research Council, listed elsewhere in this volume. The Wharton School graciously provided access to conference facilities and more through its Impact Conference funding. Additional financial support was received from the Pension Research Council, the Boettner Center for Pensions and Retirement Research, and the Ralph H. Blanchard Memorial Endowment at the Wharton School of the University of Pennsylvania. The manuscript was expertly prepared and carefully edited by Matthew Rosen and Andrew Gallagher, with oversight and direction from Hilary Farrell.

Our work at the Pension Research Council and the Boettner Center of the Wharton School of the University of Pennsylvania has focused on aspects of pensions and retirement security for more than 50 years. This fine volume will be a welcome addition to the libraries of all concerned with retirement security.

Olivia S. Mitchell

Executive Director, Pension Research Council
Director, Boettner Center for Pensions and Retirement Research
The Wharton School, University of Pennsylvania

Contents

Part III Innovations in Retirement Risk Financing

List of Figures

List of Tables

Notes on Contributors

Steven G. Allen is Associate Dean for Graduate Programs and Research in the College of Management at NC State University, where he holds appointments in the Departments of Economics and Management. He also is a research associate of the National Bureau of Economic Research and a fellow of the Employee Benefits Research Institute. Allen has taught courses in microeconomics, labor economics, and human resource management at NC State. His research in those fields has focused on absenteeism, employee benefits, labor turnover, productivity, retirement, unions, technological change, and wage determination. He earned his PhD in Economics from Harvard University and BA and MA from Michigan State University.

John Ameriks is a Vanguard principal and head of Vanguard's Investment Counseling and Research Group, where he works on retirement advice, retirement income management, and other investment issues. His current research interests include target date funds, managed payout funds, income generating strategies for retirees, and the financial behavior and decisions of individual investors. Previously, he was a senior research fellow at the TIAA-CREF Institute. He received his PhD in Economics from Columbia University and AB from Stanford University.

Igor Balevich is a director in the Pension Solutions Group at Barclays Capital, where he is responsible for developing and implementing strategies to help clients meet their objectives for managing the financial impacts of sponsoring pension plans. Previously he worked in the Pension Advisory Group at JPMorgan and served as an actuarial consultant at Hewitt Associates. He holds a BSc in applied mathematics and a BSc in actuarial science from the University of Calgary, Alberta; he is also a fellow of the Society of Actuaries (FSA), an enrolled actuary (EA), and a chartered financial analyst (CFA).

Aaron Bernstein is a senior research fellow at the Labor and Worklife Program at Harvard Law School and the Editor of *Global Proxy Watch*, a corporate governance newsletter. Previously, he was an editor and senior writer at *BusinessWeek* magazine, where he covered workplace topics such as labor rights, social responsibility, and corporate governance. He received a BA in politics and economics from the University of California at Santa Cruz and also took graduate studies in political and legal theory at Oxford University.

Robert L. Clark is Professor of Management, Innovation, and Entrepreneurship as well as Professor of Economics at North Carolina State University, where his research interests include retirement decisions, the choice between defined benefit and defined contribution plans, the impact of pension conversions to defined contribution and cash balance plans, the role of information and communications on 401(k) contributions, government regulation of pensions, and Social Security. He is currently the principal investigator on a project examining the influence of employer-provided preretirement planning programs on financial literacy and retirement decisions. Professor Clark is also writing a history of the development of state retirement plans and has another project examining retiree health plans for public sector employees. He serves on the Advisory Board of Wharton's Pension Research Council; he is also Fellow of the Employee Benefit Research Institute and the TIAA-CREF Institute; he is a member of the American Economic Association, the Gerontological Society of America, International Union for the Scientific Study of Population, and the National Academy of Social Insurance. He earned his MA and PhD from Duke University and a BA from Millsaps College.

Craig Copeland is a senior research associate with the Employee Benefit Research Institute, where he is the Director of the Social Security Reform Evaluation Research Program. His research also includes employment-based retirement plans and individual retirement accounts. He previously taught economics at Southern Illinois University, Carbondale. He received his PhD in economics from the University of Illinois at Urbana-Champaign and BS in economics from Purdue University.

Joelle H.Y. Fong is a doctoral candidate in the Department of Insurance and Risk Management at the Wharton School, University of Pennsylvania, where her research interests include pensions, risk management, and public policy. Previously, she worked in various government agencies within the Singapore Civil Service. She has an MSc in applied finance from the Singapore Management University and a BA (Honors) in accountancy from Nanyang Technological University; she is also a certified public accountant (CPA).

Sterling Gunn is responsible for supporting the Canada Pension Plan's Investment Board total portfolio approach to risk and portfolio management, including asset–liability management, investment policies, risk budgets, and risk and performance measurement methodologies. Previously he was a manager at Ontario Power Generation and CIBC, a major Canadian bank. He holds an MBA from the University of Toronto, an MSc in experimental space science from York University, and a BSc in physics and applied mathematics from the University of Toronto.

P. Brett Hammond is a managing director and chief investment strategist for TIAA-CREF Asset Management, where he is responsible for asset allocation modeling and institutional advising, economic and market commentary, and investment product and portfolio research. Previously, he held positions at the National Academy of Sciences, UCLA, and UC Berkeley. He received his PhD from the Massachusetts Institute of Technology and AB degrees in economics and political science from the University of California at Santa Cruz.

Michael Hess is a project manager in the Investment Counseling and Research Department at Vanguard Group in Valley Forge, Pennsylvania, where he is responsible for research and investment methodology supportive of advisory services, products, and strategies offered to institutional and high net worth clients. His research interests include target date funds and retirement income solutions. He holds a BS from the University of Dayton and is currently pursuing his MBA at St. Joseph's University.

R. Hall Kesmodel, Jr. is a senior manager at Ernst and Young, LLP, where he focuses on employee financial education and counseling. His interests include 401(k) participant education and advice-related issues. He holds a BA from Washington and Lee University and the certified financial planner (CFP) designation.

Benedict S.K. Koh is an associate professor of finance and Director of the MSc in applied finance at the Singapore Management University. Previously he served as Vice Dean of the National University of Singapore Business School. Prior to joining academia, he was a corporate banker at the Chase Manhattan Bank N.A. His interests include investment management and personal financial planning, financial markets, and pension systems. He received his PhD in finance from the Wharton School of the University of Pennsylvania and his BBA from the National University of Singapore.

Tracy Livingstone is a senior adviser in the Investment Risk Management Group at the Canada Pension Plan, where she is responsible for the risk policies and standards of practice governing investment activities of the CPP Investment Board. Previously she worked at Ontario Power Generation, first on the trading floor and later on enterprise risk management; she also worked in risk management at TD Securities. She received an MBA from Wilfrid Laurier University and an BA (Honors) in economics from the University of Guelph. She holds the financial risk manager designation from the Global Association of Risk Professionals.

Raimond Maurer holds the endowed Chair of Investment, Portfolio Management, and Pension Finance in the Finance Department at the Goethe University of Frankfurt, where his research focuses on asset management, lifetime portfolio choice, and pension finance. He received his habilitation, PhD, and Diploma in Business from Mannheim University. He serves in professional capacities for the Society of Actuaries, the Association of Certified International Investment Analysts, and he sits on Wharton's Advisory Board for the Pension Research Council.

Olivia S. Mitchell is the International Foundation of Employee Benefit Plans Professor of Insurance and Risk Management at the Wharton School, University of Pennsylvania. Her main areas of interest are private and public insurance, risk management, public finance and labor markets, and compensation and pensions with both a US and an international focus. She received her PhD in economics from the University of Wisconsin–Madison and a BA in Economics from Harvard University.

Melinda S. Morrill is a research assistant professor in the Department of Economics at North Carolina State University, where her research interests focus on economic demography and labor economics. Her current work focuses on preretirement financial literacy and education as well as topics in the economics of child health, female labor supply and occupation choice, and the financial impacts of divorce. Morrill received her PhD from the University of Maryland, College Park.

Lynn Pettus is a national tax partner and serves as Director for the Employee Financial Services practice at Ernst and Young, LLP, where she works on financial education and counseling programs focused on company benefit plans. She is a graduate of Converse College and holds a Bachelor's degree in accounting. She is a certified public accountant and earned the personal Financial Specialist designation granted by the American Institute of certified public accountants; she also earned the designation of certified investment management analyst through the Investment Management Consultants Association.

Anna M. Rappaport is an actuary, consultant, author, and speaker with Anna Rappaport Consulting; her interests focus on the impact of change on retirement systems and workforce issues. Previously she was at Mercer Human Resource consulting as a senior fellow on pensions and retirement, appointed by the Conference Board. She has served as President of the Society of Actuaries, is on the Board of the Women's Institute for a Secure Retirement (WISER), and sits on the Advisory Board of Wharton's Pension Research Council. Ms. Rappaport is a fellow of the Society of Actuaries and a member of the American Academy of Actuaries. She received an MBA from the University of Chicago.

Liqian Ren is an investment analyst in the Investment Counseling and Research Department at Vanguard Group in Valley Forge, Pennsylvania.

Previously she worked as an economist in the macro group preparing FOMC briefs and developing the Chicago Activity Index at the Federal Reserve Bank in Chicago. She received her MBA and PhD in business economics from the University of Chicago, an MA in economics from Indiana University–Purdue University Indianapolis, and a BS from Peking University.

David P. Richardson is Principal Research Fellow at the TIAA-CREF Institute. Prior to joining the Institute, he served as Senior Economist for Public Finance at the White House Council of Economic Advisers and held the New York Life Chair in Risk Management and Insurance at Georgia State University. His research interests focus on public pensions, employer plans, and household financial security, including retirement preparedness, retiree health care, and the allocation of retiree risk burdens. He earned his MA and the PhD in economics from Boston College, and a BBA from the University of Georgia.

Ralph Rogalla is an assistant professor for investments, portfolio management, and pension finance at the Goethe University of Frankfurt. His research interests include portfolio management and allocation, and pension topics. He studied economics at Technical University Berlin and received his PhD in finance from the Goethe University of Frankfurt.

Damon Silvers is an associate general counsel for the AFL-CIO, where he is responsible for bankruptcy, corporate governance, and pension and general business law issues. Mr. Silvers is a member of the Public Company Accounting Oversight Board Standing Advisory Group and the Financial Accounting Standards Board User Advisory Council. He is also a member of the US Treasury Department Investor's Practice Committee of the President's Working Group on Financial Markets, and chairs the Competition Subcommittee of Treasury's Advisory Committee on the Auditing Profession. Previously he served as law clerk at the Delaware Court of Chancery for Chancellor William T. Allen and Vice-Chancellor Bernard Balick. Mr. Silvers received a JD with honors from Harvard Law School and an MBA with high honors from Harvard Business School; he is a graduate of Harvard College and studied history at Kings College, Cambridge University.

John A. Turner is a Social Security and pension policy consultant. Previously, he worked in the AARP Public Policy Institute and the International Labor Office; he has also worked at the US Social Security Administration and the US Labor Department, where he was the Deputy Director of the pension research office. He has served as Adjunct Lecturer in Economics at George Washington University and at Georgetown University in the Public

Policy School. He earned his PhD in economics from the University of Chicago.

Jack VanDerhei is Research Director of the Employee Benefit Research Institute where he directs the Defined Contribution and Participant Behavior Research Program as well as the Retirement Security Research Program. His research interests focus on employee benefits and insurance, and on financial aspects of private defined benefit and defined contribution retirement plans. He received his MA and PhD from the Wharton School of the University of Pennsylvania and a BBA and MBA from the University of Wisconsin–Madison.

Abbreviations

AAUP	American Association of University Professors
AIR	Assumed Interest Rate
ASR	asset/salary ratio
COLAs	Cost-of-Living Adjustments
CPF	Central Provident Fund
CPP	Canada Pension Plan
CPPIB	Canadian Pension Plan Investment Board
DB	defined benefit
DC	defined contribution
EBRI	Employee Benefit Research Institute
EBRI/ERF	Employee Benefits Research Institution/Education and Research Fund
EBRI/ICI	Employee Benefit Research Institute/Investment Company Institute
EPDV	Expected Present Discounted Value
ERISA	Employee Retirement Income Security Act
FAB	Field Assistance Bulletin
FAS	Financial Accounting Statement
GASB	Governmental Accounting Standards Board
GDP	Gross Domestic Product
GLWB	Guaranteed Lifetime Withdrawal Benefits
GM	General Motors
IVA	Immediate Variable Annuities
IRS	Internal Revenue Service
ISG	International Steel Group Incorporated
MINT	Model of Income in the Near Term
MS	Minimum Sum
MSS	Minimum Sum Scheme
MWR	money's worth ratio
NAV	Net Asset Value
NUA	Net Unrealized Appreciation
OLS	ordinary least squares
PBGC	Pension Benefit Guaranty Corporation
PPA	Pension Protection Act
PRC	Pension Rights Center
QDIA	Qualified Default Investment Alternatives
QPP	Quebec Pension Plan

RMDs	Required Minimum Distributions
RR	replacement rate
SIPP	Survey of Income and Program Participation
SOA	Society of Actuaries
TIAA-CREF	Teachers Insurance and Annuity Association, College Retirement Equities Fund
UAW	United Auto Workers
UPS	United Parcel Service
USCB	United States Census Bureau
USDOL	United States Department of Labor
USGAO	United States Government Accountability Office
VEBA	Voluntary Employee Benefit Association

Chapter 1

The Evolution of Retirement Risk Management

Robert L. Clark and Olivia S. Mitchell

Retirement risk management will require significant modification if it is to be effective in helping position retirees to withstand the challenges of the future. Recent economic events, including the massive upheaval in global financial markets, have altered the landscape in which pension and endowment funds operate. Plummeting retirement asset values, along with employers' and employees' inability to make pension contributions, are contributing to sharp drops in retirement plan funding. In many countries, government social security systems are also facing insolvency. These factors, in tandem with an aging population and rising longevity, are giving rise to serious questions about the future of retirement in America and around the world.

This volume explores how workers and firms can reassess the risk associated with retirement saving and make creative adjustments to adapt to these new risks and realities. Our effort is grouped into three areas. First, we take up the key role for financial knowledge, implying a need for greater financial education programs. Second, we show how employers, acting as plan sponsors, and workers, must reconsider pension plan design so as to help them better address the new realities. Third, we argue that novel financial products will be required to help retirement plans innovate in the financing arena. The chapter authors of this volume, each an expert in his or her field, take up all these important aspects of retirement planning, providing new research and policy recommendations, and showing how retirement plans can be amended to better meet the retirement needs of workers and firms. This introductory chapter provides an orientation and a brief overview of key findings.

Revisiting retirement saving and dissaving

The last 2 decades have brought about a global shift from defined benefit (DB) pensions to defined contribution (DC) plans. According to Brett

Hammond and David Richardson (2010), this will require new ways of conceptualizing retirement saving adequacy. In traditional DB pensions, participants can project what future benefits will be as a percent of salary using their plan formulas; such formulas usually depend on a generosity parameter (e.g., 1.5 percent) times years of service, multiplied by final average salary. Accordingly, an employee with 30 years of service would have a pension replacement rate of 45 percent, which – along with Social Security benefits – can then be evaluated as to whether it is sufficient to retire on. By contrast, participants in DC plans may know their asset accruals but generally will be unable to convert these into benefit payout amounts.

To help approach this problem, the authors devise a measure they call the 'asset/salary ratio' (ASR), which accounts for future salary growth, rates of return, discount rates, the number of years expected in retirement, and estate planning needs. The most important inputs are contribution rates and the number of years contributed, notwithstanding popular emphasis on asset allocation, fund choice, and consultants. Next, using information from Teachers Insurance and Annuity Association, College Retirement Equities Fund (TIAA-CREF) data files on 3.5 million people, Hammond and Richardson measure how well funded participants are, by comparing the value of assets accumulated against likely future spending patterns in retirement. Their analysis indicates that, on average, the participants they study were more than adequately funded for retirement. The authors conclude that achieving sufficient retirement saving requires early and continuous contributions to retirement accounts, relatively high contribution rates, tilting allocations toward greater use of equities, and using catch-up contributions to increase account balances. Thus, pension plans that encourage early participation and provide strong incentives for increased contributions raise the likelihood that participants will be secure in retirement.

Retirement security also depends on financial literacy, and there is mounting evidence that many employees lack basic information about their retirement plans and financial mathematics. To counter this, the work by Robert Clark, Melinda Morrill, and Steven Allen (2010) examines the effectiveness of employer-provided financial education and preretirement planning programs. As individuals begin to transition from full-time work into retirement, they confront several key decisions that will affect their well-being in retirement. Without appropriate knowledge and information, many will make incorrect choices. Important retirement-related questions include when to retire from one's career job, whether to take a lump-sum distribution from a DB plan, whether to annuitize a 401(k) account, and when to claim Social Security payments. Many of these decisions are irreversible and will have profound impacts on financial well-being throughout retirement.

Recognizing the difficulty of making these decisions, several larger employers have recently sponsored educational programs to help with the decision process. Clark and colleagues examine nine large companies and chart characteristics of the financial education sessions offered; some are conducted in-house, while others are offered by outside financial education groups. The sessions range in length from 1.5 hours to 2.5 days. Seminar participants were asked to respond to a short survey on financial planning both before and after the education sessions. The authors show that the sessions did enhance financial knowledge, and as a result of the programs, employees changed their planned retirement behavior. Plans to annuitize 401(k) accounts and or take lump-sum distributions also changed.

When employer education is unavailable, people may instead turn to retirement calculators to help them with retirement planning. In their chapter, Anna Rappaport and John Turner (2010) examine how well computer calculators do in projecting future retirement income needs and accumulations. Their review suggests that many of these programs are too simple and provide misleading information about retirement saving. Furthermore, the programs often fail to address key retirement risks; instead, the information presented frequently masks risks that can fundamentally alter expected retirement income flows. The programs also differ in the ways they treat economic and personal variables: for instance, some ignore owner-occupied housing as an asset, while others compute the annuity value of housing, assuming the asset is fully liquid. Most calculators fail to address residential market risk, and none handles variable rate mortgages. The programs also do a poor job of estimating expected returns on retirement saving accounts, with many overestimating future rates and ignoring investment fees. A related problem is that few of the retirement advice programs properly model Social Security, though the government-provided benefit is the most important component of retirement income for many. Indeed, many calculators do a poor job of predicting Social Security benefits; for example, one uses the same payment regardless of the worker's age or length of work life. Further, the software packages differ dramatically in their assessments of retirement readiness, often taking too short a time horizon and underestimating longevity. Thus, many who follow the advice given by the programs may ultimately run out of money.

Nevertheless, the authors point out that using retirement planning software can help users to begin thinking about their long-term financial needs, even if the programs have some shortcomings. And these programs are now easier to use than were the earlier versions of financial planning programs. Finally, the software used by professional financial planners can be substantially more sophisticated, with some including Monte Carlo simulation approaches (rarely included in free consumer-oriented online programs).

Turning to retirement planning advice offered by employers, Lynn Pettus and Hall Kesmodel (2010) not that this is easier now than before, due to the passage of the Pension Protection Act (PPA) in 2006. The law sought to address concerns about whether employers would be in violation of the Employee Retirement Income Security Act (ERISA) by taking on a fiduciary role if they provided services to employees to help them learn about retirement saving and investment. Thus, the PPA was intended to increase the availability of high-quality advice to employees, and in fact some progress has been made: plan provider alliances now cover at least 43 million participants and more than half of those plan sponsors offer advice. The primary delivery model for employer-provided financial education programs is through online computer models and support programs with financial advisors acting as intermediaries.

Nevertheless, online computer models may not be the best method of providing actionable advice since some prefer to work with an advisor face to face. Moreover, computer programs intended to help with retirement saving plans often do not take into account the participant's larger financial situation. For example, a model may endorse the employee's decision to increase 401(k) contributions from 3 to 4 percent, yet for a worker carrying credit card debt with high interest rates, it might be more sensible to pay down those obligations. On the other hand, a financial advisor may face conflicts of interest; thus, some advisors could favor one financial product over another based on commissions, and financial advisors working in an employee education program may appear to have the employer's tacit endorsement. For these reasons, plan sponsors may wish to consider expanding financial planning education to cover more than just retirement saving and take into account housing, overall debt, and tax considerations as well, and to be alert to possible conflict of interest issues.

The environment for retirement plan redesign

While it seems clear that labor income risk should be a central determinant of one's retirement saving path, this topic is often overlooked in practice. For this reason, Raimond Maurer, Olivia Mitchell, and Ralph Rogalla (2010) undertake an analysis of how this form of risk can be mitigated in DC pension plans, taking into account social security as well. The authors find that human capital is many peoples' single most important asset and, as such, it should be included in any analysis of retirement portfolios. The authors argue that those with stable incomes and DB pensions will optimally develop a different asset mix than would investment bankers with highly variable and volatile earnings.

To examine what this means in practice, the authors construct a simulation model to derive recommended portfolio allocations, taking into account social security, labor income certainty, endogenous retirement ages, and differences in individual risk aversion. Their results imply that, for most people, it will be optimal to gradually purchase annuities over the life cycle. That is, people with very low labor income risk and high social security benefits should hold high equity positions while working, and begin to buy payout annuities around age 55. Those with higher labor income and low social security benefits should start to purchase payout annuities earlier, at around age 40. By doing so, people can build up their own individualized DB plan. The authors also point out that people who have purchased annuities have a steady stream of secondary income to buffer against labor income risk, which then permits them to hold more equity.

To further examine the interaction between pension benefits and pension plan type, Craig Copeland and Jack VanDerhei (2010) evaluate how pension freezes can influence retirement incomes. Their specific objective is to quantify the amount of potential retirement income foregone when employers freeze their DB plans, a phenomenon that has become quite prevalent following the 2006 passage of the Pension Protection Act, which added new funding requirements. It is important to note that some employers simply froze their DB programs, but others enriched their DC contributions in the process. The chapter draws on employer-provided survey data and a retirement projection model to gauge benefit generosity. The researchers report that when DB plans freeze accruals for new employees, expected nominal replacement rates fall by less than 1 percent for employees under age 25 and over 55, and 2 percent for those aged 30–34. Next, Copeland and VanDerhei show that 40 percent of DB participants aged 20–24 would have better replacement rates with an enhanced DC plan, but the figure falls below 10 percent for people over 55. The chapter concludes that, as companies move away from 'paternalistic' DB plans, employers will provide automatic enrollment in saving plans to encourage participation.

A different model for plan design is offered by Damon Silvers (2010), who sees voluntary individualized retirement accounts as a failure, in part because people are allowed to extract assets from their DC plans. Instead, he argues that new formats for collective retirement plans are needed to address the disconnect between short-term market volatility and the long-term needs of pension funds. He has proposed a new plan structure whereby a demographically diverse workforce could unite to set up a pension that would buy portfolio insurance issued in the form of a derivative that would keep plan assets stable, even as the value of the underlying portfolio fluctuated. Yet the financial crisis has suggested that precisely when this type of risk management solution is needed, it will not be available. This may mean that government plans would have to be expanded to address three forms of risk. Investment risk can be handled by a collective professional management of assets with no more than 10 percent of a portfolio in company stock. Longevity risk can be addressed with mandatory annuitization and tougher limits on the ability to withdraw saving. Employer credit risk could be diminished with universal pension portability and a shift away from employer-sponsored plans.

A key element of retirement income security involves annuitization, with some governments moving gradually to increase retiree participation in such longevity protection. In Singapore, the government has ordered that mandatory annuitization will be rolled out as part of the compulsory Singaporean Central Provident Fund (CPF) scheme. Joelle Fong, Olivia Mitchell, and Benedict Koh (2010) explore this proposal and discuss the implications of requiring participants to purchase annuities. Clearly, mandatory annuitization will help avoid adverse selection, but how important this is, is an empirical question. After evaluating the private annuity market in Singapore, the authors conclude that private insurance offers good value for the money and the relatively low fraction of participants currently purchasing voluntary annuities is mainly attributable to inertia and financial illiteracy. Therefore, the new program may crowd out private offerings, though retirees may benefit due to limitations on withdrawals and mandatory annuitization.

Innovations in retirement risk financing

As noted at the outset, novel financial products will also be required to help retirement plans confront and manage risks innovatively. In his chapter, Igor Balevich (2010) discusses longevity risk and explores how pension plans might outsource longevity protection. While expected life spans have risen steadily in the last century, there is still much debate about whether the pace of longevity improvement will continue, in the face of rising obesity and related health risks. Balevich outlines three main approaches to the problem: plan design, risk transfer to insurers, and hedging. The shift from DB to DC plans has already moved longevity risk – and many other uncertainties – from the employer to the employee, particularly when retirees take lump sums instead of annuitizing with their employers. Risk transfer to an insurer permits a pension plan to eliminate its exposure to longevity by purchasing annuities; in the United Kingdom, several companies have already moved into this business, challenging traditional insurance companies. In the United States, the US Treasury Department and Internal Revenue Service essentially banned noninsurance-based risk transfers in the United States as of mid-2008. Another way to cope with longevity risk, rather than attempting to eliminate it entirely, is to hedge the risk through derivative products such as longevity swaps. A longevity swap allows a plan to make fixed payments based on mortality expectations and receive floating payments tied to the mortality experience of the underlying population. The contract would be for a shorter period of time than the full term of the pension payout, but multiple contracts could be staggered with varying maturity dates. Since this hedge is not perfect, firms could be left with basis risk associated with the difference in mortality in their own population versus the national population.

In addition to building retirement assets, a major concern of retirement planning is how to best utilize assets in retirement. The mutual fund industry has been working actively to offer products that compete with the insurers, and John Ameriks, Michael Hess, and Liqian Ren (2010) assess several payout products currently available on the market. The global financial crisis has introduced many new uncertainties into retirement planning, particularly with guaranteed products facing difficult times. The researchers explore mutual fund products that involve a mechanism to provide periodic drawdowns, identifying are two main types: the 'endowment' style that seeks to provide payouts in perpetuity and the 'time-horizon' style where payments are scheduled over a set period. Neither type of plan offers guaranteed payments or returns; instead, they offer targeted or formula-driven distributions of assets along with a professionally managed investment portfolio. One criticism of these plans is that investors could construct similar evaluations themselves, raising the question of whether bundling by fund managers is worth 50 or 60 basis points.

To understand how payout funds and other retirement income vehicles perform over time, the authors simulate a 30-year time-horizon fund with an initial target payout rate of 5 percent. They compare this plan to other schemes including systematic distribution from a balanced mutual fund, a fixed lifetime income annuity, a variable immediate annuity, a variable annuity with a guarantee, a required minimum distribution plan, and combination strategies. They present a range of outcomes including income volatility, the probability of exhausting funds, the residual portfolio value, and internal rate of return. Their analysis shows that all strategies produce a wide variety of outcomes, including payouts and the wealth remaining to be bequeathed.

Another innovation in retirement finance is risk budgeting. The Canada Pension Plan (CPP) portfolio is managed according to this principle, as described by Sterling Gunn and Tracy Livingstone (2010). The authors point to three key points concerning risk budgeting. First, it is not an 'off-the-shelf' solution, but must be tailored to each fund. Second, it is also a way to reinforce investment decisions with total portfolio objectives. Third, it challenges an organization to quantify its risk and accept that number. CPP is a three-tiered plan made up of a basic old-age supplement, a contributory pension, and voluntary saving. The scheme underwent major reforms in 1997 to enhance retirement saving adequacy, including setting contribution rates at the current rate of 9.9 percent. Interestingly, when the CPP Investment Board (CPPIB) was created in 1999, its establishment was coupled with limitations on federal government intervention; in exchange, the government made it clear to pension officials that contribution rates could not be raised again. As a result of this compromise, risk budgets have become part of the annual business planning process and require set expectations for the amount of risk needed to achieve return targets; the Board must annually approve an active risk limit, explaining exactly how much discretion management has to deviate from the reference portfolio. In practice, this has been particularly challenging in evaluating real estate and infrastructure investments.

Another interesting way to manage retirement risk is the Voluntary Employees' Beneficiary Association (VEBA), a scheme that seeks to preserve workers' health-care benefits even as companies offering them are restructuring. Aaron Bernstein (2010) explores the benefits and risks of these plans in his chapter, which notes that the VEBA is a century-old concept. VEBAs are essentially trust funds – originally set up to help pre-fund retiree health obligations. Today, there are about 12,000 of these flexible, tax-advantaged funds that, until now, were considered to be 'humdrum' internal funding schemes. They became nationally prominent in 2007, however, when the United Auto Workers (UAW) negotiated with Detroit automakers and succeeded in placing the retiree health obligations in VEBAs. Since VEBA is an independent trust fund responsible for retiree health care for a specified number of people, if it runs short of money, there will be insufficient funds to cover the health care of the participants. And the employer is absolved of responsibility for providing additional monies to cover shortfalls. While Bernstein believes these funds have some shortcomings, given the plight of the automakers, VEBAs may have helped save jobs because they allowed employers to shift pension obligations off their books, laying the groundwork for deeper restructuring. Today, VEBAs are mainly found in the heavily unionized sectors, because union-directed funds are not subject to limits imposed by Congress in 1984 designed to prevent employers from using VEBAs as tax shelters.

Following the global economic slump and sharp downturns in sales triggering bankruptcy filings by General Motors and Chrysler, VEBAs have now given employees a seat at the table during their employers' restructurings. For instance, financed in part by company stock at Chrysler, VEBAs gave employees an important position in bankruptcy proceedings; the union has gained 55 percent of the company as a result of its VEBA obligations, and union employees are now placed ahead of bondholders and creditors in court proceedings.

Conclusion

The global financial crisis has brought unpredictable capital markets, widespread unemployment, poor corporate earnings, and weak global economies. These factors will continue to threaten the future of retirement security for older workers and retirees for years to come. Yet the crisis also affords an opportunity to revisit, reexamine, and adjust the institutions and programs on which we have relied in the past for retirement saving. In doing so, we have reconsidered the opportunities these plans provide for workers to accumulate sufficient monies to finance retirement. Equally important, we have examined the methods of payouts and the patterns of decumulation embedded in these programs. The new realities of financial markets and the greater recognition of risk and uncertainty make it imperative to develop a new structure to enhance future retirement security. This volume informs the debate by exploring how workers and firms can reassess the risk associated with retirement saving and respond creatively to the new risks and realities.

The studies included in this volume highlight several key points central to enhancing retirement risk management, in order to reduce some of the uncertainty surrounding the retirement saving process, the accumulation of sufficient assets for retirement, funding of retirement plans, and managing assets in retirement. Most salient is the urgent need for greater financial education, financial literacy, and support for financial advice and planning. Individuals who have inadequate or incorrect information about their retirement plans and general financial mathematics will make retirement decisions that undermine their economic well-being. An important policy concern is whether older workers can, in fact, boost their financial literacy to make better retirement choices. Plan sponsors also have a key role to play, as do financial advisors, in their role of finding innovative solutions to the uncertainties of aging. And last, but certainly not least, new financial products including longevity risk financing will be invaluable in making retirement more secure for millions of today's workers.

References

Ameriks, John, Michael Hess, and Liqian Ren (2010). 'Comparing Spending Approaches in Retirement,' in R.L. Clark and O.S. Mitchell, eds., *Reorienting Retirement Risk Management.* Oxford: Oxford University Press.

Balevich, Igor (2010). 'Outsourcing Pension Longevity Protection,' in R.L. Clark and O.S. Mitchell, eds., *Reorienting Retirement Risk Management.* Oxford: Oxford University Press.

Bernstein, Aaron (2010). 'Can VEBAs Alleviate Retiree Health Care Problems?,' in R.L. Clark and O.S. Mitchell, eds., *Reorienting Retirement Risk Management.* Oxford: Oxford University Press.

Clark, Robert L., Melinda S. Morrill, and Steven G. Allen (2010). 'Employer-Provided Retirement Planning Programs,' in R.L. Clark and O.S. Mitchell, eds., *Reorienting Retirement Risk Management.* Oxford: Oxford University Press.

Copeland, Craig and Jack VanDerhei (2010). 'The Declining Role of Private Defined Benefit Pension Plans: Who Is Affected, and How,' in R.L. Clark and O.S. Mitchell, eds., *Reorienting Retirement Risk Management.* Oxford: Oxford University Press.

Fong, Joelle H.Y., Olivia S. Mitchell, and Benedict S.K. Koh (2010). 'Longevity Risk and Annuities in Singapore,' in R.L. Clark and O.S. Mitchell, eds., *Reorienting Retirement Risk Management.* Oxford: Oxford University Press.

Gunn, Sterling and Tracy Livingstone (2010). 'Risk Budgeting for the Canadian Pension Plan Investment Board,' in R.L. Clark and O.S. Mitchell, eds., *Reorienting Retirement Risk Management.* Oxford: Oxford University Press.

Hammond, P. Brett and David P. Richardson (2010). 'Retirement Saving Adequacy and Individual Investment Risk Management Using the Asset/Salary Ratio,' in R.L. Clark and O.S. Mitchell, eds., *Reorienting Retirement Risk Management.* Oxford: Oxford University Press.

Maurer, Raimond, Olivia S. Mitchell, and Ralph Rogalla (2010). 'The Effect of Uncertain Labor Income and Social Security on Life-cycle Portfolios,' in R.L. Clark and O.S. Mitchell, eds., *Reorienting Retirement Risk Management.* Oxford: Oxford University Press.

Pettus, Lynn and R. Hall Kesmodel, Jr. (2010). 'Impact of the Pensions Protection Act on Financial Advice: What Works and What Remains to Be Done?' in R.L. Clark and O.S. Mitchell, eds., *Reorienting Retirement Risk Management.* Oxford: Oxford University Press.

Rappaport, Anna M. and John A. Turner (2010). 'How Does Retirement Planning Software Handle Post-Retirement Realities?' in R.L. Clark and O.S. Mitchell, eds., *Reorienting Retirement Risk Management.* Oxford: Oxford University Press.

Silvers, Damon (2010). 'Rebuilding Workers' Retirement Security: A Labor Perspective on Private Pension Reform,' in R.L. Clark and O.S. Mitchell, eds., *Reorienting Retirement Risk Management.* Oxford: Oxford University Press.

Part I
Revisiting Retirement Saving and Dissaving Advice

Chapter 2

Retirement Saving Adequacy and Individual Investment Risk Management Using the Asset/Salary Ratio

P. Brett Hammond and David P. Richardson

The defined contribution (DC) pension has become the dominant type of retirement plan in the United States. Its widespread adoption has required individuals to take more responsibility for lifetime financial security, and has led to the development of many tools intended to help people manage their retirement saving, investment, and income risks. These tools range from expensive and highly customized advice to inexpensive target-date maturity funds, automatic enrollment, and generic calculators, all intended to encourage appropriate retirement saving, asset allocation, rebalancing, and retirement income. Their purpose is to provide individuals with recommendations on how much to save and what to do with that saving, and implicitly, the notion is that if people follow those recommendations, they will be more likely to have an adequate income stream in retirement. In effect, the tools are intended to help them better manage their own retirement income risk.

Despite the growth and popularity of such tools, rules of thumb, and direct advice, it remains unclear as to what actually works well. Often people fail to follow these 'rules' and experts' recommendations, saving too little and suffering from poor asset allocation and investment choices. Indeed, exacerbated by myopic choices about retirement withdrawals, the bulk of the economics literature suggests that many will end up with inadequate retirement income (Poterba, Venti, and Wise 1998, 2008; Poterba et al. 2007). A notable exception is Scholz, Seshadri, and Khitatrakun (2006).

So if the prevailing wisdom is correct, it is important to examine whether the DC model can be modified to make it more effective for the increasing proportion of covered participants. In the US case, the Pension Protection Act of 2006 made feasible provisions such as automatic enrollment and target-date maturity funds to enhance pension sponsors and providers willingness to boost DC saving. Yet more remains to be done, to make the

DC model simpler despite the system's multiple decision points, knowledge requirements, and now well-known participant behavioral tendencies.

In this chapter, we take up two points. First, we ask what simple feedback can be provided to help participants estimate whether they are on target to generate adequate retirement income. Second, we explore the right balance between retirement income adequacy and allowing for individual choice. We outline our proposed measure, called the asset/salary ratio (ASR), which we argue offers a robust metric for gauging participant success. The underlying algorithm for computing the ASR is sophisticated, and similar to the full funding ratio for a defined benefit (DB) plan, yet the exercise provides a single number that at any point in time allows the participant to measure saving adequacy against a set of benchmarks. We show, using a sample of Teachers Insurance and Annuity Association, College Retirement Equities Fund (TIAA-CREF) participants, that certain individual decisions are particularly important in achieving adequate resources for generating sufficient retirement income. These include, in order, contribution or saving rates, tenure or length of participation, and asset allocation. The latter has received considerable attention in the research literature and among practitioners, but the first two elements are often downplayed when considering DC pension design.

The ASR

Our goal is to determine whether a plan participant is on track to accumulate sufficient assets so as to hit a target income replacement rate (RR) after retirement. Using reasonable assumptions about future asset returns, future contributions, and a retirement income goal (e.g., funding a guaranteed income stream), the ASR reflects concepts and methods widely used to measure the overall funding status of a DB pension plan. In concept, the plan's funding ratio (FR) is defined as

$$FR_t = \frac{Assets_t}{PV\ Future\ Liabilities_t} \times 100 \qquad (2.1)$$

where FR at any point in time equals the plan assets divided by the present value (PV) of the plan's future liabilities (Leibowitz et al. 2002). A DB pension plan's liabilities are essentially the sum of what it is obligated to pay individual participants over time in order to replace a certain percentage of their preretirement salaries or incomes.[1] For any individual participant, the RR (the percentage of preretirement salary he or she will receive in retirement) will depend on length of service, size of preretirement salary or income, and a multiplication factor set by the plan. Theoretically, when $FR_t \geq 100$, the plan is considered well funded, as long as the investment and actuarial assumptions that underlie it continue to be validated by subsequent experience. In contrast, when $FR_t < 100$, the plan is considered to be underfunded, in which case the plan sponsor may be required to make contributions in order to bring the required level of assets up to match the estimate of discounted future liabilities. In other words, the funding ratio acts as a signal to the plan sponsor, indicating whether the plan is on track to meet obligations, or when circumstances have changed and action is needed. In this sense, the funding ratio serves as an easily understandable metric for determining whether the plan is on a path to generate adequate retirement income for the participants.

In addition, the funding ratio has an intertemporal dimension that reflects changes in current conditions, something we call 'passage risk.' Since a pension plan is a long-horizon entity, the risk of a long-term plan inability to meet its targets ('outcome risk') should be of primary concern. But a sponsor should also be concerned about a sudden drop in market returns reducing the funding ratio, since this may determine whether the plan can recover. In this sense, the funding ratio can be used to examine how the plan fares or 'passes' through time.

Similarly, our objective in creating the ASR is to incorporate a target based on a utility function and a 'risk passage' assessment that is easy for an individual to understand. This is especially important in the DC context because, in the absence of the plan sponsor taking responsibility for funding adequacy, DC plan participants can be thought of as being their own plan sponsors, and therefore they are in charge of managing the risks associated with maintaining their own retirement solvency. In the spirit of the DB funding ratio, the ASR can indicate to an individual whether he or she is 'on track' for achieving a personal retirement income goal.

In practice, the challenge for developing an ASR is to ascertain each individual's implied future liability stream and to develop assets to meet the target. But the DC plan sponsor does not typically make a specific pension income promise (unlike the DB sponsor), so determining the liability target is difficult. One approach would be to draw on economic life-cycle theory (Ando and Modigliani 1963; Browning and Crossley 2001), where the utility of consumption is smoothed across working and retirement years. Yet analysts have raised questions about how forward-looking households are or, if they are, to what degree consumption smoothing is compatible with actual behavior (Bullard and Feigenbaum 2007). Nevertheless, inspired by the life-cycle concept, we can employ as a goal for retirement saving and investment the RR, which we define here as the proportion of preretirement income that an individual is able to replace through purchasing a guaranteed annuity at the time of retirement (Heller and King 1989, 1994). The RR is, of course, closely related to the notion of a DB funding ratio, in that for any individual at the point of retirement,

retirement income is dependent on salary growth, investment returns, annuity purchase costs, contribution rates, and length of covered employment.

In higher education, calibrating an appropriate RR objective might be done by reference to a policy statement from the American Association of University Professors (AAUP) and American Association of Colleges that suggests that educational institutions design pension plans that enable their employees to replace about two-thirds of their preretirement, inflation-adjusted, annual salary through a combination of pension income, Social Security, and other personal saving (AAUP 2006: 174). This target is roughly consistent with other research that suggests that retirees aim to replace 70–80 percent of preretirement income on average (Reno and Lavery 2007). Therefore, a target RR of 75 percent seems to be a reasonable objective.

Considering first the Social Security component, one's individual Social Security RR is inversely related to preretirement income. Thus, for long-term labor-force participants, Social Security was calculated to replace about 40 percent of a $40,000 preretirement income, 35 percent of a $60,000 income, and about 20 percent of a $120,000 preretirement income (Reno and Lavery 2007). The higher salary amount is roughly representative of incomes provided to older faculty in higher education (*The Chronicle of Higher Education* 2009). It should be noted that such a replacement rate assumes people are paid at this rate over their entire lifetimes; in reality, actual lifetime earnings in higher education are lower earlier on and rise in later life, making actual Social Security replacement rates somewhat higher.

In what follows, we make the conservative assumption that Social Security benefits replace about one-quarter of preretirement income. In this case, employer-sponsored pensions and other household saving must be capable of generating a 50 percent RR on average, to meet the 75 percent average RR standard. We acknowledge that many low-income workers might elect a lower RR target, while higher income workers might desire a higher RR. Individuals with substantial personal saving dedicated to retirement could use those assets to offset required pension saving. For most Americans, though, non-pension saving tends to be held in relatively illiquid housing, so it may not be easily accessible as a source of income.

On the presumption that the employer pension must provide a 50 percent replacement rate, it is now necessary to account for other important factors including contribution rates, years of service, investment earnings, and salary growth rates. Pulling these together, we have

$$\text{ASR}_t = \frac{A_t}{S_t} \tag{2.2}$$

which says that the ASR is equal to the level of pension assets divided by the individual's annual salary (S) at the point t years before retirement.

There are in fact two variants of the ASR: a worker's existing ASR at date t, and what we call the Par ASR, or what is *required* to achieve a target income replacement rate. It is worth noting that the required or Par ASR is dynamic: because of the role of future contributions, the Par ASR must rise over time in order to arrive at the final ratio of assets to liabilities needed to fund the required retirement income. If there were to be no future contributions, then today's assets must be sufficiently large to fund a future guaranteed income that will replace the required portion of the future income. The opportunity to make future contributions, however, means that today's assets can be smaller by the amount of the discounted future value of those contributions and any earnings on those contributions. So the Par ASR will rise over time by the increase in contributions.[2]

In any event, if an individual knows his or her current ASR and can roughly estimate the Par ASR required to fund retirement income years into the future, then he or she can evaluate whether the current ratio is adequate for retirement planning purposes. An individual who has an actual ASR equal to his required Par ASR, all else equal, could be considered to be on track for retirement adequacy. A person whose ASR is currently higher than the Par ASR now enjoys a cushion to protect against unforeseen trends or events (e.g., larger-than-expected stock market declines or better-than-expected retiree life spans). On the other hand, someone whose ASR is lower than his required ratio should consider corrective action, including increasing plan contributions, starting to save in other retirement vehicles, changing investment strategies, and rethinking retirement plans, so as to increase assets and the ASR.

To illustrate these concepts, we display in Figure 2.1 a family of Par ASR curves for an individual who seeks to remain fully funded (at the Par ASR) at each age through the retirement date; different RR targets are depicted. In this figure, we assume an employee seeks to fund a 25-year fixed annuity at age 65 in 2007. Alternatively, the employee could have funded a lifetime fixed annuity for about 6 percent less than a comparable 25-year annuity.[3] We chose to use the higher-cost option in order to eliminate any differences in life expectancy among the longest-lived individuals. Therefore, the ASR threshold calculation used in this chapter is more stringent relative to a calculation that uses a life annuity assumption.

The figure makes several additional assumptions, including constant nominal annual salary growth of 4 percent and annual investment returns of 6 percent. Note that the Par ASR starts close to zero (early in the working career) and rises to about seven (at the retirement date). Over this period, both income and assets are rising, but in order to adequately fund a retirement annuity through a combination of contributions and returns,

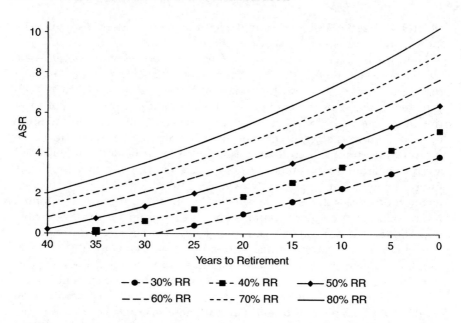

Figure 2.1 Personal funding ratios for 30–80% replacement rate (RR) targets. *Notes*: Computations assume 6% asset returns, 25-year annuity at 6%, 4% nominal salary growth, and 10% contribution rate. *Source*: Authors' calculations; see text.

assets must grow faster than salary. Naturally, this example is hypothetical; next we turn to an examination of whether individuals in the real world achieve these ratios in practice.

ASR patterns in practice

We examine retirement saving adequacy of a sample drawn from the TIAA-CREF participant population, namely those covered by institutional DC plans in 2007 and managed by the TIAA-CREF system. This is a nonprofit DC retirement system owned by its 3.2 million individual participants, and it manages over 15,000 tax-deferred plans for employer and employee contributions and diversified investments. Unlike many 401(k) providers, TIAA-CREF also offers and encourages lifetime annuities, enables pension portability, and provides extensive financial education and advice.

From this system, we gathered data on assets, sex, tenure, and contribution rates for a sample of about 77,000 active employees at 71 institutions that varied by size, contribution rate, and employer type. We calculated

TABLE 2.1 Descriptive statistics for analysis sample

Variable	Unrestricted		Restricted	
	Mean	Standard Deviation	Mean	Standard Deviation
Age (years)	48.1	11.0	48.6	10.8
Tenure (years)	12.2	9.2	12.8	9.0
Estimated salary ($)	72,107	49,757	73,158	49,992
Total assets ($)	306,577	381,406	321,989	385,227
Asset/salary ratio	2.9	42.8	2.8	10.3
Total contributions	11,854	10,003	12,178	10,111
RA contributions[a]				
Employer ($)	6,547	4,640	6,836	4,570
Employee ($)	2,821	4,368	2,951	4,443
SRA contributions[b]				
Employer ($)	45	1,205	48	1,237
Employee ($)	2,260	5,455	2,372	5,570
Contribution as percent of salary (%)	16.9	44	16.9	14.1

[a] Stands for Retirement Account.
[b] Stands for Supplementary Retirement Account.

Notes: Sample size for unrestricted group is 72,067 (36,372 male, 32,041 female, 3,654 missing). Sample size for restricted group is 68,373 (36,354 male and 32,019 female).

Source: Authors' calculations; see text.

ASRs for this sample. We note that the wealth and income figures include only accumulations inside the TIAA-CREF system, which probably understates participants' total assets and income (especially for participants who have some other pension, as well as those who hold retirement-related pensions with other providers). In addition, these data include primary pension plans, some of which have voluntary features, as well as supplemental plans, all of which are voluntary. Participant account balances may include assets from multiple accounts that may represent jobs at many different institutions, each of which had different required and voluntary contribution rates. Specifically, our estimate of contribution rates pertains only to the current employer. Fortunately, because we have access to individual plan document information, we have reconstructed employer match and voluntary plan contribution rates.

As is shown in Table 2.1, the average age of participants in the full sample is 48 with average tenure (number of years employed) at about 12 years. The sample is about 51 percent males, 44 percent females, with 5 percent unknown. Average salary stands at about \$72,100 and average retirement assets are about \$307,000. In our sample, the average actual ASR we computed was about 2.9, resulting from employer and/or employee contributions to Retirement Annuity (RA) and/or Supplemental Retirement Annuity (SRA) accounts. Annual employer contributions averaged about \$6,550 to an RA and \$2,900 to an SRA. Participant contributions averaged about \$2,800 and \$2,300 to the RA and SRA, respectively. Total contributions averaged about \$11,900, with an average total contribution rate of about 16.9 percent of salary.

For the analysis sample, we trimmed the data in a few regards. First, we omitted those with sex not available in the file. Second, we omitted a handful of participants with extremely high asset levels but very low salary on the grounds that they are mostly retired. Third, we restricted the sample to those with salary of at least \$5,000. And last, a handful of observations was omitted due to negative contribution values (because of record-keeping corrections). The resulting sample of 68,373 participants is described in the second column of Table 2.1: it is slightly older, higher income, and wealthier (but not significantly so), and the ASR is less dispersed.

Correlates of ASR

Next we explore the relationship between the ASR and various sample population characteristics. Table 2.2 shows average ASR by age cohort. As expected, contributions and income rise with age, since plan rules set contributions as a percentage of income. In addition, the average ASR increases with age, suggesting that the decision to delay retirement may have a strong effect on the ASR. Figure 2.2 provides additional information

TABLE 2.2 Distribution of mean sample characteristics by age group

Age	N	Contributions ($)	Assets ($)	Tenure (years)	Salary ($)	ASR[a]
<25	320	3,999	6,562	1.8	29,922	0.2
25–34	7,877	6,796	26,506	4.1	48,431	0.6
35–44	17,590	9,791	77,011	8.0	64,625	1.3
45–54	21,589	12,356	180,402	13.2	75,259	2.5
55–64	17,087	15,414	371,162	18.7	85,515	4.5
65–74	3,613	19,096	765,318	25.2	98,842	8.7
75–84	291	21,767	1,216,903	31.5	103,715	18.8
≥85	6	14,641	1,198,079	21.7	66,636	13.5

[a] Stands for asset/salary ratio; see text.

Note: Sample size is 68,373.

Source: Authors' calculations; see text.

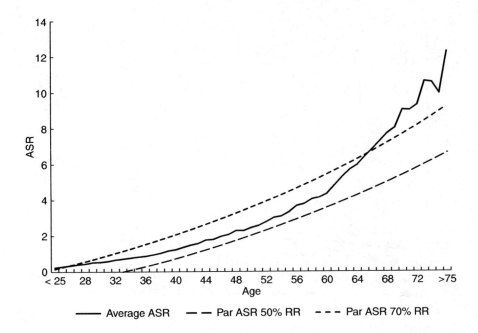

Figure 2.2 Average asset/salary ratio (ASR) by age. *Note*: See Figure 2.1 for definitions. *Source*: Authors' calculations; see text.

on average ASR by age, displaying actual average ASRs along with required
Par ASRs for the 50 and 70 percent target RRs (Par ASRs are similar to
those in Figure 2.1, but have been arrayed by age rather than years to
retirement).

The results show that the entire average ASR curve lies entirely above the
50 percent Par ASR curve, suggesting that, at the end of 2007, this sample
had more assets than needed to be on track for replacing more than 50 percent of its preretirement income. Older participants are doing even better
in providing a cushion for unexpected portfolio shocks. For those aged
61 and above, the actual ASR rises rapidly, and for those above 65 it is
consistently above the 70 percent Par ASR.

Figure 2.3 splits the ASR by age and sex. For younger participants, there
is no significant difference between male and female ASRs. For older
cohorts the results diverge: among baby boomers (those in their mid- to
late 40s or older), females are significantly below males, with ASRs averag-
ing about 75 percent of those for the men. The gap increases substantially
for older cohorts, with females in the oldest cohort having ASRs of

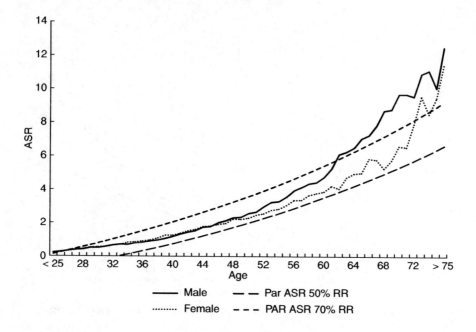

Figure 2.3 Average asset/salary ratio (ASR) by age and sex. *Note*: See Figure 2.1 for definitions. *Source*: Authors' calculations; see text.

approximately half those of their male counterparts. Nonetheless, older women's ASRs are still consistent with adequate financial resources. In other words, cohort sex differences in this sample are similar to those of the population as a whole.

We also identify differences by years of service, or what we call years of tenure in the TIAA-CREF system. Figure 2.4 shows that, on average, all participants enjoy ASRs capable of funding an RR of 50 percent or more, and participants with longer tenure have substantially higher ASRs. Strikingly, those with tenure of 15 years or more have ASRs above the 70 percent Par ASR curve, reaching ASRs of 10 or more for those with at least 32 years of service.

Figure 2.5 shows differences by sex and tenure in the system, and once again, males and females with less tenure have, on average, similar ASRs. But a comparison of Figures 2.3 and 2.5 shows a smaller tenure–sex difference than the age–sex divergence. ASRs for males with at least 27 years of participation are modestly higher than their female counterparts, while a sharp and persistent tenure–sex distinction only emerges for cohorts with more than about 36 years of participation.

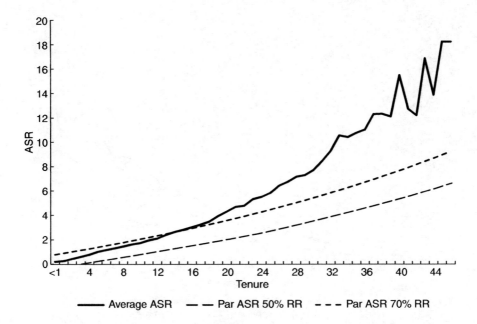

Figure 2.4 Average asset/salary ratio (ASR) by tenure. *Note*: See Figure 2.1 for definitions. *Source*: Authors' calculations; see text.

We want to emphasize that tenure comparisons are complex because some people have only participated in TIAA-CREF over their entire work-ing lives, while others might have the same, more, or less total retirement assets from working job with different plans. Nevertheless, the sex differ-ences remain interesting: women and men with similar tenures had similar opportunities to save and invest in the TIAA-CREF system, while women and men of similar ages might not. For instance, older women are more likely than men to have spent time out of the higher education labor force due to family reasons. What is harder to explain is why long-tenure women and men diverge; different family circumstances may play a role.

Table 2.3 presents information on average ASRs by salary and, as ex-pected, average ASRs rise with salary, though less sharply than by either age or tenure. One explanation for this might be faculty salary compression, with younger faculty receiving starting salaries close to (or on occasion in excess of) those of their older-tenured colleagues. This effect is suggested by the tight grouping of average age and average tenure with the various salary bands. While average ASRs rise slowly with salary, the effect does not appear to be very strong.

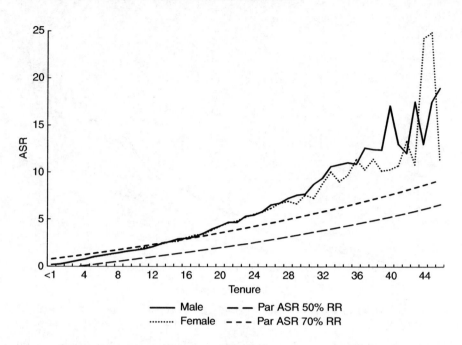

Figure 2.5 Average asset/salary ratio (ASR) by tenure and sex. *Note*: See Figure 2.1 for definitions. *Source*: Authors' calculations; see text.

TABLE 2.3 Distribution of mean sample characteristics by annual salary

Salary ($)	N	Age (years)	Contributions ($)	Assets ($)	Tenure (years)	ASR
<40,000	15,473	45	4,738	62,202	8.9	2.8
40,000–59,999	17,158	46	8,183	107,742	10.5	2.1
60,000–79,999	13,974	49	11,625	183,766	13.0	2.6
80,000–99,999	8,663	52	15,395	304,534	15.9	3.4
100,000–119,999	4,741	53	18,851	401,485	17.5	3.7
≥120,000	8,364	55	27,937	598,758	18.9	3.6

Note: See Table 2.2.

Source: Authors' calculations; see text.

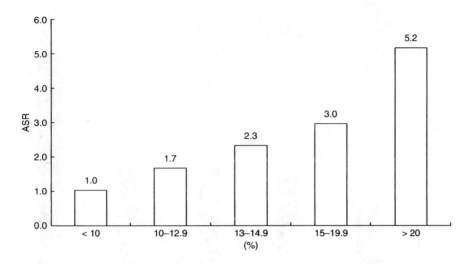

Figure 2.6 Average asset/salary ratio (ASR) by contribution rate. *Note*: See Figure 2.1 for definitions. *Source*: Authors' calculations; see text.

Next we turn to an examination of average ASRs by contribution rates; Figure 2.6 depicts average ASRs by total contribution rates, and Figure 2.7 decomposes contributions into the basic RA and the SRA. Defining the total contribution rate as the sum of all employer and employee contributions divided by salary, we see that the average ASR rises strongly with total contribution rates, increasing more than five times between the lowest and highest savers. Even comparing the top two saving groups, the average ASR is 75 percent higher for the highest savers relative to the next group. It is interesting that, as with overall contributions, the ASR for RAs and SRAs rise dramatically with contribution rates. But the SRA effect is particularly striking: at every level, contributions to the SRA have a greater effect on average ASR than comparable RA contributions. This is likely due to the SRA's role as a supplementary plan, where SRA participation is almost always conditional on prior or concurrent participation in the basic RA plan.

To summarize, different cuts of the data support the hypothesis that the average TIAA-CREF participant was 'on track' in 2007 for having sufficient assets to fund a 50 percent RR. This holds for participants of all ages, but older men seem to have more of a cushion for unexpected shock relative to older women. Several other factors are correlated with retirement saving adequacy, including contribution rates, age, tenure, and, to a lesser extent, salary.

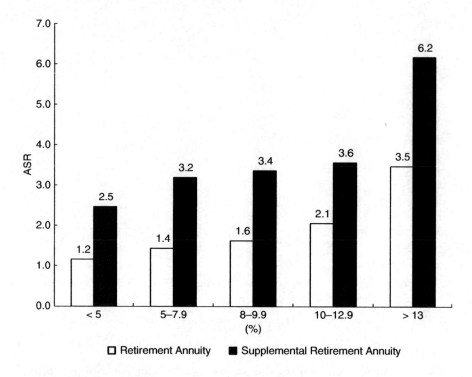

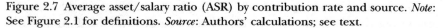

Figure 2.7 Average asset/salary ratio (ASR) by contribution rate and source. *Note*: See Figure 2.1 for definitions. *Source*: Authors' calculations; see text.

Multivariate analysis of retirement funding adequacy

Next we analyze in a multivariate setting the ways in which ASRs vary across the sample, both in absolute and deviation terms. For the first set of models, we use ordinary least squares (OLS) regression to link the dependent variable, the natural log of the ASR (ln (ASR)),[4] with a vector of explanatory variables, including age and age squared, tenure and tenure squared, sex (female), the natural log of the total contribution rate relative to salary (ln (TC percent)), the natural log of the proportion of assets held in equity (ln (Eq percent)) and the natural log of the TIAA traditional account (ln (TIAA percent)), dummy variables for participant contributions to a Retirement Annuity (RAemployee) or a Supplemental Retirement Annuity (SRAemployee), and interacted variables of female with tenure (tenure * female), and age with SRA contributions (age * SRAemployee).[5]

One of the strongest findings from the vast prior literature on asset allocation is that differences in portfolio returns are overwhelmingly determined by differences in portfolio allocations among major asset classes (Brinson, Hood, and Beebowerr 1986). So it may be that differences in the ASR could be explained by differences in asset allocation across participants. To explore this question, we use both the percent of participant's total portfolio invested in equity (ln (Eq percent)) and the percent of total portfolio invested in the TIAA Traditional Annuity (ln (TIAA percent)), which is backed by a broadly diversified portfolio of fixed-income assets. These variables leave out allocations to bond funds and accounts as well to direct real estate, but in fact, bonds and real estate comprise a small portion of most participants' portfolios. We explore whether the ASR might be affected by employee RA and SRA contributions, separate from employer contributions. In many cases, and universally so for the SRA, employee contributions depend on the individual participant decision to save additional amounts out of salary. While employee contributions are constrained by IRS limits and affected by employer matching, in the case of the RA they can be mandated, while in the case of the SRA they are completely voluntary. In essence, we are interested in seeing whether different types of contributions are associated with being on track for a secure retirement.

Results for ASR levels

Regression results appear in Table 2.4, where we see that the explanatory variables account for about 82 percent of the variance observed, and all independent variables except age squared and ln (TIAA percent) are significant at the 99 percent level (the latter is significant at the 95 percent level). Estimated elasticities for most variables are relatively small, partly reflecting the fact that the ASR for the restricted sample averages 2.8 with a standard deviation of about 10 (see Table 2.1).

It is of interest to note that variations in total contribution rates (ln (TC percent)) have by far the most important influence on the ASR. This is sensible, since for younger participants, larger contribution rates should naturally result in higher assets, while for older participants, the interaction of lifetime contribution rates and rates of return become important. Both basic pension plan RA contributions (RAemployee) and voluntary supplemental contributions (SRAemployee) have positive effects on the outcome; also SRA contributions have a much larger impact except for older SRA contributors. We believe that the negative relationship with age can be explained by 'catch-up' contributions: older participants with low ASRs have recognized that they are behind target and are more likely to maximize the RA contributions and to also contribute to their SRAs in an attempt to catch up with others in their age cohort.

TABLE 2.4 Multivariate OLS regression analysis of asset/salary ratio (ASR): dependent variable ln (asset/salary ratio)

Variable	Parameter estimate	Standard error	t value	Probability > $|t|$
Intercept	−0.158	0.044	−3.59	0.0003
Age	0.012	0.002	6.48	<.0001
Age squared	0.000	0.000	−0.65	0.5153
Tenure	0.153	0.001	161.31	<.0001
Tenure squared	−0.002	0.000	−81.12	<.0001
Female	0.031	0.008	4.15	<.0001
ln (TC percent)[a]	0.748	0.005	142.36	<.0001
ln (Eq percent)[b]	0.051	0.003	16.55	<.0001
ln (TIAA percent)[c]	0.007	0.002	2.79	0.0052
RAemployee	0.076	0.005	15.97	<.0001
SRAemployee	0.254	0.022	11.49	<.0001
Tenure * female	−0.003	0.000	−6.89	<.0001
Age * SRAemployee	−0.006	0.000	−14.83	<.0001
Root MSE	0.44			
Dependent mean	0.60			
Coefficient of Variance	73.67			
R-square	0.83			
Adjusted R-square	0.83			

[a] Stands for the natural log of the total contribution rate relative to salary.
[b] Stands for the natural log of the proportion of assets held in equity.
[c] Stands for the natural log of the TIAA traditional account.
Note: See Table 2.2.
Source: Authors' calculations; see text.

Tenure is also positively associated with larger ASRs. Going from 0 to 10 years of participation increases ASR by about 1.3, with the tenure effect reaching a maximum at about 38 years of service. Evidently participating for a long time in an institution's plan is a good way to build a healthy retirement nest egg. Interestingly, the female effect is small and positive, while the longer-tenured female effect is small but negative. We surmise that this is due to the increased probability that females had work stoppages in their past careers, leading to lower lifetime contribution rates and hence lower ASRs. We also find that for this population, having a high equity share (ln (Eq percent)) is associated with higher ASRs; whether this will hold in the future is uncertain.

In sum, individual participants who participated longer, saved more, and allocated more to equities enjoy higher ASRs than those who did not. While this may seem relatively unsurprising, this simple formulation explains over 80 percent of the variation in the ASR for our sample of TIAA-CREF participants.

Results on deviations from the Par ASR

Next we assess what influences observed deviations from the Par ASR, which we think of as the 'on-track' or 'target' ASR. To this end, we measure the tracking error around the Par ASR by defining ASRs over five threshold ranges: those with an ASR greater than or equal to 80 percent, 70 to less than 80 percent, 60 to less than 70 percent, 50 to less than 60 percent, and less than 50 percent. As before, the sample includes only participants aged 25 to 75, with 48,788 usable observations.

Table 2.5 presents the results of an ordered probit regression with the target Par ASR (Threshold ASR) as the dependent variable; the same independent variables used earlier are employed. Results indicate that all variables are highly statistically significant and all coefficients but age have coefficients with similar magnitudes and signs. As before, contribution rates and tenure have the largest effect on participants' likelihood of moving up into the next highest ASR threshold. The overall contribution rate has the largest effect, with employee contributions to an RA or SRA increasing the probability that a participant will reach the higher threshold. As before, the exception is for the interaction of SRA with age, suggesting that older participants making SRA contributions are playing catch-up with their retirement saving.

One important difference with the prior results is that here the coefficient on age is negative. This is because the proportion of individuals in the lower ASR thresholds starts low for young cohorts, rises for middle-aged cohorts, and then falls for older cohorts, a pattern perhaps attributable to student loan debt, child rearing, and home purchases early on, which do not persist into late middle-age but may crowd out retirement saving. Tenure increases the probability that a participant crosses into the next higher threshold. As before, longer-tenured females are less likely to cross into higher thresholds, perhaps because they did not contribute at the same rate as men over time. As before, the asset allocation mix is important, with higher equity fractions boosting the likelihood of achieving the next threshold. Likewise, fixed income (ln (TIAA percent)) is also significant, slightly increasing the likelihood of reaching the next threshold. Nevertheless, the effect of asset allocation proves rather small, relative to the impact of contributions and tenure. The main implication is that chasing returns is no substitute for adequately funding a retirement plan over time.

TABLE 2.5 Multivariate ordered probit analysis of threshold asset/salary ratio
(ASR): dependent variable threshold ASR

Variable	Parameter estimate	Standard error	Chi-square	Probability > chi-square
Intercept 1	11.092	0.131	7,202.3	<.0001
Intercept 2	0.629	0.008	6,187.0	<.0001
Intercept 3	1.480	0.011	19,365.9	<.0001
Intercept 4	2.522	0.013	37,857.4	<.0001
Age	−0.411	0.006	5,513.5	<.0001
Age squared	0.003	0.000	2,455.9	<.0001
Tenure	0.286	0.003	7,826.1	<.0001
Tenure squared	−0.002	0.000	850.4	<.0001
Female	0.091	0.022	17.4	<.0001
ln (TC percent)	1.658	0.017	9,909.0	<.0001
ln (Eq percent)	0.156	0.008	347.3	<.0001
ln (TIAA percent)	0.038	0.006	37.1	<.0001
RAemployee	0.180	0.013	189.9	<.0001
SRAemployee	0.290	0.057	25.7	<.0001
Tenure * female	−0.009	0.001	42.6	<.0001
Age * SRAemployee	−0.008	0.001	49.2	<.0001
Log likelihood	−50,951			

Note: See Tables 2.2 and 2.4.

Source: Authors' calculations; see text.

Conclusion

We use the ASR to highlight factors associated with retirement saving
adequacy in a large DC pension system. On average, our sample participants in a range of TIAA-CREF plans appear to be on track for funding a
fixed retirement annuity that, with Social Security, will replace at least 70
percent of preretirement income. Furthermore, many appear able to do
better, buying themselves higher replacement rates or having a significant
cushion against economic shocks. Factors most predictive of success are
contribution rate, years of participation in the system, and the fraction of
equities in the retirement portfolio. Also those employees who contributed
to their SRAs had substantially greater chances of meeting ASR targets.

One caveat to this analysis is that our dataset was collected in 2007, when
equity markets were near all-time highs and many other assets, including
bonds, real estate, and other alternatives were providing solid returns.
In 2008 and 2009, financial markets were highly volatile; equity markets

dropped by more than half and then rose again by about 60 percent through the end of 2009. Looking only at the period of decline from the beginning of 2008 through February 2009, aggregate TIAA-CREF assets lost roughly 17 percent of their value (equity losses were tempered by investments in a guaranteed account and fixed income). We estimate that, if the average sample participant lost 17 percent, his or her ASR would have declined by a similar proportion. An average participant with 30 years tenure would have had an ASR of 8 at year-end 2007, consistent with a Par ASR of over 100 percent RR. This 17 percent decline in assets would have left that hypothetical participant with an ASR of over 6.6, still well above the 70 percent ASR. Recall that our PAR ASRs assume a constant annual 6 percent investment return from a diversified portfolio of assets. At the end of 2007, the average TIAA-CREF participant's portfolio consisted of about 52 percent equities, 39 percent guaranteed and fixed income, 5 percent direct real estate, and 4 percent money market assets. Over the last 10 years (through the end of September 2009), a portfolio constantly maintained at these asset allocations would have returned about 3.1 percent per year, about half of the assumed total rate of return. A steady 3 percent rate of return would place a considerable burden on participants saving for retirement. One way to look at this is that the required ASR 15 years before retirement would rise from 3.5 times salary using the 6 percent return assumption to 5.8 times salary using a 3 percent return assumption, an increase of more than 65 percent. Another way to look at it is that a sustained multi-decade period of subpar returns would leave many participants unable to fund their target replacement incomes in retirement. In order to explore these and other issues, we intend to track what actually happened to TIAA-CREF participants in future work.

We would note that many other DC plans are less generous than most TIAA-CREF plans, so participants and policymakers must not be overly sanguine regarding these results. For instance, contribution rates across the private sector plan universe range from 6 to 8 percent of salary, rather than the 10 to 20 percent seen in many TIAA-CREF plans. Furthermore, high contribution rates are a key determinant of being able to hit one's Par ASR as we have shown. And even in our sample, employees contributing less than 10 percent had average ASRs of 1.0, far less than the number needed to fund an adequate retirement income. Another feature of many 401(k) plans is people have shorter plan tenure; private sector 401(k) plans have only existed since the early 1980s and did not achieve deep market penetration until the mid-1990s. By contrast, TIAA-CREF has been in existence for over 90 years.

In sum, we have shown that it is possible to design robust DC plans that considerably increase the likelihood of achieving sufficient saving for generating adequate retirement income. We believe that our proposed measure, the ASR, can help individuals do a better job setting saving goals as well as gauge whether they are on track for retirement in a dynamic way. All too often, workers lack incentives or feedback mechanisms they can use to judge their progress to a goal. Providing interim and easily understandable feedback could be useful in helping participants link future goals to current conditions and make adjustments as necessary.

Appendix 2A More Detail on the ASR[6]

We define the ASR as the ratio of current retirement assets (A) to current salary (S) at time t years before retirement:

$$\text{ASR}_t = \frac{A_t}{S_t} \tag{2A.1}$$

where S is the salary earned over the previous year. In the chapter, we explain two different versions of this measure. Without any future contributions (i.e., pension premiums) beyond the current moment, the *required* current level of assets or initial principal would be equal to the discounted present value of the cost of an annuity at retirement divided by future salary growth:

$$A_t(\text{No contributions}) = \frac{\text{FV}_A}{(1+r)^t} \tag{2A.2}$$

where FV_A is the discounted present value of the cost of an annuity at retirement that would be sufficient to produce the desired RR, and r is the rate of investment return on the existing assets. If we allow positive future pension contributions and other incremental saving, then required current assets is reduced accordingly to

$$A_t(\text{With contributions}) = \frac{\text{FV}_A - \text{FV}_P}{(1+r)^t} \tag{2A.3}$$

where FV_P is the accumulated value of annual premium payments (and any other retirement saving) at retirement. These in turn depend on initial salary, salary growth, and investment return on premiums such that

$$\text{FV}_p = \sum_{n=1}^{t} PS_t(1+w)^{n-1}(1+r)^{t-n} \tag{2A.4}$$

and $w =$ nominal salary increase rate, including a real salary increase and an inflation component.

Substituting Equation (2A.4) into Equation (2A.3), the required assets size becomes

$$A_t = \frac{FV_A - \sum_{n=1}^{t} PS_t(1+w)^{n-1}(1+r)^{n-t}}{(1+r)^t} \quad \text{(2A.5)}$$

Now the future value of an annuity can be recast in terms of the RR, salary, salary growth, and an annuity purchase cost:

$$FV_A = [S_t(1+w)^t RR]AC \quad \text{(2A.6)}$$

where

$$AC = \frac{\left[1 - \left(\frac{1}{(1+r_{AN})^K}\right)\right]}{r_{AN}}$$

r_{AN} = investment rate of return on annuity assets
K = total number of years in the annuity
RR = income replacement rate
Substituting Equation (2A.6) into Equation (2A.5) yields

$$A_t = \frac{S_t}{(1+r)^t}[[RR(1+w)^t AC] - \sum_{n=1}^{t} P(1+w)^{n-1}(1+r)^{t-n}] \quad \text{(2A.7)}$$

Simplifying further yields the expression

$$\frac{A_t}{S_t} = \frac{RR(1+w)^t AC}{(1+r)^t} - \frac{P(1+w)[(1+r)^t - (1+w)^t]}{(r-w)(1+r)^t} \quad \text{(2A.8)}$$

or

$$ASR_t = \frac{A_t}{S_t} = RR * AC\left(\frac{1+w}{1+r}\right)^t - \frac{P(1+w)}{r-w}\left[1 - \left(\frac{1+w}{1+r}\right)^t\right] \quad \text{(2A.9)}$$

Two things should be noted about this characterization of the ASR. First, the annuity value is based on a date certain rather than a life annuity. If a life annuity is used, then the annuity cost (AC) depends on the annuity's interest rate, i, the probability of a person's age b at retirement of living to age $b + h$ (hPb), and on the last age in a mortality table, m, as follows:

$$AC_b = \sum_{h=0}^{m-b} \frac{hPb}{(1+i)^h} \quad \text{(2A.10)}$$

Second, the preretirement investment return, annuity investment return, and salary growth terms may all be different. If any of them are similar, the ASR equation is further simplified. For example, if the preretirement investment rate of return and the salary growth rate are equal, then

$$\text{ASR}_t = \frac{A_t}{S_t} = \text{RR} * \text{AC} - P * t \qquad (2\text{A}.11)$$

Notes

[1] For present purposes, it suffices to acknowledge that several different approaches may be taken to compute DB funding ratios, some of which depend on how plan liabilities are defined. For example, liabilities may be defined as though the plan were to close today, with the need to pay all currently accrued liabilities but no future liability buildup would be booked. Alternatively, they can be defined to include an estimate of the buildup in future liabilities (including assumptions about how long employees will continue to work, what they will get paid, etc.). For further detail, see McGill et al. (2005).

[2] The Appendix 2A provides a detailed description of the mathematical relationships among the elements that make up the required Par ASR: the desired income replacement rate (RR), pension contribution rate, investment rate of return on pension contributions, salary growth rate, investment rate of return on annuity assets, and the respective number of years remaining prior to and following retirement.

[3] The 25-year fixed annuity is actually more expensive than a life annuity because it does not fully leverage pooled mortality risk the way a life annuity does. Under our assumptions, it is about 6 percent more expensive to buy the 25-year fixed annuity than the pure life annuity beginning at age 65.

[4] The OLS models eliminate cases where the ASR was over 50 on the grounds that there might be measurement errors or temporarily low incomes reported in our sample snapshot. We also exclude individuals over the age of 75 and under the age of 25. The resulting sample has 67,324 observations.

[5] Because of zero values for some percentages, only 48,778 observations are used in the final regression.

[6] This appendix is derived from Leibowitz et al. (2002).

References

American Association of University Professors (AAUP) (2006). *Policy Documents & Reports, 10th Edition*, Baltimore, MD: Johns Hopkins University Press.

Ando, Albert and Franco Modigliani (1963). 'The "Life Cycle" Hypothesis of Saving: Aggregate Implications and Tests,' *The American Economic Review*, 53(1): 55–84.

Brinson, Gary P., L. Randolph Hood, and Gilbert L. Beebower (1986). 'Determinants of Portfolio Performance,' *Financial Analysts Journal*, 42(4): 45–51.

Browning, Martin and Tom Crossley (2001). 'The Life-Cycle Model of Consumption and Saving,' *Journal of Economic Perspectives*, 15: 3–22.

Bullard, James and James Feigenbaum (2007). 'A Leisurely Reading of the Life-Cycle Consumption Data,' *Journal of Monetary Economics*, 54(8): 2305–20.

Heller, Michael and Francis P. King (1989). 'Estimating Real Income Replacement Ratios in Defined Contribution Retirement Plans,' *Research Dialogues 23*. New York: TIAA-CREF.

——— (1994). 'Replacement Ratio Projections in Defined Contribution Retirement Plans: Time, Salary Growth, Investment Return, and Real Income,' *Research Dialogues 41*. New York: TIAA-CREF.

Leibowitz, Martin L., Benson Durham, P. Brett Hammond, and Michael Heller (2002). 'Retirement Planning and the Asset/Salary Ratio,' in O.S. Mitchell, Z. Bodie, P.B. Hammond, and S. Zeldes (eds.), *Innovations in Retirement Financing*. Philadelphia, PA: University of Pennsylvania Press, pp. 106–31.

McGill, Dan, Kyle Brown, John Haley, and Sylvester Schieber (2005). *Fundamentals of Private Pensions*, 8th Edition. Oxford, UK: Oxford University Press.

Poterba, James M., Steven Venti, and David Wise (1998). '401(k) Plans and Future Patterns of Retirement Saving,' *American Economic Review*, 88(2): 179–84.

—— Joshua Rauh, Steven F. Venti, and David A. Wise (2007). 'Defined Contribution Plans, Defined Benefit Plans, and the Accumulation of Retirement Wealth,' *Journal of Public Economics*, 91(10): 2062–86.

—— Steven Venti, and David Wise (2008). 'New Estimates of the Future Path of 401(k) Assets,' in J.M. Poterba (ed.), *Tax Policy and the Economy, Volume 22*. Chicago, IL: University of Chicago Press, pp. 43–80.

Reno, Virginia P. and Joni Lavery (2007). 'Social Security and Retirement Income Adequacy,' *Social Security Brief No. 25*. Washington, DC: National Academy of Social Insurance.

Scholz, John Karl, Ananth Seshadri, and Surachai Khitatrakun (2006). 'Are Americans Saving "Optimally" for Retirement?' *Journal of Political Economy*, 114(4): 607–43.

The Chronicle of Higher Education (2009). *AAUP Rating Scale*. Washington, DC: The Chronicle of Higher Education. http://chronicle.com/stats/aaup/ratingscale/2009aaupratingscale.htm

Chapter 3

Employer-Provided Retirement Planning Programs

Robert L. Clark, Melinda S. Morrill, and Steven G. Allen

Millions of baby boomers will make the transition from full-time work to complete retirement over the next decade. As retirement approaches, these older workers must make a series of important decisions, some of which will be irreversible. These choices will determine, in part, their income levels in retirement, the sensitivity of their income to economic fluctuations, and their ability to maintain consumption through retirement. To make the transition into retirement successfully, people will need to rely on their own financial literacy and knowledge about retirement programs offered by employers and the government. Without accurate information and sufficient financial literacy, many may make inappropriate employment and investment choices that could have significant consequences in their retirement years.

Economists and other social science researchers have recently examined the level of financial literacy and its role in economic decision-making to determine whether and how individuals can improve their knowledge base. This chapter presents evidence from a unique new study of the retirement planning and financial literacy programs offered by employers to their older employees. Our initial findings indicate that participants can enhance their financial literacy and knowledge and, on the basis of this new information, many tend to alter their retirement plans. Consequently, employers can facilitate the transition into retirement by providing the means for workers to increase their understanding of key retirement concepts, enabling their employees to achieve a more desirable retirement.

Retirement decisions and knowledge requirements

When individuals enter the labor force, they must immediately begin making important choices about their lifetime consumption and saving profiles. Life-cycle theory suggests that individuals will set retirement goals or targets early on, and select saving and investment behavior that should allow them to achieve their goals. As new information becomes available, people will re-optimize their consumption and saving patterns, and they may alter their retirement expectations. The primary retirement goals that workers must set include the retirement age and their level of retirement income. A fundamental principle in retirement planning is that younger retirement ages and higher retirement incomes require more saving and less consumption throughout the working life.

While considerable attention has been paid to American workers' under-saving, by contrast, much less attention has been focused on how older workers make decisions concerning the allocation of their resources as they enter into retirement. Workers must decide when and how to enter into retirement, and how to best use the resources available to them. The limited evidence available suggests that older workers do not have sufficient knowledge or the financial literacy needed to make the many choices that must be made as they transition from work to retirement (Bernheim 1995, 1998; Hilgert and Hogarth 2002; Lusardi and Mitchell 2006, 2007). Incorrect or insufficient knowledge can lead to suboptimal choices. For this reason, programs that increase financial literacy and retirement program knowledge can improve retirement decisions and produce better retirement outcomes (Clark and d'Ambrosio 2003; Clark et al. 2006; Lusardi 2008). In addition, preretirement planning seminars can efficiently address the numerous questions and concerns that individuals approaching retirement share, thereby reducing human resources (HR) costs.

Some of the most important decisions older workers must make are as follows

- When to retire from their career jobs
- Whether to take a lump-sum distribution from a defined benefit (DB) pension plan or to accept the annuity option
- When to claim Social Security benefits
- Whether to annuitize all or part of 401(k) and/or 403(b) account balances
- How to manage investments in retirement

For workers to make these important choices, they must have an appropriate level of financial literacy, understand financial mathematics, and have accurate knowledge about their employers' and national retirement programs. Workers can acquire the needed knowledge to make these key decisions in various ways and one resource often available is employer-sponsored preretirement planning programs.

Many large employers offer some type of planning seminar for retirement-eligible employees. Sabelhaus, Brogdan, and Holden (2008) report that

46 percent of pension participants covered by defined contribution (DC) plans work for companies that provide resources to assist participants in retirement choices. Thirty percent of participants have the opportunity to attend employer seminars and workshops, and almost 85 percent of these rely on this information to 'some' or a 'great' extent in making their retirement decisions. In a plan sponsor survey, Wray (2008) finds that 31 percent of employers offer seminars focusing on retirement assets and income planning. While not universal, employer-provided retirement planning programs are common, accessible to perhaps one-third of the labor force.

Although many believe this type of program is beneficial to employees, relatively little is known about the effectiveness of these programs in enhancing the knowledge of, and altering the retirement decisions of, employees. In this chapter, we examine the preretirement programs of five large national employers to assess whether these are successful in improving workers' knowledge base as they near retirement. We also assess whether, on the basis of this learning, employees alter their retirement plans. Finally, we explore employee views of these programs, including whether they thought the programs were worthwhile and whether the seminars are seen as a valuable employee benefit.

Our key findings are that participants do learn, alter retirement behavior, and appreciate the programs offered by their employers. Knowledge gained varies with age, sex, income level, education, tenure, and wealth. Participants also reported that they had changed retirement plans, including altering their expected retirement ages, plans to take lump-sum pension payouts, and when they anticipated claiming Social Security benefits. Employees value these programs and report that the programs enhance their opinion of their employers.

Methodology

To evaluate employer-provided preretirement planning programs, we assembled a team of five large employers ranging in size from 8,000 to 40,000 employees. Our employer partners are Becton, Dickinson, and Company (BD); North Carolina State University; Progress Energy; Weyerhaeuser; and the Williams Companies.[1] Four of the firms have sites throughout the United States; their home offices are in New Jersey, North Carolina, Oklahoma, and Washington. Each of the employers offers DB plans (three employers have cash balance plans), health insurance to active and retired workers, and supplemental DC plans (although not all have an employer match). The employee populations of these companies vary by gender, education, earnings, and geographic location.

Each of the employers offered a series of preretirement planning programs to their older employees during the second half of 2008. The usual process is that retirement-eligible employees are invited individually to participate in these programs by their employer: invitations are issued, attendance is tracked, and there are usually high participation rates. The firms track attendance and may limit participation by employees in these programs to once every 5 years or so. These programs are usually ongoing, and the employers expect that over a number of years, most eligible employees will attend one of these programs. Thus, the participants in the programs we observe should reflect the population of older workers at these employers.

The financial education literature has focused in depth on possible selection issues, suggesting that one might overstate the impact of financial education seminars if one only focuses on those who voluntarily attend. This is exacerbated by the fact that few, if any, records of attendance are kept. By contrast, the programs we examine are more structured; while attendance is voluntary, employees receive specific invitations from their employers and attendance is recorded. Given that most eligible employees attend one of these company-provided programs once they become retirement-eligible, the selection bias should be considerably less in our study.[2] Nevertheless, as we observe seminars offered between June and December 2008, we have not been able to monitor behavior over a long time period. For this reason, it is possible that these programs may have attracted a nonrepresentative sample of the workforce.

We worked with each employer in the spring of 2008 to develop an evaluation process for their preretirement planning programs. Our methodology included the development of two surveys,[3] the first of which was to be completed by each participant prior to the start of the program. The objective was to obtain baseline socioeconomic data about the individual and his/her household, as well as information concerning retirement plans and investment strategies. Employees also completed questions about their financial literacy and their knowledge of employer and national retirement programs. Two financial literacy questions similar to those developed by Lusardi and Mitchell (2006) for the Health and Retirement Study were included along with a series of knowledge questions about Social Security, Medicare, and the characteristics of company retirement plans.

At the conclusion of the seminar, participants were asked to complete a second survey. This time, participants answered questions concerning the program, the employee's assessment of the seminar, and its value. The knowledge and literacy questions were repeated, to see if the participants' overall knowledge of retirement programs and financial markets had improved. Seminar participants were also asked if they had changed any of their important retirement-related decisions.[4]

Some of the employers used hard-copy surveys (BD, Progress Energy, and Weyerhaeuser). The program leaders at each of these companies extended the length of their programs to allow participants 15–20 minutes prior to the start of the seminar to complete Survey One and similar time at the end of the program to complete Survey Two. Other employers (North Carolina State University and Williams) used electronic surveys; in this case, a link to the electronic Survey One was sent via e-mail to participants about a week prior to the seminar and a link to Survey Two was e-mailed to the participants immediately following the seminar. Attendees were given approximately 2 weeks to complete the surveys. In what follows, we review the results of 28 seminars that incorporated our surveys into their programs between June and December 2008. For this chapter, we restrict our analysis to participants born between 1943 and 1959 (approximately age 50–65 at the time of the seminars).[5] This yields a total sample with usable responses of 395 employees (see Table 3A.1).

In the following sections, we describe these employers and their preretirement programs, as well as the responses of seminar participants. Our analysis highlights three areas. First, we examine how the participants evaluated the program. Second, we determine whether these employees improved their basic understanding of employer retirement programs, Social Security, and Medicare. Finally, we determine whether individuals altered their retirement plans on the basis of the program.

Survey design

While Surveys One and Two were customized for each employer, the framework was similar across firms. Usually, both surveys mentioned the specific employer by name, where appropriate, and people were asked about their own employer-specific retirement schemes. Questions concerning retirement saving accounts differed somewhat between private-sector versus public/nonprofit employers (i.e., questions concerned 401(k) plans in the private sector and 403(b) and 457 plans in the public sector). In addition, several employers requested that specific questions be added to the survey to help them better understand how their employees were using the HR programs and accessing the help lines offered by their 401(k) and 403(b) providers.

The objectives of Survey One were to determine employee understanding levels regarding their employer's pension and health benefits, their knowledge of national retirement plans such as Social Security and Medicare, their financial literacy, and their current retirement plans. To assess the current level of knowledge regarding national retirement plans, the survey asked about Social Security early and normal retirement ages as well as early retirement penalties, cost-of-living increases, and the age of eligibility for Medicare. In addition, participants were asked benefit and eligibility questions concerning their employer DB plans and their own 401(k) or 403(b) accounts. This survey also included several questions related to basic financial literacy. Survey One also asked participants the age that they expected to retire, when they expected to start Social Security benefits, what the expected level of benefits would be, and what benefits they expected to receive from their employer-provided retirement plans. Questions probed employee intentions concerning annuitization of pension assets and work plans after they retired from their current employer. Finally, Survey One contained a series of economic and demographic questions concerning current income, wealth, age, marital status, and the work, income, and retirement benefits of any spouse or partner.

The primary objectives of Survey Two were to determine how participants evaluated the seminar, whether they enhanced their knowledge of retirement programs, and whether the new information changed their retirement plans. To assess the employees' impression of the seminars, the first section of Survey Two asked respondents if the program provided useful information, if the information was presented at the right level for them, if the presenters were of high caliber, if they felt better able to make retirement decisions after completing the program, and whether they valued the program as an employee benefit. The next two sections of Survey Two repeated many Survey One questions concerning retirement intentions and knowledge. By comparing the answers given across both surveys, we assess the change in the respondent's knowledge about retirement programs, financial literacy, and whether participants changed their retirement plans.

Did participant financial literacy rise?

We seek to learn whether these employer-provided programs are effective in increasing financial literacy and knowledge about company and national retirement programs, and if financial literacy is increased, how this affects worker behavior. To measure financial education program impact, we merge responses from the five employers into a single data file;[6] means of various demographic, economic, and retirement plans characteristics appear in Table 3.1. The sample is composed of workers aged 50–65 with a mean age of 57.8 years. Two-thirds of the employees are men, 82 percent are married, and they have an average of almost 25 years of service with their current employer. In general, these are relatively high earners with above-average wealth.

TABLE 3.1 Sample descriptive statistics

	Value
Age (years)	57.8
Male (%)	66.3
Married (%)	81.9
Years of service	24.6
Some college (%)	89.2
Covered by a pension plan (%)	94
Own home (%)	95
Self-assessed knowledge (1–7)	4.3
Years from planned retirement	3.9
Wealth and earnings variables:	
Medium earnings ($50,000–100,000) (%)	47.6
High earnings (>$100,000) (%)	43.1
Medium 401(k) account balance (1–5 years of current salary) (%)	72.6
High 401(k) account balance (>5 years of current salary) (%)	19.5
Plans prior to seminar:	
Planned retirement age (years)	62.0
social security receipt age (years)	63.9
Work after retirement (%)	46.8
Intend to annuitize DC plan (%)	16.9
Undecided on annuitization of DC plan (%)	56.9
Intend to take lump-sum pension (%)	30.7
Undecided on lump-sum pension (%)	50.0
Plans after seminar	
Planned retirement age (years)	62.2
social security receipt age (years)	64.1
Work after retirement (%)	56.9
Intend to annuitize DC plan (%)	26.6
Undecided on annuitization of DC plan (%)	46.0
Intend to take lump-sum pension (%)	31.3
Undecided on lump-sum pension (%)	46.1

Note: The table presents the mean values for the questions in the surveys from participants that participated in the employer-provided preretirement planning programs in 2008.

Source: Authors' calculations; see text.

To examine the level of financial literacy and knowledge of retirement programs prior to the seminar, the participants were asked several questions of which 10 are analyzed here. The questions, along with a summary of correct answers, appear in Table 3.2. The average number of correct responses prior to the seminar was 7.1; afterward the average number of correct answers rose to 8.4, indicating a substantial level of learning among program participants. The average knowledge score after the seminar for the entire sample was significantly higher than the average score prior to the seminar, and the improvement in knowledge and literacy for participants from each employer was significantly higher after the seminar. Figure 3.1 shows the distribution of participants' knowledge scores (the number of correct answers). Prior to the seminar, 20 participants scored a perfect 10 while 57 participants had scores of 5 or lower. After the seminar, 61 participants gave correct answers for all 10 questions and only seven had a score of 5 or less.

Figure 3.2 shows the change in knowledge achieved during the seminar. Overall, 171 participants (69 percent) improved their knowledge scores with the score remaining unchanged for 57 individuals (23 percent of the sample). Panel B illustrates the knowledge gain sorted by the base level of financial knowledge from Survey One. Most importantly, those with initial low scores achieved substantial increases in their knowledge of retirement plans. For this reason, we conclude that the preretirement planning seminars did increase financial literacy for almost all participants, with large gains among those with relatively little knowledge prior to the event.

It should not be surprising that many older workers do not know the basic eligibility and plan characteristics of national retirement programs. Key parameters of Social Security, Medicare, and pension regulations are based on legislation passed at different points in time and have different objectives. As a result, many alternative ages are specified in these programs that determine access to retirement income. A recent study (USGAO 2007) summarized these many different retirement age-related rules ranging from age 55, the age of eligibility for drawing certain pensions without penalties if leaving an employer, to 70.5, which is the age for mandatory withdrawals from pension plans to avoid tax penalties. While confusion over these ages is understandable, the retirement income of workers depends on their knowledge of these ages and the timing of their retirement decisions.

It is also worth noting that the gains in knowledge were observed across all economic and demographic characteristics of the participants. Table 3.3 shows the knowledge index by various employee characteristics. There was a 1.38 gain in the mean score of the entire population. Younger participants, those aged 50–58, had a greater increase in their knowledge scores

TABLE 3.2 Participant knowledge before and after the seminar: percentage of participants (number) answering each question correctly and the average number of correct answers to the 10 questions

		F1[b]	F2[b]	P1[c]	P2[c]	P3[c]	P4[c]	P5[c]	P6[c]	C1[d]	C2[d]	Total correct
BD[a]	Before	100	86	86	62	28	72	44	76	90	58	7.0
N = 50	After	100	88	84	90	60	94	50	94	98	96	8.5
NCSU[a]	Before	93	79	86	64	21	79	43	86	22	86	6.6
N = 14	After	100	93	86	79	36	93	64	100	29	100	7.9
PE[a]	Before	97	92	81	50	40	71	33	75	77	92	7.1
N = 95	After	98	95	93	72	50	82	57	86	84	99	8.2
WEY[a]	Before	100	92	73	38	46	85	58	92	83	79	7.5
N = 48	After	100	96	98	88	85	94	98	96	85	85	9.3
WLM[a]	Before	100	100	71	69	29	81	38	79	67	45	6.8
N = 42	After	100	100	81	88	50	98	50	86	90	76	8.2
Total	Before	98	91	79	54	36	76	42	80	76	74	7.1
N = 249	After	99	94	90	82	58	90	63	90	86	92	8.4

[a] Employers included in the table are Becton, Dickinson, and Company (BD); North Carolina State University (NCSU); Progress Energy (PE); Weyerhaeuser (WEY); and the Williams Companies (WLM).

[b] Financial knowledge questions:

F1: True or false? 'Buying a single company stock usually provides a safer return than a diversified portfolio.'

  Answer: False

F2: Assume that your retirement income increases by 2 percent per year and that the annual rate of inflation is 4 percent per year. After 1 year, will you be able to

  a. buy more goods and services?

  b. buy fewer goods and services?

  c. buy exactly the same amount of goods and services?

  d. don't know.

  Answer: b

[c] Public programs knowledge questions:

P1: What is the earliest age that you can start social security benefits?

Answer: 62

P2: What is the age that you can receive a full or unreduced social security benefit ('normal retirement age')?

Answer: 66

P3: If you start social security benefits at the earliest possible age, you will receive a benefit that is __percent of the benefit you would have received at the normal retirement age. (multiple-choice question)

Answer: 75

P4: Is the reduction in social security benefits for early retirement permanent or does the reduction end when you reach the normal retirement age?

Answer: Permanent

P5: After you start receiving social security benefits, these benefits are

   a. the same for the rest of my life

   b. increased annually by the rate of inflation

   c. increased annually but by less than the rate of inflation

   d. increased annually but by more than the rate of inflation

   e. don't know

Answer: b

P6: What is the earliest age that you will be eligible for Medicare?

Answer: 65

[d] Company-specific questions:

C1: Can you take a lump-sum distribution of some or all of your pension plan (do not include income for your 401(k) account)?

Answer: Yes (all five companies)

C2: Does your company offer you the opportunity to stay in the company health plan after you retire?

Answer: Yes (all five companies)

Note: The average knowledge score after the seminar is significantly higher for participants from all employers at the 1-percent level except for NCSU, where the increase is significant at the 5-percent level.

Source: Authors' calculations; see text.

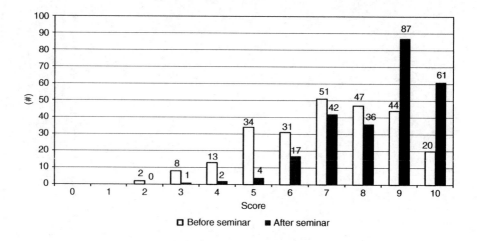

Figure 3.1 Knowledge score before and after seminar. *Source*: Authors' calculations; see text.

than the older participants and virtually eliminated the age difference in knowledge observed prior to the program. Women had larger gains in knowledge than men but still had a lower knowledge score after the program. Interestingly, people with lower self-assessed knowledge scores prior to the seminar had a much larger gain in mean scores, than those with a higher initial self-assessed level of knowledge (1.61 compared to 1.06). This is another indication that the programs were beneficial to those with relatively little knowledge of their retirement plans. Improvements in knowledge scores for the entire sample and for each of the various demographic characteristics are statistically significant.

Next we attempt to determine differences in initial knowledge and learning by estimating multivariate regressions that appear in Table 3.4. The first two columns have as a dependent variable the number of correct answers out of the 10 questions shown in Table 3.2.[7] Not surprisingly, the first column indicates that, prior to the seminar, older workers (presumably closer to retirement) are more knowledgeable, as are men and the more educated. When measures of earnings and wealth are included in the regression, we find that high earners are more knowledgeable and that the male coefficient is no longer significantly different from zero. Similar results are found in the regression indicating the level of knowledge post-seminar. The only statistically different coefficient between the before and after regressions is age, which is not statistically significant in the prediction of knowledge after the seminar.

(A)

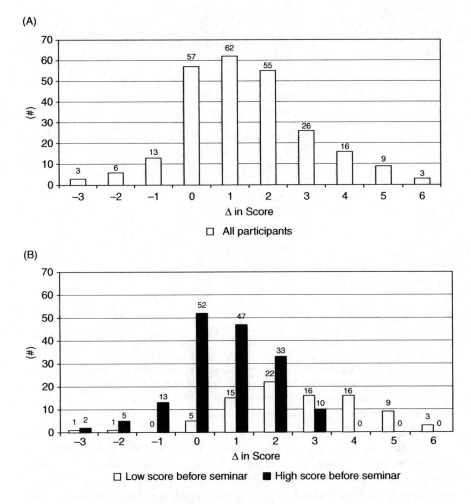

(B)

Figure 3.2 Change in knowledge score before and after seminar. Panel A: All participants. Panel B: Arrayed by knowledge before seminar. *Notes*: Low scores were 6 or below; high scores were 7 or more. *Source*: Authors' calculations; see text.

Did greater knowledge change retirement plans?

Next we ask whether more knowledge is likely to translate into planned behavior change. In particular, we examine the age of planned retirement from the current employer, as well as plans to start Social Security benefits, work after retirement from the current employer, desires to annuitize account balances in supplemental retirement plans, and expectations

TABLE 3.3 Participant index of knowledge before and after seminar

Participant characteristics	Categories	Before seminar[a]	After seminar[a]	Difference
Full sample		7.06	8.44	1.38
Age	50–58	6.86	8.40	1.54
	59–65	7.37	8.50	1.13
Sex	Male	7.34	8.61	1.27
	Female	6.50	8.11	1.61
Education	HS or less	6.00	7.41	1.41
	Some college	7.18	8.56	1.38
Earnings	≤$50,000	6.34	7.88	1.54
	>$50,000	7.34	8.68	1.34
Years of service	≤20	6.86	8.38	1.52
	>20	7.15	8.46	1.31
Self-assessed knowledge	1–4	6.56	8.17	1.61
	5–7	7.70	8.76	1.06
Years from planned retirement	<5	7.48	8.69	1.21
	≥5	6.48	8.10	1.62

[a] Columns indicate the mean number of questions answered by the participants in each category. Sample sizes may vary for particular rows due to missing information on some characteristics. All differences are statistically significant at the 1-percent level.

Note: The number of observations with a valid index is 249.

Source: Authors' calculation; see text.

concerning lump-sum distributions from DB plans. Table 3.5 reports pre- and post-seminar estimates, where we see that mean and median responses to expected retirement age and age for starting Social Security benefits are unchanged by the program. Interestingly, there is a 10 percentage point increase in the proportion of employees planning to work after retiring from their current employer. Prior to the seminar, there was considerable uncertainty concerning whether to annuitize account balances in supplemental retirement plans or to take lump-sum distributions from the DB plans, with about half the respondents indicating that they had not yet decided on these options. Before the seminar, only 16.9 percent of the sample planned to annuitize some or all of their supplement plan funds; this increased to 26.6 percent after the seminar, with the proportion that had not decided declining by roughly the same 10 percentage points. Nevertheless, almost half of the participants were still undecided on annuitization. Nearly one-third of the employees planned to take a lump-sum distribution prior to the program; afterward, this percentage increased slightly. Once again, almost half of the participants were undecided on the choice of a lump sum. This implies that

TABLE 3.4 Estimated coefficients from multivariate OLS knowledge equation: before and after seminar

	Knowledge score before		Knowledge score after	
	(1)	(2)	(3)	(4)
Age	0.100	0.126	0.021	0.029
	(0.034)**	(0.036) **	(0.025)	(0.026)
Male	0.716	0.297	0.521	0.341
	(0.281) *	(0.323)	(0.203) *	(0.234)
Married	0.014	−0.078	−0.063	−0.266
	(0.321)	(0.331)	(0.232)	(0.240)
Tenure	0.010	0.010	0.010	0.006
	(0.014)	(0.015)	(0.010)	(0.011)
Some college	1.003	0.932	0.971	0.803
	(0.373) **	(0.388) *	(0.270) **	(0.281) **
Medium earnings		0.552		0.733
		(0.467)		(0.338)*
High earnings		1.110		0.951
		(0.505) *		(0.366) **
Medium 401(k) account balance		0.400		0.584
		(0.511)		(0.370)
High 401(k) account balance		0.492		0.670
		(0.603)		(0.436)
Number of observations	249	239	249	239
R-square	0.13	0.15	0.19	0.22

* Implies significance at the 5-percent level.
** Implies significance at the 1-percent level.

Notes: The coefficients are from a regression with the dependent variable being the knowledge index. The knowledge index indicates the number of questions out of 10 that the participant answered correctly. Each of the equations includes dichotomous variables indicating the employer of the participant. Standard errors are in parentheses. Note that all specifications include company fixed effects and a constant term. Comparing across the corresponding columns, Column (1) versus (3) and Column (2) versus (4), only the coefficients on age and the company fixed effects are significantly different.

Source: Authors' calculations; see text.

only about one-quarter of these employees were certain that they want to receive a lifetime benefit from their DB plan.

Table 3.6 presents the results of models examining planned retirement ages, before and after the seminar. The first two columns report Survey One estimates, while the next two focus on Survey Two. Prior to the seminar, the age of planned retirement was significantly higher for older employees and lower for those with more years of tenure, no doubt reflec-

TABLE 3.5 Respondent retirement plans: before and after seminar

	Before seminar	After seminar
Median planned retirement age (years)	62.0	62.0
Mean planned retirement age (years)	62.0	62.2
Median social security receipt age (years)	64.0	63.0
Mean social security receipt age (years)	63.9	64.1
Work after retirement (%)	46.6	56.9
Undecided on working after retirement (%)	30.9	21.5
Intend to annuitize DC plan (%)	16.9	26.6
Undecided on annuitization of DC plan (%)	56.9	46.0
Intend to take lump-sum pension (%)	30.5	31.3
Undecided on lump-sum pension (%)	49.8	46.1

Note: 24.4 percent of respondents changed their planned retirement age and 30.9 percent of respondents changed their planned age to start receiving social security benefits.
Source: Authors' calculations; see text.

tive of sample selection: those who had wanted to retire early have already done so. The tenure effect, once controlling for age, is a proxy for pension wealth from the DB plans offered by all of the employers; variation across the employers is captured by employer dichotomous variables included in the regression. Adding earnings and 401(k) account balances to the regression does not affect the size or significance of these effects. Estimated coefficients are similar in the post-seminar equation as the age and tenure effects remain significant and have only small changes in magnitude.

The relationship between knowledge and retirement plans is complex and depends on the direction of knowledge errors. For example, some employees believe that they can start employer retirement benefits or Social Security benefits, or are covered by Medicare at younger ages than is realistic. On learning that their expectations are wrong and benefit receipt must be delayed, these employees are now likely to plan to retire at an older age. In this way, an improvement in knowledge leads to later retirement. But conversely, if an employee believed that benefits were only available at older ages, learning that he or she could retire younger may lead to earlier retirement. In this way, an improvement in knowledge would lower the planned retirement age. Further research is needed to disentangle these two effects.

Assessment of the programs by participants

Employers who offer these programs as an employee benefit are naturally seeking to ensure that these programs are effective and valued by employ-

TABLE 3.6 Estimated coefficients from multivariate OLS from planned age of retirement equation: before and after seminar

	Planned retirement age before seminar		Planned retirement age after seminar	
	(1)	(2)	(3)	(4)
Age	0.540	0.540	0.507	0.497
	(0.056) * *	(0.061) * *	(0.059) * *	(0.062) * *
Male	−0.249	−0.179	0.194	0.267
	(0.457)	(0.539)	(0.474)	(0.565)
Married	−0.707	−0.577	−0.878	−0.953
	(0.529)	(0.559)	(0.555)	(0.587)
Tenure	−0.071	−0.075	−0.066	−0.067
	(0.022) * *	(0.024) * *	(0.024) *	(0.026) *
Some college	−0.902	−0.743	−1.437	−1.433
	(0.775)	(0.812)	(0.814)+	(0.854)+
Knowledge score (before/after)	−0.294	−0.237	−0.457	−0.485
	(0.114) *	(0.121) *	(0.165) * *	(0.177) * *
Medium earnings		−0.128		1.121
		(0.774)		(0.824)
High earnings		−0.597		0.515
		(0.875)		(0.925)
Medium 401(k) account balance		−0.233		−0.356
		(0.809)		(0.853)
High 401(k) account balance		−0.087		−0.723
		(0.996)		(1.050)
Number of observations	172	165	172	165
R-square	0.45	0.46	0.45	0.47

* Implies significance at the 5-percent level.
* * Implies significance at the 1-percent level.

Notes: The dependent variable is the planned retirement age before and after the seminar. The knowledge index indicates the number of questions out of 10 the participant answered correctly. Each of the equations includes dichotomous variables indicating the employer of the participant. Standard errors are in parentheses. All specifications include company fixed effects and a constant term.

Source: Authors' calculation; see text.

TABLE 3.7 Participant evaluation of program

Question	Responses (%)
The program provided all or most of the information needed for retirement	96.8
Overall very good or excellent program	92.8
Overall very good or excellent presenters and program leaders	96.4
Will be able to make better choices	88.3
Plan to change some retirement plans because of program	80.2
Participation raised awareness of benefits provided	77.2

Note: Responses indicate the percentage of participants giving the specific answer to questions about the seminar.
Source: Authors' calculations; see text.

ees. Table 3.7 indicates that program participants had a very positive experience and believed that the seminars were helpful; some 97 percent of respondents stated that the programs provided all or most of the information needed for them to make important retirement decisions. Ninety-three percent rated the programs as very good or excellent, and 96 percent found the presenters and program leaders to be very good or excellent. Finally, 88 percent of employees believed that they would be able to make better retirement choices after participating in the seminar. Importantly, for companies considering whether to provide such programs to their employees, 77 percent of individuals reported that the programs raised their awareness of the benefits provided by their employers. Accordingly, participants gave high marks to the quality of the programs, believing that the programs provided the information they needed, and gave their employers credit for offering these programs.

Conclusion

Many older workers have a rather low level of financial literacy and understanding of their retirement programs. Limited or inaccurate information may lead them to make poor retirement decisions, undermining their ability to achieve retirement income adequacy. Our project has examined how preretirement planning programs offered by five large employers changes employee perspectives. The analysis reveals that program participants increased their financial knowledge, changed their retirement plans, and decided to handle their retirement money differently. Participants also expressed satisfaction with the quality of the programs and credited their employers for offering the seminars.

The results of this study should provide encouragement to employers considering whether to adopt preretirement planning programs. Based on our assessment of this initial data, employer-provided financial education programs can increase employee knowledge of retirement programs and assist them in making better retirement choices. In future work, we will seek to develop a template for evaluating these programs so that other employers can monitor and improve their own offerings.

Acknowledgments

We would like to thank Kristin Bunn, Michael Qingliang Fan, Qi Guo, Myongju Kim, Mehtab Randhawa, Ruirui Sun, and Jinjing Wang for excellent research assistance. We appreciate the cooperation and support of each of our employer partners, the seminar presenters, and the participants. This research is funded by a grant from the FINRA Investor Education Foundation and has been conducted in close collaboration with the employer partners who sponsor the preretirement benefit programs examined in this research.

Appendix 3A Employer Characteristics and Overview of Survey Responses

This appendix briefly describes each of the five employers, their retirement benefits, and their preretirement planning programs for retirement-eligible employees. Mean responses from key survey questions for each employer are discussed; tables of full results by employer are available upon request. This information provides an overview of the type of workers included in the analysis and their employers. In comparing these results to other studies of financial knowledge and the impact of financial education programs, one should remember that all of participants in these seminars work for large employers who offer their employees retirement plans. In general, all employees of a given employer are covered by the same DB pension, thus variation in pension wealth among participants at each employer is due to differences in annual earnings and tenure. Also, participants from an employer are offered the same supplemental saving plan with the same characteristics; however, variation in the account balances in these plans also reflect individual choices to participate, the contribution rate, and the investment allocations of each employee.

Becton, Dickinson, and Company

Becton, Dickinson, and Company (BD) is a global medical technology company. According to their web site, their focus is on 'improving drug delivery, enhancing the diagnosis of infectious diseases and cancers, and advancing drug discovery.' BD develops, manufactures, and sells medical supplies, devices, laboratory instruments, antibodies, reagents, and diagnostic products through its three segments: BD Medical, BD Diagnostics, and BD Biosciences. It serves health-care institutions, life science researchers, clinical laboratories, the pharmaceutical industry, and the general public. BD was founded in 1897 and is headquartered in Franklin Lakes, New Jersey. BD employs approximately 28,000 people in approximately 50 countries throughout the world.

BD converted its traditional DB plan to a cash balance plan in April 2007. The traditional plan was integrated with Social Security and had a formula of 1 percent per year of service for earnings up to the average final covered compensation plus 1.5 percent times years of service times any average excess earnings over the Social Security earnings limit. All employees hired prior to the conversion date were given a choice to remain in the old plan or shift to the new plan. This recent pension choice may have stimulated employees to learn more about their retirement benefits and enhanced financial literacy among BD employees. BD also offers a Saving Income Plan with a company match that was increased from $0.50 per each dollar of employee contribution up to 6 percent of salary prior to 2007 to a match of $0.75 per dollar of employee contributions up to 6 percent of salary. Retirees are eligible to participate in the company health plan, provided they are aged 55 with 10 years of service or 65 with 5 years of service.

BD offers a preretirement planning program that is presented by the Ayco Company. The typical program is 4 hours long and has on average 20 employees attending per session. Thus far, our evaluation tool was used in conjunction with four seminars completed in September 2008. From these programs, we have 69 completed surveys. The median age of the respondents was 58, 64 percent were women, 70 percent were married, 62 percent had a college degree, and more than half had 24 or more years of service. Among these employees, the median annual earnings were between $75,000 and $100,000. All of the participants were enrolled in the Savings Incentive Plan and had a median account balance equal to 3–5 years of salary. In addition, the participants reported a median financial wealth of $100,000–250,000 and 91 percent reported owning their own home with a median equity value of over $200,000. In general, the seminar participants represented middle- and upper-income households who had substantial assets as they approached retirement.

The participants gave the seminar and the presenter high marks for developing and executing a valuable event. Ninety-three percent of respondents indicated that the program included all or most of the information they needed, 99 percent stated that the material was presented at a level that they could understand and incorporate into their retirement planning, and 93 percent rated the program as very good or excellent in terms of increasing their understanding of the retirement decisions they were facing. Eighty-four percent of participants indicated that they could now make better retirement choices and 83 percent stated that they would now change some of their retirement choices. Participants thought the seminar was a valuable benefit, that it enhanced their positive feelings about BD, and that it raised their awareness of the benefits that BD provides.

One key question in evaluating these programs is whether the participants learned. We might expect that an individual's improved understanding of the level of pension benefits should facilitate better retirement planning. To assess the learning acquired during the seminars, the surveys included eight general financial knowledge and Social Security and Medicare questions and two questions specific to BD benefits. By comparing the answers to the 10 questions concerning the BD retirement programs, Social Security, Medicare, and general financial literacy given before the seminar to those after the seminar, we are able to assess whether the respondents substantially increased their knowledge of these issues. In addition, by comparing their before and after responses to planned retirement decisions, we are able to determine if, based on the new knowledge, participants altered their retirement plans.

Virtually, all of the participants correctly answered the two general financial knowledge questions before the seminar. This indicates that BD employees had a much higher level of knowledge compared to the general population (Lusardi and Mitchell 2006). In general, BD workers were fairly knowledgeable of the characteristics of Social Security and Medicare; however, substantial learning did occur. There were large increases in the proportion of participants that correctly answered the questions on the normal retirement age for Social Security (a 21 percentage point increase in correct answers), the age of eligibility for Medicare (an 18 percentage point increase), and the reduction for starting Social Security benefits early (a 33 percentage point increase). The mean number of correct answers increased from 5.5 before the seminar to 6.6 after the seminar.

Prior to the seminar, 56 percent of the sample indicated that they did not know how large their pension benefits would be relative to their final salary. After the seminar, this declined to 31 percent. Based on the information gained during the seminar, individuals were more optimistic with 42 percent stating that they expected to be able to maintain their standard of living in retirement. This is compared to only one-third of the participants prior to the seminar, with nearly an identical number unsure before and after. This increased optimism is reflected in the higher expected income replacement rates reported after the seminar as well.

Median planned ages for retirement from BD (age 62) and starting Social Security benefits (age 65) did not change; however, the proportion of participants who anticipate working after retirement from BD rose from 35 to 50 percent. An interesting result we find here is that after the seminar, more individuals planned to annuitize funds in the Savings Incentive Plan but more also planned to take a lump-sum distribution from their pension.

North Carolina State University

With more than 31,000 students and nearly 8,000 faculty and staff, North Carolina State University (NC State) is a comprehensive, public land-grant university. NC State is located in Raleigh, NC. Faculty and staff of NC State are employees of the state of North Carolina and are eligible to participate in Teachers' and State Employees' Retirement plan (TSERs). The benefit formula is 1.82 percent of average salary during the employee's 4 consecutive highest-paid years of employment times years of service. Faculty also have the option of enrolling in an Optional Retirement Plan (a DC plan) instead of the state plan; however, the seminar was restricted to employees enrolled in TSERs. The university offers employees several supplemental retirement plans (401(k), 457, and 403(b) plans), but does not provide any employer match. Retirees are eligible to remain in the state health plan after retirement without any retiree premium as long as they are receiving a monthly pension benefit. Prior to the start of this project, the HR division of NC State offered several short retirement planning programs; however, an all day program was developed in 2008 for employees enrolled in the state retirement plan. In the fall of 2008, two of the daylong preretirement planning programs were offered to participants in TSERs.

The median age of the respondents was 59, 73 percent were women, 60 percent were married, 57 percent had a college degree, and the median tenure was 28 years of service. Among these employees, the median annual earnings were $25,000–50,000. In addition to being covered by the state DB plan, 67 percent of participants had established a 403(b) or 457 accounts; however, these balances tended to be relatively small with the median account balance averaging less than 1 year of salary. Most of these employees made annual contributions but they were less than the maximum contribution allowed. The participants had a median financial wealth of between $50,000 and $75,000 and 87 percent reported owning their own home with a median equity value of between $100,000 and $150,000. In general, the seminar participants represented middle-income households in NC.

The participants reported strong approval of the seminar and the presenters. Ninety-eight percent of respondents indicated that the program included all or most of the information they needed, 100 percent stated that the material was presented at a level that they could understand and that they could incorporate into their retirement planning, and 95 percent rated the program as very good or excellent in terms of increasing their understanding of the retirement decision they were facing. All of the participants indicated that they were better informed about their retirement programs, 88 percent thought that they could now make better retirement choices, and 67 percent stated that they would now change some of their retirement plans. Participants thought the seminar was a valuable employee benefit, that it enhanced their positive feelings about NC State, and that it raised their awareness of the benefits that the university provides.

Did the participants learn? The survey responses show that 76–87 percent of the participants correctly answered the general financial knowledge questions before the seminar. In general, many of these employees lack basic knowledge of the characteristics of Social Security and Medicare; however, substantial learning did occur. There were large increases in the proportion of participants that correctly answered the questions on the normal retirement age for Social Security (a 23 percentage point increase in correct answers), the age of eligibility for Medicare (a 29 percentage point increase), and the reduction for starting Social Security benefits early (a 13 percentage point increase). The mean number of correct answers increased from 4.5 before the seminar to 5.7 after the seminar.

Prior to the seminar, 27 percent of the sample indicated that they did not know how large their pension benefits would be relative to their final salary. After the seminar, this declined to 3 percent. Based on the information gained during the seminar, individuals were more optimistic with 50 percent stating that they expected to be able to maintain their standard of living in retirement compared to only 37 percent of the participants prior to the seminar. Planned ages for retirement from NC State (age 56) and starting Social Security benefits (age 62 before, 63 after) changed only slightly; however, the proportion of participants who anticipate working after retirement from NC State rose from 67 to 83 percent. Interestingly, there was a drop in the proportion of participants planning to take a lump-sum distribution from the state pension while there was an increase in those planning to annuitize some of the 403(b) or 457 account balances.

Progress Energy

Progress Energy is a Fortune 250 energy company with more than 21,000 megawatts of generation capacity, $9 billion in annual revenues, and over

10,000 employees. The company has a cash balance pension plan that was established in 1998 for all new employees. Employees hired before the conversion were previously in a traditional DB plan. They were moved to the cash balance and provided conversion credits from the old plan. The company also offers active employees a 401(k) plan with an employer match, health insurance, and they allow retirees to remain in the company health plan.

For some years, this employer has provided daylong seminars to its retirement-eligible employees. The programs are conducted by company personnel; however, several outside experts and representatives are used to augment the program. Retirement-eligible employees are invited to attend the program; however, employees can attend a preretirement planning program only once every 5 years. Each year, the company offers a series of programs at various sites between July and September. In 2008, our survey was incorporated into all 15 programs offered by the company covering 201 employees participating in nine different locations. From all of the seminars, we received a total of 157 completed surveys for a response rate of 78 percent. Fifty of the participants provided contact information and indicated that they would be willing to complete Survey Three.

The median age of the respondents was 57, 84 percent were men, 85 percent were married, 56 percent had a college degree, and more than half had 30 or more years of service. Among these employees, their median annual earnings were between $75,000 and $100,000. Virtually, all of the participants had established a 401(k) account with a median account balance of between 3 and 5 years of salary. In addition, participants reported other savings and financial assets worth between $50,000 and $75,000 and 96 percent reported owning their own home with a median equity value of between $100,000 and $150,000. In general, the seminar participants represented middle-and upper-income households who had substantial assets as they approached retirement.

The participants strongly endorsed the seminars and presenters. Ninety-eight percent of respondents indicated that the program included all or most of the information they needed, 98 percent stated that the material was presented at a level that they could understand and that they could incorporate into their retirement planning, and 91 percent rated the program as very good or excellent in terms of increasing their understanding of the retirement decision they were facing. Seventy percent of the participants indicated that they were better informed about their retirement programs, 91 percent thought that they could now make better retirement choices, and 80 percent stated that they would now change some of their retirement choices. Participants thought the seminar was a valuable employee benefit, that it enhanced their positive feelings about the company, and that it raised their awareness of the benefits that the company provides.

Did the participants learn? The survey responses show that 88–96 percent of the participants correctly answered the general financial knowledge questions before the seminar. Prior to the seminar, many of these employees lacked basic knowledge of the characteristics of Social Security and Medicare; however, substantial learning did occur. There were large increases in the proportion of participants that correctly answered the questions on the normal retirement age for Social Security (a 21 percentage point increase in correct answers), the age of eligibility for Medicare (a 13 percentage point increase), and the reduction for starting Social Security benefits early (an 18 percentage point increase). The mean number of correct answers increased from 5.4 before the seminar to 6.3 after the seminar.

Prior to the seminar, 55 percent of the sample indicated that they did not know how large their pension benefits would be relative to their final salary. After the seminar, this declined to 33 percent. Based on the information gained during the seminar, individuals were more optimistic with 43 percent stating that they expected to be able to maintain their standard of living in retirement compared to only 37 percent of the participants prior to the seminar. Planned ages for retirement from the company (age 62) and starting Social Security benefits (age 62) did not change; however, the proportion of participants who anticipated working after retirement from the company rose from 50 to 59 percent. There was a small increase in the proportion of participants planning to take a lump-sum distribution from the cash balance plan and a similar increase in those planning to annuitize some of the 401(k) account balances.

Weyerhaeuser

Weyerhaeuser is one of the world's largest forest products companies. They have offices or operations in 13 countries and have customers worldwide. As of December 31, 2007, Weyerhaeuser had 37,900 employees, primarily in the United States and Canada. They employ a variety of workers, from scientists, engineers, architects, and financial specialists to forestry, trade, and craft workers. Weyerhaeuser offers a DB pension plan that is integrated with Social Security. The benefit formula is 1.1 percent times final average salary time years of service plus 0.45 percent times excess earnings over the Social Security integration level times years of service. Weyerhaeuser also offers retirees the opportunity to remain in the company medical plan. The company offers a 401(k) plan with a $0.70 company match for each dollar of employee contributions up to 7 percent of salary. Weyerhaeuser has offered a preretirement planning program for a number of years. The company offers 2.5-day programs that are conducted by Weyerhaeuser personnel with outside experts used to complement the program. Programs are offered monthly. Our surveys have been incorporated into five seminars completed in 2008.

The median age of the respondents was 57, 35 percent were female, 81 percent were married, 79 percent had a college degree, and the median tenure was 23 years of service. Among these employees, their median annual earnings were between $100,000 and $150,000. All of the participants had established a 401(k) account with a median account balance of between 3 and 5 years of salary and all were included in the company pension plan. In addition, they reported other savings and financial assets worth between $100,000 and $250,000, and 96 percent reported owning their own home with a median equity value of over $200,000. In general, the seminar participants represented middle-and upper-income households who had substantial assets as they approached retirement.

The participants gave the seminar and presenters high marks for developing and presenting a valuable event. Ninety-nine percent of respondents indicated that the program included all or most of the information they needed, 99 percent stated that the material was presented at a level that they could understand and that they could incorporate into their retirement planning, and 96 percent rated the program as very good or excellent in terms of increasing their understanding of the retirement decisions they were facing. All of the participants indicated that they were better informed about their retirement programs, 99 percent thought that they could now make better retirement choices, and 88 percent stated that they would now change some of their retirement choices. Participants thought the seminar was a valuable employee benefit, that it enhanced their positive feelings about Weyerhaeuser, and that it raised their awareness of the benefits that Weyerhaeuser provides.

Did the participants learn? Survey responses show that 92 to 100 percent of the participants correctly answered the general financial knowledge questions before the seminar. Prior to the seminar, many of these employees lacked basic knowledge of the characteristics of Social Security and Medicare; however, substantial learning did occur. There were large increases in the proportion of participants that correctly answered the questions on the normal retirement age for Social Security (a 25 percentage point increase in correct answers), the age of eligibility for Medicare (a 3 percentage point increase), and the reduction for starting Social Security benefits early (a 37 percentage point increase). The mean number of correct answers increased from 5.8 before the seminar to 7.5 after the seminar.

Prior to the seminar, 24 percent of the sample indicated that they did not know how large their pension benefits would be relative to their final salary. After the seminar, this declined to 9 percent. Based on the information gained during the seminar, individuals were more optimistic with 53 percent stating that they expected to be able to maintain their standard of living in retirement compared to only 47 percent of the participants prior to the seminar. Planned ages for retirement from Weyerhaeuser (age 60 before, 62 after) increased but the age for starting Social Security benefits (age 65 before, 63 after) declined. The proportion of participants who anticipated working after retirement from Weyerhaeuser rose slightly from 53 to 60 percent. There was a small increase in the proportion of participants planning to take a lump-sum distribution from the cash balance plan and a similar increase in those planning to annuitize some of their 401(k) account balances.

The Williams Companies, Inc.

Williams is an integrated natural gas company that produces, gathers, processes, and transports natural gas to heat homes and power electric generation across the country. The company operates approximately 14,600 miles of interstate natural gas pipeline with a capacity of more than 11 billion cubic feet per day. Williams transports enough gas to heat 30 million homes on a winter day and delivers approximately 12 percent of the natural gas consumed in the United States. Prior to the start of this project, Williams did not offer a formal preretirement planning program. To assess the desire of their employees for such a program, Williams allowed us to survey all of their retirement-eligible population. There was overwhelming support by their employees for a more comprehensive program. The findings from this survey are reported in Clark, Morrill, and Allen (2009). As a result, the HR staff developed a daylong program and their first seminars were offered in November and December 2008. Our surveys were used to evaluate these initial programs.

Williams offers a cash balance pension plan to its employees with company credits as a percentage of compensation rising with age. Company contributions are greater on pay exceeding the Social Security taxable wage base. As such, the account balances are reported in a lump sum and not as a monthly benefit. Employees are eligible to participate in the Williams Investment Plus Plan, a 401(k) plan, and Williams matches employee contributions dollar for dollar up to 6 percent of salary. Retirees are eligible to remain in the company health plan.

The median age of the respondents was 57, 47 percent were women, 69 percent were married, 78 percent had a college degree, and the median years of service was 10 years. Among these employees, their median annual earnings were between $100,000 and $150,000. All of the participants had established a 401(k) account with a median account balance of between 1 and 2 years of salary. In addition, they reported other savings and financial assets worth between $100,000 and $150,000, and 94 percent reported owning their own home with a median equity value of between $100,000 and $150,000. In general, the seminar participants represented middle- and upper-income households, who had substantial assets as they approached retirement.

Even though the program was brand new, the participants gave very complimentary evaluations of the seminar and presenters. Ninety-one percent of respondents indicated that the program included all or most of the information they needed, 100 percent stated that the material was presented at a level that they could understand and that they could incorporate into their retirement planning, and 86 percent rated the program as very good or excellent in terms of increasing their understanding of the retirement decisions they were facing. Ninety-eight percent of the participants indicated that they were better informed about their retirement programs, 79 percent thought that they could now make better retirement choices, and 77 percent stated that they would now change some of their retirement choices. Participants thought the seminar was a valuable employee benefit, that it enhanced their positive feelings about Williams, and that it raised their awareness of the benefits that Williams provides.

Did the participants learn? Survey responses show that 96–98 percent of the participants correctly answered the general financial knowledge questions before the seminar. Prior to the seminar, many of these employees lacked basic knowledge of the characteristics of Social Security and Medicare; however, substantial learning did occur. There were large increases in the proportion of participants that correctly answered the questions on the normal retirement age for Social Security (a 22 percentage point increase in correct answers), the age of eligibility for Medicare (an 8 percentage point increase), and the reduction for starting Social Security benefits early (an 18 percentage point increase). The mean number of correct answers increased from 5.3 before the seminar to 6.3 after the seminar.

Prior to the seminar, 45 percent of the sample indicated that they did not know how large their pension benefits would be relative to their final salary. After the seminar, this declined to 29 percent. Based on the information gained during the seminar, individuals were more optimistic with 43 percent stating that they expected to be able to maintain their standard of living in retirement compared to only 29 percent of the participants prior to the seminar. Planned ages for retirement from Williams (age 64 before, 65 after) increased slightly but the age for starting Social Security benefits (age 66) did not change. The proportion of participants who anticipated working after retirement from Williams rose from 35 to 55 percent. There was an increase in the proportion of participants planning to take a lump-sum distribution from their plan and a larger increase in those planning to annuitize some of the 401(k) account balances (see Table 3.A1).

TABLE 3A.1 Seminars and participants in 2008

Employer	Number of employer seminars[a]	Number of participants with valid birth year[b]	Number of participants with valid knowledge scores[c]
BD	4	69	50
NCSU	2	30	14
PE	15	170	95
WEY	5	77	48
WEL	2	49	42
Total	28	395	249

[a] This column indicates the number of seminars held by each employer during 2008, which incorporated our surveys into the program.
[b] This column indicates the number of participants at each company born between 1943 and 1959; the ages included in our analysis.
[c] This column indicates the number of completed surveys where the participants answered all of the financial literacy and retirement program questions.
Note: For employer code, see Table 3.2.
Source: Authors' calculations; see text.

Notes

[1] In addition to these employer partners, we are also examining the financial education programs for older employees at Branch Banking and Trust (BB&T), WakeMed, a large national insurance company, and a large western public university.
[2] The programs offered by Weyerhaeuser, Progress Energy, and BD have been presented over a number of years. In contrast, the programs by North Carolina State and Williams are relatively new and thus a full cycle of retirees has not had a chance to attend one of the programs.
[3] Copies of the questionnaires are available from the authors upon request.
[4] As part of the long-range objectives of this research project, seminar participants will be sent a third survey in approximately 1 year to determine whether the learning achieved at the seminar has been retained and how their retirement plans have unfolded.
[5] The age restriction was applied to limit the sample to individuals approaching retirement decisions. Most of the employers only invite retirement-eligible employees to these programs so, in fact, this results in only a few seminar participants being deleted from the sample. The upper age limit was applied to limit the sample to those who had not yet attained the normal retirement age for Social Security. In addition, we felt that workers over age 65 had already made the decision to delay retirement and that they would most likely have very different responses to these programs than workers aged 50 to 65.

[6] Appendix 3A provides information on each of the five employers, their retirement plans, their financial education programs, and the responses of their older workers to the survey.

[7] Dichotomous variables for the employers are also included in each of these regressions.

References

Bernheim, Douglas (1995). 'Do Households Appreciate Their Financial Vulnerabilities? An Analysis of Actions, Perceptions, and Public Policy,' in *Tax Policy and Economic Growth*. Washington, DC: American Council for Capital Formation, pp. 1–30.

—— (1998). 'Financial Illiteracy, Education and Retirement Saving,' in O.S. Mitchell and S. Schieber, eds., *Living with Defined Contribution Pensions*. Philadelphia, PA: University of Pennsylvania Press, pp. 38–68.

Clark, Robert and Madeleine d'Ambrosio (2003). 'Ignorance Is Not Bliss: The Importance of Financial Education,' *TIAA-CREF Research Dialogue 78*. New York: TIAA-CREF Institute.

———— Ann McDermed, and Kshama Sawant (2006). 'Retirement Plans and Saving Decisions: The Role of Information and Education,' *Journal of Pension Economics and Finance*, 5–1: 45–67.

Clark, Robert, Melinda Morrill, and Steven Allen (2009). 'The Role of Financial Literacy and Knowledge in Determining Retirement Plans,' Forthcoming Working Paper. Raleigh, NC: North Carolina State University.

Hilgert, Marianne and Jeanne Hogarth (2002). 'Financial Knowledge, Experience and Learning Preferences: Preliminary Results from a New Survey on Financial Literacy,' *Consumer Interest Annual*, 48.

Lusardi, Annamaria (ed.) (2008). *Overcoming the Saving Slump: How to Increase the Effectiveness of Financial Education and Saving Programs*. Chicago, IL: University of Chicago Press.

—— and Olivia Mitchell (2006). 'Financial Literacy and Planning: Implications for Retirement Wellbeing,' MRRC Working Paper No. 2007-157. Ann Arbor, MI: Michigan Retirement and Research Center.

———— (2007). 'Baby Boomer Retirement Security: The Roles of Planning, Financial Literacy, and Housing Wealth,' *Journal of Monetary Economics*, 54: 205–24.

Sabelhaus, John, Michael Brogdan, and Sarah Holden (2008). *Defined Contribution Plan Distribution Choices at Retirement: A Survey of Employees Retiring Between 2002 and 2007*. Washington, DC: Investment Company Institute. http://www.ici.org/pdf/rpt_08_dcdd.pdf

Wray, David (2008). 'Testimony Before the ERISA Advisory Council Working Group on Spend Down of Defined Contribution Plan Assets at Retirement.' Chicago, IL, July 16.

United States Government Accountability Office (USGAO) (2007). *Federal Policies Offer Mixed Signals on When to Retire*. Washington, DC: USGAO.

Chapter 4

How Does Retirement Planning Software Handle Postretirement Realities?

Anna M. Rappaport and John A. Turner

Good retirement planning and management requires building assets and deploying them well over a period of years. In the postretirement period, there are many potential risks requiring that assets be used to generate income under a range of uncertain outcomes. Retirement planning software offers individuals and advisors the opportunity to perform a range of calculations to help them in retirement planning. In this chapter, we first offer an overview of postretirement risks, including information on how they are perceived and understood by the public. Next we provide insights into how retirement planning software assists individuals and their advisors in evaluating these risks.[1]

The risks of retirement

A 2008 Society of Actuaries (SOA) study (2008c) identifies and describes 15 postretirement risks that span financial risks, changes in family status and needs, changes in housing needs, policy changes, and risks from bad advice, theft, and fraud. In this chapter, we focus on major financial risks, in as much as these are the risks analyzed by planning software. Over the period 2001–7, the evidence presented in the SOA study shows that pre-retirees have consistently been more concerned about risk than retirees. Furthermore, retirees have shown relatively little change in the level of concern about risk over the four risk surveys. By contrast, preretirees indicated growing concern from 2001 to 2003, but levels dropped back to 2001 levels by 2007. Rising concerns between 2001 and 2003 are believed to reflect a combination of the terrorist event in September 2001 as well as poor market conditions during that period (SOA 2008c). Top risk concerns over the full period include inflation as well as health and long-term care costs. Longevity is seen as a major risk concern by experts. These risks are discussed below.

Longevity risk

There are two sides to longevity risk: the problem of outliving one's assets and the problem of dying early and not providing adequately for dependent family members. Longevity can be predicted quite accurately in the aggregate for a group of people, but it is impossible to predict accurately for an individual. Table 4.1 shows the probability that one or both members of a couple, both of whom are initially aged 65, will live to ages 80, 90, and 100. Public attitudinal research shows that many people underestimate longevity risk – 40 percent underestimate population life expectancy by 5 years or more, and another 20 percent by 1–4 years (Cowell and Rappaport 2006).

Family history and own health are the key factors used by retirees and those near retirement in estimating personal life expectancy, accounting for over 80 percent of the top considerations (Cowell and Rappaport 2006). It appears unlikely that most people understand the variability of longevity and have evaluated options for managing this risk. Some options include investment strategies that preserve principal, payout annuities with income guaranteed for the life of the survivor, and longer-term payouts without lifetime guarantees. The choice of a strategy for managing the payout period involves trade-offs between more versus less income, lifetime guarantees, availability of a bequest, and control of assets (Rappaport 2008). For lower- and lower-middle-income retirees, deferring retirement

TABLE 4.1   Probability of survival (%) from age 65 to 80, 90, and 100: status quo projections

	Female	Male	Both	One only
Panel 1: Probability of survival from age 65 in 2005				
To age 80	75.30	64.70	48.70	91.30
To age 90	37.00	23.50	8.70	51.80
To age 100	4.20	1.50	0.10	5.60
Panel 2: Probability of survival from age 65 in 2025				
To age 80	78.00	71.80	56.00	93.80
To age 90	41.20	29.80	12.30	58.70
To age 100	5.00	2.00	0.10	6.90
Panel 3: Probability of survival from age 65 in 2045				
To age 80	80.40	77.80	62.60	95.60
To age 90	45.30	36.20	16.40	65.10
To age 100	5.70	2.50	0.10	8.10

Note: Calculations are based on UP 1994 Tables projected.
Source: Cowell and Rappaport (2006:16).

and receipt of Social Security benefits is the most available strategy. The strategies that retirees cited as most common for managing longevity risk were elimination of consumer debt, paying off mortgages, trying to save as much as possible, and cutting back on spending (Cowell and Rappaport 2006). Most try to manage this risk themselves rather than insuring it (Cowell and Rappaport 2006). It appears that many individuals handling their own retirement assets will be unable to manage their resources so as to not outlive them, and financial advisors may not present a full range of options.

Inflation risk

Inflation risk was the top concern of retirees in 2007, with 57 percent very or somewhat concerned about inflation compared to 52 percent concerned about having enough money to pay for a long stay in a nursing home, and 51 percent concerned about having enough money to pay for adequate health care. Among preretirees, the corresponding levels of concern were 63, 63, and 69 percent, respectively (SOA 2008*c*). As with longevity, averages do not tell the story well. The United States experienced double-digit inflation in 1947, 1974, and 1979–81 (SOA 2008*b*).

Understanding and managing inflation risk requires better long-term thinking and understanding of the time value of money than many retirees have. Focus groups conducted with retirees having at least $100,000 of assets to manage indicated that many of them had a shorter-term focus, and did not factor in inflation, market volatility, or longevity risk when deciding if they could afford to retire (Greenwald, Bryck, and Sondergeld 2006: 6). Questions included in the 2004 Health and Retirement Study show very low levels of financial literacy among individuals at retirement ages. Only 18 percent of baby boomers were able to answer the following question correctly: 'Let's say you have 200 dollars in a savings account. The account earns 10 percent interest per year. How much would you have at the end of two years?' (Lusardi and Mitchell 2007).

Delaying receipt of Social Security benefits is a relatively easy way to increase inflation-indexed monthly income benefits, yet more than half of Americans take Social Security at the earliest claiming age. Treasury Inflation-Protected Securities (TIPS) and inflation-indexed annuities are strategies for investing to hedge inflation risk, but neither are commonly used. Many retirees have invested in housing and common stocks, but neither are good hedges against inflation as shown during 2008.

Investment risk

Also important are interest rate risk and stock market risk. Lower interest rates tend to reduce retirement income because workers need to save more to build up assets, retirees earn less income on investments such as certificates of deposit and bonds, reinvested income earns less, and annuities are more expensive when long-term interest rates are low. Stocks offer the potential for significant gain or loss, and have been a major source of investment of defined contribution (DC) plan assets. Experts disagree about the desirability of investing such assets in common stocks, and the lineup of opinions is likely to change after the global financial crisis of 2008 and beyond. In any event, individuals tend to overestimate future investment returns. One study found that 401(k) participants anticipated a 5-year average return of 10.9 percent from US equities, 8.1 percent returns on corporate bonds, 7.7 percent from money market funds, and 7.6 percent from stable-value funds (Sondergeld and Greenwald 2005: 21).

Research by the John Hancock Life Insurance Company has shown consistent misunderstanding of the features and characteristics of different investments. For example, when asked what money market funds include, only 9 percent correctly replied that a money market fund includes only short-term investments. Further, respondents believed that the stock of their employer was less risky than a diversified portfolio of stocks, and they did not understand the relationship between changes in interest rates and bond prices (SOA 2008c).

Health care and long-term costs

Paying for health and long-term care are consistently identified as top retirement risk concerns. It is interesting that these are ranked similarly, despite the fact that after age 65, Medicare pays for a substantial part of acute health care while there is no universal program to pay for long-term care services. Costs of both health care and medical care also vary greatly across individuals, with a few users accounting for a great deal of the cost.

Long-term care is a serious issue. As shown in Table 4.2, men aged 65 and older can expect to spend 1.5 years with mild or moderate disability on average, and 1.5 years with severe disability. For women, the anticipated periods of disability are 3.0 and 2.8 years. Most long-term care is provided by family members or friends at home, but long-term care may also be provided by paid caregivers at home, in nursing homes, in continuing care retirement communities, in assisted living facilities, and at adult care centers. For those with virtually no assets, Medicaid is a primary source of financing long-term care. Privately purchased long-term care insurance and private saving provide advance financing for the better-off. Relatively

TABLE 4.2 Expected periods of long-term care need and expected costs for long-term care

Age	All	Healthy	Mild/moderate disability	Severe disability
Panel 1: Remaining life expectancy in years by age, sex, and disability status				
Male 65	15.3	12.3	1.5	1.5
85	5.7	2.9	1.0	1.8
Female 65	19.4	13.6	3.0	2.8
85	7.2	2.5	1.7	3.0
Panel 2: Estimated average lifetime costs of long-term care ($2,000)				
	All[a]	Users of long-term care services[b]		
Male	29,000	127,000		
Female	82,000	158,000		

[a] 92% of these amounts are expected to be incurred during periods of severe disability.
[b] Highest lifetime costs average $300,000–750,000.
Source: Derived from SOA (2008*a*: 18, 20, 21).

few buy insurance; however, only 28 percent of retirees say they have purchased long-term care insurance, and 9 percent say they plan to, in the 2007 Risks and Process of Retirement survey (SOA 2008*c*). Seventeen percent of preretirees (age 45 and older) say they have purchased long-term care insurance, and 23 percent say they plan to. This survey provides higher positive responses compared to other sources.

Health care costs are much more likely to be covered by insurance than are long-term care costs. Virtually, all Americans aged 65 and over have Medicare coverage, and many purchase additional supplemental coverage. In the 2007 Risks and Process of Retirement survey, 61 percent of retirees say they have purchased supplemental health insurance or participate in an employer's postretirement health plan, and 14 percent say they plan to obtain coverage (SOA 2008*c*). Twenty-eight percent of preretirees (age 45 and older) indicate they have purchased supplemental health insurance or participate in an employer's health plan; 50 percent say they plan to do so. The most commonly cited strategy to protect against financial health shocks is to maintain healthy habits: 75 percent of retirees say they do this currently, and 23 percent say they plan to; among preretirees, 69 percent say they do now, and 29 percent say they plan to. Of course, as SOA (2008*a*: 8) notes, 'maintaining healthy lifestyle habits is an admirable goal, [but] in light of ... increases in obesity, these high percentages may be more indicative of wishful thinking than tangible action.'

Health spending varies greatly by individual. It has been estimated that 10 percent of the population each year accounts for 60 percent of spending on health services, and the half of the population with the lowest health spending accounts for only 3 percent of health costs. At age 65, the expected present value of lifetime health costs (in excess of Medicare) per couple, where both are aged 65 and excluding long-term care, has been estimated at $225,000 in 2008; these costs are projected to rise to $284,000 by 2020 (SOA 2008a).

Incorporating nonfinancial assets

Housing is an extremely important component of wealth among middle-income Americans. Among households aged 55–64 in the 25th–85th percentiles by wealth, nonfinancial assets accounted for 68–75 percent of their wealth (not including Social Security and defined benefit (DB) pensions; Abkemeier and Hamann 2009). Table 4.3 shows both financial and nonfinancial assets for middle-income individuals (in the 25th–75th percentiles) and the well-off (75th–85th percentiles). For both groups, nonfinancial assets (mainly residential housing) are two to three times as large as financial assets (excluding pensions and Social Security; Abkemeier and Hamann 2009). Despite this, existing planning software is incomplete, in that it usually does not take explicit account of how housing wealth fits

TABLE 4.3 Wealth of middle-income, middle-aged households (age 55–64)

Household type	Number of households (M)	Median annual income ($)	Median net worth ($)	NonFinancial assets ($)	Financial assets ($)	NonFinancial assets as % of net worth
Panel 1: Middle mass household segments (25–75% of all households)						
Married	5.2	75,000	348,000	240,000	108,000	69
Single female	2.5	28,000	111,000	75,000	36,000	68
Single male	1.4	41,000	125,000	89,000	36,000	71
Panel 2: Mass affluent household segments (75–85% of all households)						
Married	1.0	132,000	1,300,000	884,000	416,000	68
Single female	0.5	58,000	415,000	299,000	116,000	72
Single male	0.3	79,000	465,000	349,000	116,000	75

Source: Derived from Abkemeier and Hamann (2009) using 2004 Survey of Consumer Finances.

into retirement planning. Even when it does, housing wealth is handled in very different ways (Sondergeld et al. 2003).

Behavioral finance provides a broader context for understanding that individuals often have incomplete understanding of risks, and that they often do not make decisions that are economically optimal. Retirement planning software could work to combat this situation, but to date, available programs do not appear to have taken due account of this opportunity.

An overview of retirement planning software

Many studies have looked at how much wealth people nearing retirement have, and analysts often disagree over whether these amounts seem adequate or inadequate.[2] Hence it may not be surprising that retirement planning software in the marketplace varies greatly in complexity, sophistication, and number of inputs required. Furthermore, retirement planning challenges differ considerably across income levels. Lower-income individuals tend to have few assets, so they rely primarily on Social Security. For them, the main retirement planning issues are when to stop working, when to take Social Security, and how to limit spending. Middle-income people with longer-term employment records may have employer-sponsored retirement programs, own homes, and must manage their saving so as to not run out of money. This group is unlikely to have financial advice beyond what employers provide at the workplace. And for those in higher-income brackets, people with more assets are still concerned about having adequate retirement income for their desired consumption, but they are also concerned about tax issues and estate planning.

Previous analyses

A small prior literature has analyzed aspects of retirement planning software. For instance, Bodie (2003) examines financial advice provided by retirement planning software available on four major web sites, and concludes that they have a pro-equity (pro-risk) bias. Kotlikoff (2006) evaluated advice provided by four well-known, reputable financial services companies, and he concludes that they all advised dramatic oversaving compared to what workers would need to maintain a constant level of consumption. Dowd, Atherly, and Town (2008) evaluate a dozen retirement planning calculators and conclude that these calculators were weak in their recognition and handling of health costs. In 2003, a joint study by the SOA, Life Insurance and Market Research Association (LIMRA), and the International Foundation for Retirement Education (InFRE) focused on a mix of consumer programs and professional programs, including both programs available for purchase by advisors and proprietary programs for use in a single organization (Sondergeld et al. 2003). And a 2009 SOA and Actuarial Foundation study brought in a mix of web-based and professional programs.

Methodology

Typically, evaluative studies chose a set of programs to provide a sense of the range of outcomes and use case studies with each program, to understand how it operates, what a user would experience, and to compare results.[3] These cases are selected with the aid of financial planners in order to reflect a mix of different situations similar to those encountered in real life.

Types of software

A lot of software is now available over the Internet for free. We group the programs evaluated into those providing advice about investments and portfolios, advice on how much to save for retirement, and advice on managing resources and risks in retirement. Some programs combine two or all three of these capabilities. Programs also differ in their target market (level of household income and complexity of household finances), with some programs intended for households with relatively simple finances, while others can handle fairly complex financial situations. The Internet has revolutionized the transmission of information, including information on retirement planning and risks. A new SOA and Actuarial Foundation study (Turner and Witte forthcoming) is addressing the changing ways that people receive computer-based assistance with retirement income planning.[4] This assistance is no longer limited to stand-alone programs, but now it includes programs at web sites seeking to tailor information to users' self-identified needs. Professional software used by financial planners allows for analysis of complex financial situations encountered by wealthy individuals. The free, web-based software, by comparison, are best viewed as educational tools to help users address major issues in financial planning, rather than for making detailed projections.

Masking or understanding risks

Modeling approaches embodied in these software programs may be deterministic, stochastic, or provide various different scenarios. The earlier SOA/LIMRA/InFRE study concluded that most of the planning tools did not recognize several key postretirement risks; in fact, often the programs mask risks instead of highlighting them. This would be true of the two-thirds of the programs that used a deterministic approach; only one-third used a stochastic approach. In a deterministic model, the program presents a single outcome, without considering other possible outcomes resulting from different circumstances (such as living longer than expected or the stock market performing worse than expected).

Of course, even in a deterministic setting, multiple alternative scenarios may be generated, but a user must take the initiative to do this which may be time consuming and awkward. Turner and Witte (forthcoming) conclude that more programs today are using Monte Carlo techniques to take into account financial market risk, but most programs still use a small number of runs (500 or 1,000), and generally the only parameter that is stochastic is the rate of return on financial markets. Thus, while Monte Carlo techniques do offer additional and valuable information on financial risks, there is room for improvement: multiple scenarios are needed to explore variations in other risks. Only one family of programs examined incorporated stochastic inflation as well as stochastic returns (including returns on bonds), while another program incorporated stochastic life expectancy and rates of return.

How the programs address postretirement risks

This section discusses how the programs evaluated differ in how they handle key aspects of postretirement risk management.

Longevity

Many people underestimate their life expectancies: two-thirds of male preretirees underestimated the life expectancy of the average 65-year-old man, and 42 percent of that group underestimated it by 5 years or more (SOA 2004). Among women, half (54 percent) of preretirees underestimated the life expectancy of the average 65-year-old woman. For this reason, there is a good chance that people will underestimate their own life expectancies if they are asked to supply this information as an input to financial planning software. Accordingly, they may need guidance from the program in estimating their anticipated longevity.

Some of the free consumer-oriented programs supply a life expectancy for the user but do not distinguish differences by sex.[5] Even when they do provide an age and sex-specific life expectancy, they tend not to recognize that about half of the population will live beyond the average life expectancy. Thus, longevity determines the length of one's planning horizon and retirement period, but it is generally not recognized as a risk. One program allows a user to estimate his or her life expectancy based on nine factors: age, gender, marital status, height, weight, blood pressure, alcohol consumption, use of tobacco products, and exercise. By varying the inputs, the user can see how changes in health habits, such as losing weight, could affect life expectancy. The software provides both life expectancy and the age to which the user has a 25 percent probability of survival. This latter is a desirable feature that most programs do not have. Given the importance of longevity in financial planning, this is an area where programs could be improved.

Length of planning horizon

Planning software programs take different approaches when determining the length of the planning period relevant to the user. One ignores life expectancy and calculates expenses to age 95; another assumes that retirement lasts 30 years (ignoring differences in life expectancy between men and women, and assuming that people who retire earlier die earlier). Still another assumes that people live to their 25 percent life expectancy, which is the age at which 25 percent of a birth cohort is still alive. And another permits the user to determine his or her own life expectancy, which then becomes the length of the planning period.

Naturally, if the planning period assumed for the computations is too short, people may be forced to curtail their consumption at older ages. If they have sufficient annuitized income (e.g., Social Security benefits), they may not be too concerned about completely running out of money – though they might run out of financial assets and have insufficient resources to maintain their accustomed level of consumption. If the planning period is set too long, people risk dying with extra resources, having given up opportunities for consumption during their lifetime, but leaving extra bequests to their heirs.

How long the planning horizon is anticipated to be relates to the question of whether people purchase annuities to protect against outliving their assets. In fact, in most developed nations, people rarely have price-indexed annuities other than Social Security. In many countries, those benefits do not provide high replacement rates (except for the low lifetime wage workers). While insurers offer annuity products to generate life income, the products tend to be complex, incorporating different trade-offs including control over investments, liquidity, guarantee of life income, guarantee of minimum returns, and level of bequest. Most existing financial planning software available to the consumer cannot analyze the range of products for providing lifetime payouts nor analyze the purchase of financial products.

Inflation

None of the free consumer programs, and few of the professional programs evaluated, treat inflation as a risk. That is, they assume that inflation is constant over the period analyzed. In the professional programs, a higher inflation rate than the default can be input, but some consumer programs specify a single inflation rate. Only one professional program examined offers the option of treating inflation as stochastic.

Medical and long-term care expenses

Some of the free web-based programs allow the user to input information about expected medical and long-term care expenses. Yet none examined by Turner and Witte (forthcoming) treats these expenses as a risk factor or alerts the user to possibly huge variations in these expenses.

Social Security benefit receipt

In the United States, most people receive more in Social Security benefits than from investments. Accordingly, the age at which the person claims benefits and the decision whether or not to postpone taking benefits becomes key. Unfortunately, most consumer-oriented programs do not highlight this issue; rather, the user simply specifies the age he or she will claim benefits.

A related point is that many financial planning tools do not accurately determine each individual's Social Security benefit. For instance, one software tool simply presumes that everyone receives the same Social Security benefit, regardless of whether it is a single or married household. Some programs require the user to provide that information, but older workers tend not to be very well apprised as to the level of their future Social Security benefits (Mitchell 1988; Gustman and Steinmeier 2003). Indeed, the research shows that many workers underestimate their Social Security benefit and overestimate how much income they will receive from pensions and work in retirement (Sondergeld and Greenwald 2005). Focusing on those within 2 years of benefit receipt, Rohwedder and Kleinjans (2004) find that about 30 percent did not know what their Social Security benefits would be, and of those who said they did, half were accurate to within 10 percent of their actual benefits. One-quarter overestimated their future benefits by 10 percent or more.

It is the case that the programs often recommend postponing the age at which Social Security benefits are taken, if retirement savings are inadequate. One web site inputs the user's age and sex, and calculates the 'break-even' point if benefit receipt were postponed from age 62 to the normal retirement age (66 for a person, currently 59 years old). It notes that a person with average life expectancy for their age and gender has a given percentage chance of living longer than the break-even point, with the likelihood of living longer than that age being higher for women than for men. It would be useful to integrate more detail on longevity risks with the discussion of the benefit claiming age. Moreover, that program does not calculate (or even note), that the optimal claiming age depends on whether the user has a dependent spouse or is a dependent spouse. More detailed information is provided in a separate document, including the option of purchasing a 5-year fixed-term annuity as a bridge from 62 to 67 in order to postpone receipt of Social Security benefits. This option of purchasing an annuity is noted in the software provided by a life insurance company.

One program suggests that everyone would be better off in terms of lifetime benefits received by postponing receipt of retirement benefits past age 62. A substantial portion of the population, however, has life expectancy less than the mean. Many of these people would not receive higher lifetime benefits by postponing retirement. In addition, many women would be better off taking Social Security at age 62 on their own earnings records and then claiming spousal benefits at a later date, with their husbands postponing retirement. Some of the consumer programs have no option for separately entering information for spouses. Thus, they are incapable of assessing the issues of whether the survivor has adequate income, economies of scale in consumption, and the decline in family consumption following the death of a spouse.

Poor planning

Financial planning software programs are designed to reduce the risk of poor planning, but few programs have checks on inconsistent or outlandish assumptions. This may be less of an issue for professional programs because a professional financial planner is inputting the data, but some internal consistency checks are important for the consumer programs. For example, many programs permit the user to specify long-term risk-free rates of return of 10 or even 20 percent.

A common problem with many consumer software programs is that most do not recognize users' low level of knowledge documented by numerous behavioral studies. That is, the programs are designed for knowledgeable users and may yield misleading results for many users. For example, users who underestimate their life expectancies and hence draw down their assets too soon will possibly outlive their assets in retirement.

Targets

A key aspect of retirement planning and retirement planning software has to do with the criteria for deciding whether retirement saving is adequate. Adequacy criteria involve the goal to be achieved and the probability that it will be achieved. Programs generally are based on the approach of determining whether the user is on the right path to meet a particular goal, with the goal either determined by the user or by the program. They have some criteria for determining whether savings are adequate. The next section discusses aspects of the target criteria for measuring success in retirement planning.

How the programs measure success

Whether one is successful in meeting one's retirement planning target depends on what measure of success is used. This will in general depend on the length of the planning period, the measure of income/asset adequacy, and the probability that adequacy will be achieved over the entire planning period. Furthermore, one's estimate of success will vary with risk aversion, rate of time preference, and mortality risk.

The software programs differ widely in what they deem success. One program that uses Monte Carlo analysis suggests that the goal is an 80 percent chance that income will last to age 95, given a 70 percent target replacement rate. A different nonstochastic program defines success as having sufficient resources to meet the user's specified target expenditure level, up to the user's specified life expectancy. A third program defines success as a 90 percent chance that the desired level of retirement income, based on an 85 percent target replacement rate, can be sustained over a 30-year retirement. Thus, for a person retiring at age 65, that would be a 90 percent chance of success up to age 95.

Sometimes, programs use measures of retirement income adequacy to measure success, including the replacement ratio. This refers to the ratio of postretirement income to the employee's preretirement pay. For some, a constant replacement ratio may make sense, but it will not be a good guide if retirement spending is anticipated to change significantly due to lifestyle choices, not needing to pay for dependent children, or having paid off a mortgage. One approach, taken by some software programs, divides retirement consumption into 'necessary' and 'desired' expenses, on the notion that people would be able to reduce desired expenses more readily than necessary expenses. Another way to measure what is 'necessary' uses the Elder Economic Security Index (Kuriansky 2007). This standard defined the elder standard per year for a single person who owned a home without a mortgage at $15,134 in 2006, for a single renter at $19,541, for a couple with a home without a mortgage at $21,658, and for a couple renting at $26,064.

Of course, what is necessary and desired is also a subjective concept, so more research is needed on ways to measure and explain different success concepts. An important question is whether the measure of success should be specified by the program or the user. Perhaps multiple outcomes would be useful to alert the user to different ways in which the goal and shortfalls can be defined.

Why projected outcomes differ

Based on what we have found thus far, it will not be surprising that retirement planning programs differ in terms of their results and advice. One reason is that their input values differ. While this explanation is obvious, the reasons behind it are not. For example, one program uses a rate of return of 10 percent on equity, while another program has a default rate of return of 5 percent on equity and a maximum allowable rate of 7 percent. Some programs recognize that the price of medical care is rising faster than other prices, while others do not. Another issue is that the measures of retirement resources differ. For example, one program asks the user to indicate expected inheritances or other onetime receipts, while others do not mention expected inheritances. Some incorporate the value of housing as a source of retirement income, while others do not. Many consumer-oriented programs ignore taxes, leading one to conclude that the user has more retirement resources than in reality. Programs that request more detail in the inputs for sources of income may tend to yield a higher probability of success because users end up specifying a higher level of expected income in retirement.

Also, as noted earlier, projected outcomes differ since measures of retirement needs also differ. One program specifies a replacement rate of 85 percent, while another program allows the user to specify the amount of income needed in retirement. Similarly, replacement rate definitions differ: some specify replacement rates relative to current income, while others specify postretirement relative to lifetime average income. Further, retirement planning periods differ across programs. One will stipulate a retirement planning period of 30 years, while another specifies a period that ends at age 95; yet another will base computations on the user's specification of life expectancy. A related point is that there is disparate treatment of surviving spouses' needs. Some programs set as a default that the surviving spouse needs half the income of a couple, while one program takes into account economies of scale in consumption, assuming that a couple needs 1.6 times as much as a single person.

Another source of differentiation is whether the models used are deterministic or stochastic. Stochastic programs recognize the possibility of worst-case scenarios, while deterministic programs do not explicitly incorporate that possibility in their methodology. And even in stochastic programs, the standard for the minimum probability of success differs. For example, one program requires that the user be successful in 90 percent of the scenarios, while other programs use lower standards.

Conclusion

This chapter has reviewed how postretirement risk is handled by widely available retirement planning software. The programs evaluated here have entailed enormous programming and design efforts, and in that sense, they represent a remarkable achievement. At the same time, these are still in the relatively early stages; and future programs will likely be greatly improved.

In overview, and not surprisingly, we find that web-based programs aimed at the general consumer are less complex than programs used by professional financial planners. The five free web-based approaches considered here provide a rough idea of whether the user is on target for retirement, how much additional, if any, he or she would need to save, and whether he or she should consider postponing retirement. Yet one has a serious flaw in that it assumes that everyone, even if married, receives the same Social Security benefit. Another is inadequate in that it determines income sufficiency based on life expectancy and overlooks the chances of living longer. Several do not even permit calculations to take spouses' benefits and needs into account. Only one includes DC plan saving but ignores DB pensions or other sources of retirement income. Programs used by financial planners are far more complex, yet none is capable of dealing with variable rate mortgages. Nor do they anticipate the situation of falling housing prices, job loss, and foreclosures. We conclude that on the whole, the tools do not highlight nor address retirement risk particularly well; rather, they mainly mask risk.

A common problem with the consumer software programs evaluated is that most do not recognize the users' low level of financial knowledge. As a result, the programs tend to be designed to work best for knowledgeable users but they may produce misleading results for many. For example, users who fail to understand their longevity may underestimate the amount of resources they need for retirement. Future programs that confront limitations in individual knowledge and understanding could check user-provided inputs and provide warnings if these seem out of line. It would also be useful to provide consumers with outcomes from running multiple scenarios, and discuss the potential impact of inflation and health risks. Having said that, it remains the case that even experts may disagree on what financial targets are best, and hence what advice may be optimal. No wonder then that software developers disagree on how to attain goals.

The global financial crisis has prompted many to pay new attention to the downside potential of investment risk. It has also revealed key weaknesses inherent in retirement planning software. Partly this is the result of deterministic approaches, which fail to prompt scenario testing. Yet even when stochastic modeling is preferred, the existing models still do not focus people on rare or 'tail' events, and how to deal with them. Furthermore, stochastic approaches currently in use tend to focus on financial market risks, but downplay or ignore other risks. An additional issue is that the crisis has induced many to consider working longer and delaying retirement, but few software models properly model and present this option. The crisis has also made it clear that housing values can fall, and variable rate mortgages can rise rapidly – yet neither eventuality is well handled by most programs. And finally, virtually no program has contemplated the possibility of all of these negative shocks happening at the same time – and just when the person loses his or her job. In short, existing retirement planning programs have a long way to go. They still underrepresent, or downplay, the impact of multiple extreme events and what to do about them. The next generation of software therefore has much to do to inform users of such uncertainties and offer new solutions.

Appendix 4A Case studies

Case studies can help researchers understand the operation and results of the software programs used in retirement planning. The question, 'Will I run out of money in retirement?' is often the most critical one for retirees and people nearing retirement. Given their circumstances and their plans for the future, how likely are they to be able to maintain their standard of living? This issue was addressed through the use of case studies developed for the 2009 SOA Research Study (Turner and Witte forthcoming) by the Project Oversight Group for comparing retirement software. They may be characterized in brief as follows:

- Case 1. Sue Singleton, a 60-year-old divorcee, still working. This case involves issues of working past age 65, changes in Social Security benefits with postponed retirement, using the home as a primary retirement asset, no employer retirement plan, reverse mortgage for retirement income, and Social Security benefits based on divorce and prior marriage.

- Case 2. Hal and Karen Middleton, ages 64 and 60, recently retired. This case involves issues of being too conservatively invested through retirement, spending a sizable part of assets early in retirement, annuity income stream reduced upon death of husband, and change in health coverage at Medicare eligibility.
- Case 3. Gary and Sandra Alterman, ages 74 and 74, retired. This case involves issues of long-term care needs, 40 percent of retirement income does not have a cost-of-living adjustment (COLA), liquidating home value through move in retirement; increasing medical, assisted living, and transportation costs as time goes on, and elimination of spousal pension benefit upon death of primary wage earner.
- Case 4. Leslie Gonzalez, a 58-year-old widow, still working, dependent mother. This case involves issues of increasing dependent costs, long life, does not own home, the majority of her retirement assets being in a taxable, low-earning account, different annuitization versus asset investment/withdrawal strategies, and health benefits from former husband's employment.
- Case 5. John and Judy Richman, ages 56 and 50, higher income, still working. This case involves issues of high credit card debt and mortgage going into retirement, college costs at the same time as the need to save for retirement, employer stock options, lack of long-term care insurance, not being able to afford retiring at age 65, and Social Security spouse benefits where spouse is a government employee not covered by Social Security.
- Case 6. Jim and Linda Goldin, ages 72 and 69, higher income, retired.

Case study results

The research used the six cases in each program to determine how long it would take to run out of money in each scenario. Results varied widely. For one case, one program assesses that when retirement occurs at age 70 the person has adequate retirement income, while another program finds the income to be insufficient. The differences are explained at least in part because the first program allows the user to set life expectancy, and uses life expectancy to determine the planning period, while the second program sets the planning period to end at age 95, 8 years later, or 47 percent longer, than in the first study.

For a case of a recently retired couple aged 60 and 64, one program finds the couple's saving to be inadequate, while another finds it to be adequate. The program that finds it to be adequate recognizes the value of the home equity as a source of retirement income, while the other software does not. The first study found that consumer programs tended to completely overlook home equity. For the couple aged 56 and 50 who were still working, one program finds the couple's saving to be inadequate, while another finds it to be adequate. The one that finds it to be inadequate sets a maximum rate of return of 7 percent on investments, while the other allows the 8 percent specified in the case. Differences in assumed rates of return are more important the younger the users and the more financial assets they have.

To further explore the difference in results between deterministic and stochastic programs, in one case the person is aged 55, plans to retire at age 62, has a life expectancy of 95, has a salary of $100,000, and annual saving of $12,000. Again, a deterministic and a stochastic program were compared. The deterministic program indicated that the person would be able to retire if he or she had already accumulated $740,000, while the stochastic program indicated that he or she would need to have already accumulated $690,000. Thus, it cannot be concluded that the stochastic programs indicate that people need greater saving than do the deterministic programs.

Software analyzed in the 2009 SOA study

Free consumer programs

- Fidelity's Retirement Income Planner http://personal.fidelity.com/planning/retirement/retiree/content/ripover.shtml
- AARP Retirement Planning Calculator http://www.aarp.org/money/financial_planning/sessionseven/retirement_planning_calculator.html
- MetLife Calculator http://www.metlife.com/Applications/Corporate/WPS/CDA/PageGenerator/0,4773,P18280,00.html
- US Department of Labor, Employee Benefits Security Administration: Taking the Mystery Out of Retirement Planning http://askebsa.dol.gov/retirementcalculator/UI/general.aspx
- T. Rowe Price Retirement Income Calculator http://www.troweprice.com/common/index3/0,3011,lnp%253D10002%2526cg%253D1270%2526pgid%253D8277,00.html

Fee-based consumer program (included with professional programs)

- ESPlanner http://www.esplanner.com/

Professional programs

- NaviPlan Standard
  http://www.eisi.com/products/us/standard/product_features.htm
- NaviPlan Extended
  http://www.eisi.com/products/us/extended/index.htm
- NaviPlan Profiles
  http://www.eisi.com/products/us/professional/index.htm
- PIE's MoneyGuidePro
- http://www.moneyguidepro.com/Default.aspx?page=products
- AdviceAmerica – AdvisorVision Retirement Income Edition
  http://www.adviceamerica.com/AAweb/RIE.htm
- Money Tree
  http://www.moneytree.com/

Notes

[1] This chapter relies on several surveys conducted by the Society of Actuaries (SOA) examining how the public views retirement risks in 2001, 2003, 2005, and 2007; the SOA also ran several focus groups on how people manage their retirement assets. Additional information was derived from a 2003 analysis by the SOA, LIMRA (a US-based marketing and research organization serving over 850 financial services companies in over 70 countries), and the International Foundation for Retirement Education on the handling of postretirement risks by planning software (Sondergeld et al. 2003). Ongoing work (Turner and Witte 2009) builds on the first study to further show how such software treats the management of postretirement risks. Results from the 2009 study are preliminary and have not yet been finally approved by the sponsoring organizations. The software used in the 2009 study is listed in Appendix 4A.

[2] For a recent review, see Mitchell and Turner (2009).

[3] The case studies for the 2009 study can be found in Appendix 4A.

[4] Programs compared in the 2009 study are listed in Appendix 4A.

[5] Other differences in longevity are also considerable, with differences of a decade or more across identifiable demographic and economic groups, for example, low-income African-American men compared to high-income Asian women (Murray et al. 2006).

References

Abkemeier, Noel and Brent Hamann (2009). *Segmenting the Middle Market: Retirement Risks and Solutions Phase I Report.* Schaumburg, IL: Society of Actuaries.

Bodie, Zvi (2003). 'An Analysis of Investment Advice to Retirement Plan Participants,' in O.S. Mitchell and K. Smetters, *The Pension Challenge: Risk Transfers and Retirement Income Security*. Oxford, UK: Oxford University Press.

Cowell, Michael and Anna M. Rappaport (2006). *Longevity: The Underlying Driver of Retirement Risk: 2005 Risks and Process of Retirement Survey Report*. Schaumburg, IL: Society of Actuaries.

Dowd, Bryan, Adam Atherly, and Robert Town (2008). *Planning for Retirement? Web Calculators Weak on Health Costs*. Washington, DC: AARP Public Policy Institute.

Greenwald, Mathew, Sally A. Bryck, and Eric T. Sondergeld (2006). *Spending and Investing in Retirement: Is There a Strategy?* Hartford, CT, and Schaumburg, IL: LIMRA International and the Society of Actuaries.

Gustman, Alan L. and Thomas L. Steinmeier (2003). 'What People Don't Know About Their Pensions and Social Security: An Analysis Using Linked Data from the Health and Retirement Study,' in W.G. Gale, J.B. Shoven, and M.J. Warshawsky, eds., *Private Pensions and Public Policies*. Washington, DC: The Brookings Institution.

Kotlikoff, Laurence L. (2006). *Is Conventional Financial Planning Good for Your Financial Health?* Boston, MA: Boston University. http://people.bu.edu/kotlikoff/Is% 20Conventional%20Financial%20Planning%20Good%20for%20Your%20Financial%20Health.pdf

Kuriansky, Joan (2007). *Written Statement Submitted to the Subcommittee on Income Security and Family Support, US House of Representatives*. Washington, DC: Wider Opportunities for Women. http://www.wowonline.org/publicpolicy/reports/ documents/Testimony-;MeasuringPovertyInAmerica8-2007.pdf

Lusardi, Annamaria and Olivia S. Mitchell (2007). 'Baby Boomer Retirement Security: The Roles of Planning, Financial Literacy, and Housing Wealth,' *Journal of Monetary Economics*, 54(1): 205–24.

Mitchell, Olivia S. (1988). 'Worker Knowledge of Pension Provisions,' *Journal of Labor Economics*, 6(1): 21–39.

——and John Turner (2009). 'Labor Market Uncertainty and Pension System Performance,' PRC Working Paper No. 2009-11. Philadelphia, PA: The Pension Research Council of The Wharton School, University of Pennsylvania.

Murray, Christopher J.L., Sandeep C. Kulkarni, Catherine Michaud, Niels Tomijima, Maria T. Bulzacchelli, Terrel J. Iandiorio, and Majid Ezzati (2006). 'Eight Americas: Investigating Mortality Disparities across Races, Counties, and Race-Counties in the United States,' *PLoS Medicine*, 3(9): e260.

Rappaport, Anna M. (2008). *Testimony delivered to ERISA Advisory Council Working Group on Spend Down of Defined Contribution Assets in Retirement*. Washington, DC, July 16.

Rohwedder, Susann and K. J. Kleinjans (2004). *Dynamics of Individual Information About Social Security*. Boston, MA: RAND Corporation. http://client.norc.org/ jole/SOLEweb/RohwedderKleinjans.pdf

Society of Actuaries (SOA) (2004). *2003 Risks and Process of Retirement Survey: Report of Findings*. Washington, DC: Mathew Greenwald and Associates. http://www.soa. org/files/pdf/Retirement_Risk_2-12_FINAL_V2.pdf

—— (2008*a*). *Health and Long-Term Care Risks in Retirement.* Schaumburg, IL: Society of Actuaries.

—— (2008*b*). *Managing Post-Retirement Risks: A Guide to Retirement Planning.* Schaumburg, IL: Society of Actuaries.

—— (2008*c*). *Understanding and Managing the Risks of Retirement: 2007 Risks and Process of Retirement Survey Report.* Schaumburg, IL: Society of Actuaries.

Sondergeld, Eric T., Robert S. Chamerda, Matthew Drinkwater, and Daniel G. Landsberg (2003). *Retirement Planning Software.* Hartford, CT, Lubbock, TX, and Schaumburg, IL: LIMRA International, International Foundation for Retirement Education, and the Society of Actuaries.

——and Mathew Greenwald (2005). *Public Misperceptions About Retirement Security.* Hartford, CT, Schaumburg, IL, and Washington, DC: LIMRA International, the Society of Actuaries, and Mathew Greenwald and Associates.

Turner, John A. and Hazel A. Witte (2009). 'Retirement Planning Software and Post-Retirement Risks.' Schaumburg, IL: The Society of Actuaries and the Actuarial Foundation.

Chapter 5

Impact of the Pension Protection Act on Financial Advice: What Works and What Remains to Be Done?

Lynn Pettus and R. Hall Kesmodel, Jr.

The US Congress addressed several issues important to both defined benefit (DB) and defined contribution (DC) pension plans with the 2006 enactment of the Pension Protection Act (PPA). Certain aspects of the PPA are widely viewed as improvements to the existing system, including changes to certain funding rules for DB plans and the explicit endorsement of auto-enrollment in DC plans, while others are more controversial (Warshawsky 2007; Sirkin and Coffin 2008). One of the most hotly debated topics is a provision expanding the delivery of plan participant investment advice.

By including participant advice provisions under the PPA, Congress effectively took the position that existing fiduciary requirements for participant advice programs were too restrictive to allow widespread plan sponsor adoption. Accordingly, relief from the prohibited transaction restrictions of the Employee Retirement Income Security Act (ERISA) was needed. In January 2009, the United States Department of Labor (USDOL) issued final regulations outlining how to comply with PPA statutory exemptions, and at the same time it created a new class exemption seeking to increase the availability of participant advice while controlling potential conflicts of interest (USDOL 2009).

Prior to the passage of the PPA, a 401(k) benchmarking survey showed that about 40 percent of 401(k) plans had offered participant investment advice programs for many years; the remainder had not offered advice due to fiduciary concerns (Smith 2006). In early 2007, the number offering advice had risen to 51 percent. Nevertheless, fiduciary concerns are still a main reason that sponsors elect not to provide financial advice (Phoenix and Dzierzak 2008). Therefore, while the PPA was somewhat successful in increasing the availability of advice, it may have failed to fully address fiduciary concerns. The Labor Department suggests that its new class exemption will do much to alleviate these fiduciary concerns, ultimately resulting in 60 percent of plan participants having access to investment advice.

This chapter addresses three important questions related to the PPA advice provisions:

- How did advice programs operating prior to PPA deliver advice to plan participants?
- Have eligible advice arrangements put forth under PPA both expanded the availability of advice and better served plan sponsors and participants thus far?
- Particularly with respect to serving the needs of plan participants, what remains to be done?

Participant investment advice: a brief regulatory and legislative history

Interpretive Bulletin 96-1

The transition to DC pension 'self-directed' plans has meant that more employees are now responsible for managing their own retirement saving. For this reason, in 1996, the USDOL released Interpretive Bulletin 96-1 to provide plan sponsors with clarifications regarding non-fiduciary participant *education* versus fiduciary investment *advice*. This release indicated that plan sponsors may educate participants on such concepts as diversification and historical return expectations for various asset classes and assist participants with estimating future retirement income needs and assessing risk tolerance. Such non-fiduciary education may go so far as to provide participants with hypothetical asset allocation models and interactive software built using 'generally accepted investments theories' and assumptions that identify a 'specific investment alternative available under the plan.' To comply, the model must identify the specific assumptions made, acknowledge the availability of other similar investment alternatives in the plan, and take into account (or ask participants to consider) individual circumstances and outside assets. Such models and related output materials are not considered a 'recommendation' and thus do not constitute fiduciary 'investment advice' under ERISA (USDOL 1996).

In defining fiduciary investment advice, USDOL stated that this would include specific recommendations to buy or sell securities, as well as discretionary control over assets or a mutual agreement that the advice will be the 'primary basis for the participant's or beneficiary's investment decisions.' The Bulletin also confirmed that providing either non-fiduciary education or fiduciary investment advice to participants would not cause the plan to violate ERISA Section 404(c), as the participant might choose to accept or disregard the investment education or advice.

SunAmerica

The next definitive action by the USDOL on investment advice came in December 2001 when USDOL issued Advisory Opinion 2001-09A to Sun-America Retirement Markets. This advisory opinion concluded that a retirement plan services provider offering its own investment options to plan participants may also render participants investment advice and discretionary managed account services, provided that an 'independent financial expert' developed the recommendations for participants using objective criteria. In so doing, USDOL determined that SunAmerica would not be in violation of ERISA Section 406(b), which prohibits a plan's investment advisor fiduciaries from receiving additional compensation resulting from participant investment advice. Some commentators (Ungurean 2004) have noted that the SunAmerica Advisory Opinion was significant, as it outlined a clear model under which retirement plan providers may now offer 'independent' investment advice and managed account programs, even with the presence of their own investment options in the plan (USDOL 2001).

Failed legislation

Over the period 2001–5, both Democratic and Republican members of Congress introduced competing legislation proposing investment advice models that would shield plan sponsors from liability related to participant advice. Notably, Rep. John Boehner (R-Ohio), Chairman of the House Committee on Education and the Workforce, introduced the Retirement Security Advice Act, which permitted advice from plan providers with disclosures. Largely in response to this legislation, Sen. Jeff Bingaman (D-New Mexico) later introduced the Independent Investment Advice Act, which required that participant advice come from independent firms not involved with the management of the plan's investments. Neither Act was ever passed into law.

The Pension Protection Act

Finally in 2006, PPA was enacted by Congress and signed into law by President Bush to address widespread pension funding issues and increase retirement security. Along with addressing certain DC plan design features such as auto-enrollment and creating Qualified Default Investment Alternatives

(QDIA), the PPA added a statutory exemption to ERISA that, if followed, permits the plan's fiduciary investment advisor to provide participant investment advice under an 'eligible advice arrangement.' The advice provisions in PPA effectively represented a compromise between the Boehner and Bingaman proposals (but much closer to the Boehner approach) by permitting a conflicted party to offer participant advice with controls.

Field Assistance Bulletin

Shortly after the enactment of PPA, USDOL issued a Field Assistance Bulletin (FAB No. 2007-01) providing preliminary guidance on implementing eligible advice arrangements under which a 'fiduciary advisor' renders advice either by using a computer model certified to produce objective advice, or by using a 'fee-leveling' approach. It also affirmed that past guidance remained effective, and that plan sponsors need not operate under a PPA-eligible advice arrangement. Additionally, it also reiterated plan sponsors' fiduciary obligations in providing participant investment advice (USDOL 2007).

USDOL final rules

In 2009, USDOL issued proposed regulations that largely followed FAB No. 2007-01, but further liberalized investment advice rules by introducing a class exemption that goes beyond the statutory exemption defined under PPA. Most significantly, under the USDOL class exemption, the fee-leveling requirement applies only to the representative (person) providing the advice to participants. It does not apply to fees received by the fiduciary advisor (firm) responsible for the eligible advice arrangement. Consistent with FAB No. 2007-01, the fiduciary advisor providing the eligible advice arrangement is not required to be registered under the Investment Advisers Act of 1940 and may be a bank, insurance company, or broker–dealer. The class exemption also allows the fiduciary advisor's representative using a computer model to render additional subjective 'off-model' advice under certain circumstances, with documentation. While these liberalized rules might conceivably make advice more available, by removing certain barriers, they also potentially increase conflicts of interest within PPA-eligible advice arrangements by removing the requirement for representatives to follow the computer-model recommendations and the requirement for firms to receive level fees for the representative's recommendations (USDOL 2009).

Final USDOL rules were filed in the Federal Register on January 21, 2009, and had an effective date of March 23, 2009. But the change in presidential administration prompted the USDOL to extend the effective date by an additional 60 days and request further comment. As of the writing of this chapter, part or all of the USDOL final rules are not expected to go into effect without substantial rewrite, due to Congressional disagreement over perceived conflicts of interest and liberalized rules that could go beyond the statutory compromise.

Participant investment advice today

Despite the availability of the new PPA statutory exemption, the market for participant investment advice today continues to be dominated by Internet-based computer models developed by independent firms registered under the Investment Advisers Act of 1940. Independent providers are distinguished in that they are not affiliated with the retirement plan's asset manager, and they do not sell financial products or provide brokerage services to plan participants.

Business and delivery models

These firms typically sell their Internet computer-model services through marketing alliances with retirement plan administrators, or directly to large DC plan sponsors. Smaller advisory firms sometimes sell services directly to individual plan participants, bypassing the plan sponsor. Some providers exclusively offer participant investment advice while others operate large diversified institutional investment advisory, research, and technology businesses.[1]

Most large retirement plan services businesses have entered into alliance agreements with at least one independent advice provider to deliver Internet-based participant advice via a computer model. Some co-market with several advice providers to offer plan sponsors a choice of tools and advice methodologies. Others have branded a single advice platform as part of a 'bundled' service with an independent advice provider's computer model ('financial expert') delivering the participant advice behind the scenes, similar to the SunAmerica approach. Few businesses, if any, currently structure their computer-model platforms as PPA-eligible advice arrangements.[2]

While retirement plan services providers may be awaiting the fate of USDOL final rules before establishing new PPA-eligible computer-model arrangements, there are several reasons that providers might retain their existing platforms. These include the widespread availability of third-party computer models, the expense of creating new models, and the presence of certification and annual audit requirements under PPA compared to no such requirements for independent advice providers and SunAmerica arrangements.

The lack of retirement plan services providers delivering participant investment advice programs via PPA-eligible fee-leveling arrangements might be due to the prevalence of mutual fund revenue-sharing agreements at the plan level, which include both the provider (fiduciary advisor) responsible for the advice arrangement, and the financial advisor intermediary (firm or representative who sold the 401(k) plan to the plan sponsor) responsible for providing investment advice to participants. Such agreements complicate the implementation of fee-leveling, particularly if the USDOL class exemption is not made effective.

Services and scope

Computer-model advice tools offer personalized asset allocation and investment recommendations based on a proprietary analysis of the retirement plan's investment options, coupled with an assessment of the participant's investment needs. These tools typically ask participants to input relevant information such as age, income, assets outside the retirement plan, and desired retirement age. The advice output includes educational materials and graphics designed to provide the participant with portfolio return and risk expectations as well as target saving levels. The output also may include a Monte Carlo analysis, which might show a range of returns representing 90–95 percent (approximately two standard deviations) of calculated possible future outcomes.[3]

In some cases, the plan provider, the advice provider, or the plan sponsor may offer telephone-based counseling related to the advice tool or managed account program. Managed account programs involve the advice provider taking the extra step of implementing ongoing investment decisions on a discretionary basis. Plan providers may also offer face-to-face meetings in conjunction with the computer model. While participants are more likely to use face-to-face advisors than any other delivery method (Helman, Copeland, and VanDerhei 2006) of advice delivery, there can be caveats to these interactions that we will explore further.

Fee structures

Independent computer-model advice providers, or plan providers operating a program similar to that of SunAmerica, collect fees from the plan sponsor, who may in turn pass through the cost of offering the advice program (and related telephone or face-to-face support) by charging a fee to each participant's account. The advice provider may charge fees on a per capita or assets-under-management basis. When an alliance relationship is involved, the retirement plan services provider may offer education and investment advice for no additional cost as part of its 'bundled' platform with an additional fee charged for managed account services. Generally, under pre-PPA delivery models, provider representatives supporting the computer model are salaried registered investment advisor representatives or employees who do not receive additional compensation or commissions from participants.

If a financial advisor intermediary (i.e., a commissioned representative affiliated with a brokerage firm, wealth management firm, or life insurance agency) is involved, there may be an informal or personal advisory relationship formed between financial advisors and certain participants, such as the business owner or its executives. Financial advisors unaffiliated with the retirement plan provider may also find their way to the employer via informal networking contacts with human resources, corporate business leaders, or individuals at company locations to offer face-to-face financial planning and out-of-plan advice services.

In these circumstances, the financial advisor might offer select plan participants ancillary investment advisory services or insurance products for assets outside of the plan's formal advice platform. The financial advisor intermediary's affiliated financial institution will dictate the extent to which fees and commissions are charged outside the context of the plan (e.g., commissions from financial product sales, fees related to assets under management, and brokerage commissions).

Limitations

Both the independent, online computer model (formal program offered in the plan) and the financial advisor intermediary (informal program offered outside of plan) have some limitations in providing participant advice, irrespective of PPA.

Today's sophisticated Monte Carlo computer models in both retirement and investment advice programs are essential for performing stochastic modeling that potentially could include all sources of retirement income (e.g., Social Security benefits, DB pensions) and invested assets (e.g., IRAs, taxable accounts). Aside from lacking Internet access at work, the issue for most participants continues to be their lack of desire or financial knowledge to accurately and confidently enter information into these tools or understand the outputs without the assistance of a trusted professional. Indeed, for most plan participants, the Internet is not the preferred method of obtaining advice (Helman, Copeland, and VanDerhei 2006). While most are comfortable seeking general information from web sites, relatively few trust the Internet for financial advice (Greenwald 2007). Fewer are inclined to input the required personal information (from all of their various accounts) to obtain investment advice, and even fewer understand advice tool outputs and investment concepts.

Such reluctance is further complicated by the behavioral tendencies of participants to trust their own investment decisions for delivering their retirement saving objectives (47 percent) over that of a professionally managed account (25 percent). In cases where participants do access advice, only 13 percent say they implement all of the advice (Helman, Copeland, and VanDerhei 2006). Finally, online advice programs are not designed to provide financial planning recommendations for participants who struggle with debt or for those near retirement who are focused on plan distribution options and long-term cash flow planning. Decisions facing today's plan participants approaching retirement include: when to commence DB pension benefits, whether to elect an annuity or a lump sum, when to begin Social Security benefits, determining the appropriate level of cash reserves versus invested assets, whether to pay off their mortgage, and ordering and timing account withdrawals to minimize taxes. Collectively, these decisions are difficult for plan participants to address without the assistance of a financial planning professional.

There are also limitations to financial advisor intermediary or commissioned representatives' roles in providing financial planning advice. Factors to be considered relate to objectivity, quality, and consistency of the advice delivered for each participant, as well as how wealth management firms compensate these financial advisors.

One major issue is that dialogue and recommendations rendered during face-to-face meetings between financial advisors and participants are seldom recorded or archived. Consequently there are few ways to control quality, consistency, or conflicts that may arise. For example, an insurance agent, acting on a suitability (non-fiduciary) standard in providing out-of-plan recommendations, might be trained by his or her field office to sell more life insurance by instructing clients (plan participants) to limit their plan contributions to the employer match level (e.g., 6 percent of salary). Whole life insurance premiums, rather than additional plan contributions, are then recommended as an alternative to additional plan contributions.

Issues also arise around the compensation structure of commission-based financial advisor intermediaries, which incents advisors to focus attention on executives and business owners rather than rank-and-file participants, who arguably need the most help and have the fewest assets. This compensation structure may therefore create inherent issues of uneven participant access as well as conflicts of interest, irrespective of the advice framework (i.e., SunAmerica or PPA).

Other problems with exposing employees to commissioned representatives in the workplace include participants' lack of ability to select the lowest-cost option when it comes to investments (Choi, Laibson, and Madrian

2010) and presumably other financial product decisions as well. Participants might also view the recommendations and products offered by financial advisors in the workplace as tacit plan sponsor recommendations. This can lead participants to believe that they should work with these advisors (Pessin 2008) even if this is not the employer's intent. Allowing commissioned representatives further access to the workplace under PPA-eligible advice arrangements will not change these dynamics, as PPA and USDOL only focus on the conflicts related specifically to plan investment advice, not financial product sales.

Participant issues

While retirement plan providers and sponsors continue to focus much attention on participant needs with respect to plan investment advice, significant problems for many participants exist outside the context of selecting investments in their 401(k) plans. One need only look at the current problems in the housing market to understand how severe resource allocation problems are relative to selecting investment options in 401(k) plans. Consider also that these serious financial problems can exist when the employee receives regular paychecks from an employer. With a lump-sum retirement benefit, the problem only worsens as these same individuals must now create their own paychecks for 30 years or more, juggling investment management, spending decisions, and unpredictable health-care expenses.

To put the relative importance of competing saving goals into perspective, the 2003 Employee Benefit Research Institute Retirement Confidence Survey showed that retirement saving was the most important long-term saving goal for only 45 percent of employees. When short-term goals are included, retirement was most important for only 30 percent of workers (EBRI and MGA 2003). Though this objective was mentioned more often than other saving goals, retirement is not considered to be the most important goal for a majority of employees. Along these lines, a recent survey conducted by The Federal Retirement Thrift Investment Board of 35,121 employees eligible for the Thrift Savings Plan found that 23 percent believe they 'do not have enough money' to contribute to the plan. However, only 4.3 percent were not contributing because of dissatisfaction with the investment options and only 2.2 percent were not contributing because the decision was 'too complex' (The Federal Retirement Thrift Investment Board 2009).

These findings suggest that, if participant education and advice is to be more effective, these must help participants understand how to allocate their limited financial resources across competing goals–rather than simply allocating their 401(k) investments.

Factors affecting 401(k) plan advice

Trust

Participant financial problems may also lead to a breakdown of trust in financial institutions, an important component in any participant's decision to participate in a plan (Agnew et al. 2007; Vanguard 2008). Participants may also question the presentation of potential investment outcomes due to recent financial shocks. As mentioned above, providers who show 90–95 percent probability calculations might not properly manage participant expectations when extreme market events become a reality, further confusing and disheartening those who relied on investment advice and stated return expectations in the past. Bodie (2003) illustrates this with a discussion of the 'fat tails' of the equity return distribution. Ironically, inertia has kept many from making changes to their allocations or contribution levels in response to recent market turmoil (Benartzi 2008), but trust in the system and in advice models may be further eroded nonetheless. In the present environment, advice programs funded in part by ancillary financial product sales could further erode participant trust in the plan sponsor and the plan provider's motives.

Automatic solutions

It is possible that participant investment advice in 401(k) plans is giving way to automatic solutions offered under the PPA, which are increasingly focused on helping participants save and diversify their investments passively.

MANAGED ACCOUNTS

For example, with the enactment of PPA, third-party advice providers won a major victory – not through the enactment of advice provisions, but through third-party advice providers' successful bid to include managed accounts as a Qualified Default Investment Alternative (QDIA) along with risk-based 'lifestyle' and age-based 'life-cycle' funds. QDIA status has given advice providers the opportunity to vastly increase the number of participants utilizing their advice through default investment managed account programs offered under auto-enrollment programs. Although managed accounts used as a plan's QDIA are still the exception rather than the rule, retirement plan services providers continue to expand their alliance relationships with third-party advice providers, delivering managed account services to more participants as a plan option and as QDIA default investments for auto-enrolled participants (Financial Engines 2008).

As a practical matter, the proliferation of managed account platforms as a plan option tends to conflict with conventional lifestyle and life-cycle fund choices, as they steer participants away from these. A plan sponsor's communication efforts might also become unmanageably complex, if advice, managed accounts, and life-cycle funds are all offered. Plan sponsors might question whether the additional fees and communications challenges are necessary when low-cost life-cycle funds (or institutional life-cycle funds customized for the plan) might provide similar results with more streamlined communications.[4]

One reason for plan sponsors to consider offering managed accounts as a plan option or as a QDIA default investment comes from work by Benartzi and Thaler (2007) that suggests that participants are not necessarily comfortable 'putting all their eggs in one basket' via a single life-cycle fund. This propensity toward multiple funds is also demonstrated by the fact that only 13 percent of participants believe a life-cycle fund is the investment option most likely to achieve retirement saving objectives, and only 11 percent believe a balanced fund will attain this end (Helman, Copeland, and VanDerhei 2006). That study, and Benartzi and Thaler (2007), help explain the misuse of life-cycle funds by over 70 percent of participants. Nevertheless, few participants can accurately explain what the various options are, or their differences. For this reason, enhancing financial literacy could help, though managed account programs may also produce better results.

Managed account programs have certain advantages and seem to yield positive results for participants (Charles Schwab 2007), but more research is needed to determine whether these programs yield superior overall results when compared to life-cycle funds. For instance, it would be useful to ask whether managed account programs adequately retain participants over the long-term and mitigate irrational investment behavior in times of extraordinary stock market losses when compared to life-cycle funds. This analysis is unfortunately complicated by the fact that aspects of managed account performance are dependent on the underlying funds available in each plan.

AUTOMATIC ENROLLMENT

Studies also show the potentially negative impact on providing 'tacit' advice to employees in areas such as plan saving levels. While some programs providing contribution auto-escalation may mitigate this issue, most employers offering auto-enrollment today continue to have a 3–4 percent fixed contribution rate (Phoenix 2008). This is often due to the significant increased match costs of automatically escalating contribution rates above these levels. Due to inertia, these 3–4 percent saving rates may prove to be a long-term challenge for employers in making sure their workforce retires with adequate replacement ratios through 401(k) plans alone–with or without investment advice.

The need to address this problem is further evidenced by a recent study by Brady (2009) who suggests that employees may achieve acceptable retirement income replacement ratios, including Social Security benefits, by saving 4–10 percent of earnings. While this might be in line with participant trends in traditional 'opt-in' programs, these rates are well above the levels of most auto-enrollment programs. For example, if the employer's match is 50 percent of the first 6 percent of contributions, total contributions for auto-enrollees are more likely 5–6 percent. The problem of inadequate retirement fund accumulations is exacerbated by the fact that auto-enrollment programs without auto-escalate features have tended to create lower overall saving rates in 401(k) plans when compared to participant saving rates in plans without auto-enrollment (Olsen and Whitman 2007).

Increasing complexity

As employers move beyond investment advice toward automated solutions, it is important to keep in mind the complexity involved in accumulating and distributing 'lump-sum' retirement assets as discussed above. Even a seemingly simple decision such as rolling over a 401(k) balance to an IRA carries with it potentially complex tax considerations, such as Net Unrealized Appreciation (NUA) on employer securities.

Another key consideration is creating a way for participants to automatically continue receiving asset allocation assistance even after leaving their employers. Since the median tenure for American workers is currently 4.1 years (USDOL 2008), the transfer of advice from one employer to the next, and for multiple accounts is a key challenge. A recent survey of Americans aged 55–75 with over $50,000 in savings found that 43 percent held more than six accounts (including employer plans, IRAs, and transaction accounts such as checking; Mottola and Utkus 2008*b*). As more future workers rely on 401(k) plan assets for retirement, the number and complexity of account management will only continue to grow.

Even if the participant's current 401(k) plan is the only retirement saving vehicle, the complexity of managing a lump sum to create a stream of retirement payments is extremely challenging given inflation and longevity risks. Relatively few elderly today rely on lump sums from employer-sponsored plans as their primary means of retirement income (Ernst & Young LLP 2008; Mottola and Utkus 2008*a*), but this will not be the case for future retirees. The transition poses significant challenges from an educational and resource perspective, going beyond what computer-model investment advice offerings can effectively achieve for participants. Consider, for example, that future advice might need to include income product selection (e.g., managed payout mutual funds versus annuities). Employers will also confront a decision on how (or if) to automate this payment process and whether to provide employees with payout options inside or outside the plan, and/or educate participants on the universe of options beyond the plan for managing retirement income derived from their 401(k).

Where do we go from here?

Several open questions still remain. For one, it is not yet clear whether programs are delivering the right kind of advice and guidance to participants given their increasingly complex financial needs, which impact their plan participation and saving levels. Investment advice programs focused on accumulating assets are only part of the picture. While there is a need for relevant financial planning assistance beyond what is delivered by investment advice tools geared toward 401(k)s, how should plan sponsors deliver these programs? Should plan sponsors be comfortable with the PPA-eligible advice arrangements and USDOL class exemption, which, if implemented, will increase the presence of commissioned financial service representatives in the workplace? Face-to-face meetings with financial advisors might help certain participants make broader financial decisions beyond their 401(k) accounts, yet plan sponsors lack oversight over their recommendations, the kinds of financial products offered, the uniformity of participant access, and the methodology of the education or advice provided.

Expanding financial planning while addressing broader conflicts

Clearly 401(k) plan automation will continue to grow in scope and popularity. In the process, employers and plan sponsors may consider whether money spent on providing investment advice could be better deployed aiding participants in understanding broader personal finance issues including guidance on allocating the paycheck to coordinate long-term goals like retirement, immediate needs such as paying bills, and mid-term goals like buying a home. Related education might include making efforts to proactively assist with coordinating W-4 withholding calculations and 401(k) contributions, so employees decrease taxes withheld from their paycheck while simultaneously increasing plan contributions, thus keeping their paycheck levels unchanged. Such calculations can be easily performed by a financial planner via an Internet calculator.

If plan sponsors demand an increased spectrum of education and advice for participants, retirement plan services providers and other independent providers might deliver these expanded financial planning services through fee-only (salaried) professionals, without relying on the USDOL class exemption for their representatives. This model might combine a high-touch approach of a professional financial planner with an independent computer model subject to fiduciary advice requirements. If delivered over recorded telephone calls, this approach would limit sponsor and participant costs, assist in quality control, and reduce both real and perceived conflicts associated with commissioned representatives. The scope of permitted financial planning might address immediate needs (e.g., how do I find money to save in the 401(k), pay off debt, how much house can I afford, etc.) in order to better assist participants with meeting their retirement saving goals.

To offer these services, financial institutions would need to train fee-only (salaried) professionals to serve their workplace or plan sponsor clients, in lieu of commissioned representatives. Such a holistic workplace financial planning model might better comport with plan sponsors' fiduciary responsibilities and sensibilities, while allowing participants to receive unbiased (or less conflicted) financial planning from a trusted source without the reliance on ancillary financial product sales to indirectly fund these arrangements. Some financial institutions have already implemented a similar model that complies with pre-PPA regulations and does not rely on the USDOL class exemption for its representatives (Tyson and Palumbo 2008). Though certain conflicts might continue to exist at the plan provider level, the most troubling conflicts, including the incentive to recommend certain financial products in lieu of additional plan contributions, could be mitigated if provider representatives are not financially motivated to market these products to participants in the workplace.

Reevaluating the relative costs of participant education and advice programs

Many plan sponsors, when seeking to move beyond traditional 401(k) education and investment advice, may be concerned about the efficacy, cost, and potentially uncertain fiduciary questions associated with these new approaches. Given the mixed results in studies on the efficacy of certain employer education programs (Hira and Loibl 2005; Benartzi and Thaler 2007; Olsen and Whitman 2007), employers will continue to ask where their resources should be allocated in these areas. In this connection, a recent study suggests employee financial stress might cost more than $15,000 per affected employee (Financial Literacy Partners LLC 2008).

Another consideration is to put the cost of providing participants with financial planning into context. According to Kopcke, Vitagiano, and Muldoon (2009), asset management fees and trading costs make up 80–90 percent of a typical large employer's plan costs. This is particularly significant given that decisions on saving levels, when to retire, and when to collect Social Security benefits – rather than asset allocation or investment selection – are often the most important factors in determining participant retirement incomes (Mottola and Utkus 2008*a*; T. Rowe Price 2009). Yet plan sponsors spend little time or money counseling participants on these key decisions. Unfortunately, commissioned representatives again may be ill-suited to provide participants with unbiased recommendations on these issues, when ancillary (out-of-plan) financial product sales weigh heavily.

In the end, the overall cost of providing broader education and advice programs through commissioned representatives might prove to be much higher than fee-only programs delivered by the plan sponsor, if we include the external commissions and fees paid by participants purchasing ancillary financial products.

Leveraging automatic solutions to reduce the need for traditional 401(k) investment advice

As plan sponsors continue to focus on automatic plan designs and QDIA default investments, this will also reduce the need for traditional 401(k) investment advice. This is because more participants will find themselves automatically invested in diversified portfolios. In this event, education programs could then focus on helping participants understand the QDIA default investments and addressing important financial planning and saving issues, rather than expending efforts to help each participant select plan investments. Only engaged participants who choose to opt out of the QDIA would require traditional investment advice, thus reducing overall costs for delivering these services to the plan.

Conclusion

The Pension Protection Act led to a modest increase in plan sponsors offering participant investment advice and managed account programs. But to date, PPA-eligible advice arrangements have yet to take hold with plan providers or sponsors, as the final rules remain in flux. Therefore, formal participant investment advice programs today, while somewhat more available than in the past, are not materially different than programs offered prior to the PPA (notwithstanding the advent of QDIA managed accounts). For this reason, advice providers seek to ensure that pre-PPA SunAmerica arrangements continue to be permitted under any future rulings.

The complexity and interconnectedness of participants' financial obligations–both immediate and long term–require effective participant education and advice programs to move beyond the narrow focus on 401(k) investment recommendations. If financial advisors can assist participants in the workplace with these broader considerations, beyond the 401(k), the regulators and plan sponsors will be able to consider the presence of broader conflicts of interest as well as the plan's ability to pay for services beyond the context of traditional plan education and investment advice.[5] More needs to be done to deliver better education and advice to participants and retirees without compromising plan sponsors' fiduciary responsibilities and sensibilities, or relying on certain participants to indirectly fund the cost of advice programs through their purchase of ancillary financial products.

Acknowledgments

The views expressed in this chapter are those of the authors and do not necessarily reflect the views of Ernst & Young LLP. The authors would like to thank Ernst & Young LLP colleagues William J. Arnone and Stuart A. Sirkin for their contributions.

Notes

[1] Examples of large independent providers who market directly to plan sponsors or partner with retirement plan service providers under SunAmerica arrangements include: Financial Engines, GuidedChoice, Ibbotson, Morningstar, and 401kToolbox. Examples of smaller independent providers marketing directly to participants include: StraightLine and Smart401k.

[2] The following retirement plan services providers who collectively serve an estimated 43,400,000 plan participants (PlanSponsor.com 2008; Financial Engines 2009) currently partner with an independent advice provider to offer plan sponsor clients access to participant investment advice under a pre-PPA or SunAmerica model: ACS, ADP, Charles Schwab, Fidelity, Hewitt, ING, J.P. Morgan, Mercer, Principal, T. Rowe Price, and Vanguard.

[3] The authors have reviewed advice tool disclosure statements from several providers. However, the description of Monte Carlo analysis is not meant to represent any specific provider's tool.

[4] Managed accounts programs typically charge 0.2 to 0.5 percent of assets under management. Retail life-cycle funds might include similar, or even higher, implicit asset allocation costs. Plan sponsors, particularly those with DB pension plans, might negotiate fees with asset managers to pool assets under management

reducing the cost of offering customized or institutional life-cycle funds to participants.

[5] USDOL final rules do not address these broader conflicts that directly affect plan participants who receive advice from commissioned representatives (USDOL 2009).

References

Agnew, Julie R., Lisa Szykman, Stephen P. Utkus, and Jean A. Young (2007). 'Literacy, Trust and 401(k) Savings Behavior,' Center for Retirement Research at Boston College Working Paper No. 2007-10. Chestnut Hill, MA: Center for Retirement Research at Boston College.

Benartzi, Schlomo (2008). 'Behavioral Finance, the Market Crisis and Retirement Savings: Comments Presented to the House Education and Labor Committee on October 22, 2008,' Washington, DC.

——and Richard Thaler (2007). 'Heuristics and Biases in Retirement Savings Behavior,' *Journal of Economic Perspectives*, 21(3): 81–104.

Bodie, Zvi (2003). 'An Analysis of Investment Advice to Retirement Plan Participants,' in O.S. Mitchell and K. Smetters, eds., *The Pension Challenge: Risk Transfers and Retirement Income Security*. Oxford, UK: Oxford University Press, pp. 19–30.

Brady, Peter J. (2009). 'Can 401(k) Plans Provide Adequate Retirement Resources?,' PRC Working Paper No. 2009-01. Philadelphia, PA: The Pension Research Council of the Wharton School, University of Pennsylvania.

Charles Schwab (2007). 'Press Release: New Schwab Data Indicates Use of Advice and Professionally-Managed Portfolios Results in Higher Rate of Return for 401(k) Participants,' San Francisco, CA: November 27. http://www.businesswire.com/portal/site/schwab/index.jsp/epi-content=GENERIC&beanID=1715635376&viewID=news_view&ndmConfigId=1002458&newsId=20071128005300&newsLang=en&vnsId=4608

Choi, James J., David Laibson, and Briditte C. Madrian (2010). 'Why Does the Law of One Price Fail? An Experiment on Index Mutual Funds,' *Review of Financial Studies*, 23(4): 1405–32.

Employee Benefit Research Institute and Matthew Greenwald & Associates, Inc. (EBRI and MGA) (2003). *Attitudes & Behaviors of Workers and Retirees: 2003 Retirement Confidence Survey*. Washington, DC: Employee Benefit Research Institute and Matthew Greenwald & Associates, Inc. http://www.ebri.org/pdf/surveys/rcs/2003/03fsatit.pdf

Ernst & Young LLP (2008). *Retirement Vulnerability of New Retirees: The Likelihood of Outliving Their Financial Assets*. New York: Ernst & Young LLP. http://www.paycheckforlife.org/uploads/2008_E_Y_RRA.pdf

Financial Engines, Inc. (2008). 'Press Release: Financial Engines Doubles Managed Accounts Business Again in 2007,' Palo Alto, CA, February 12. http://corp.financialengines.com/press_room/press_releases/2008/20080212.html

——(2009). *Who We Work With*. Palo Alto, CA: Financial Engines, Inc. http://corp.financialengines.com/corp/who_we_work_with.html

Financial Literacy Partners LLC (2008). *Employee Financial Stress Is Costing Your Company a Bundle*. New York: Financial Literacy Partners LLC. http://www.finlitinc.com/images/Employee_Financial_Stress_is_Costing_Your_Company_A_Bundle.pdf

Greenwald, Mathew (2007). 'Mathew Greenwald Remarks: 2007 Retirement Confidence Survey Briefing, April 11, 2007.' Washington, DC. http://www.ebri.org/pdf/surveys/rcs/2007/RCS07_MG_Comments.pdf

Helman, Ruth, Craig Copeland, and Jack VanDerhei (2006). 'Will More of Us Be Working Forever? The 2006 Retirement Confidence Survey.' *EBRI Issue Brief 292*. Washington, DC: Employee Benefit Research Institute.

Hira, Tahira K. and Cazilia Loibl (2005). 'Understanding the Impact of Employer-Provided Financial Education on Workplace Satisfaction,' *Journal of Consumer Affairs*, 39(1): 179–94.

Kopcke, Richard W., Francis Vitagiano, and Dan Muldoon. (2009). 'The Structure of 401(k) Fees.' *Issue Brief 9-3*. Chestnut Hill, MA: Center for Retirement Research at Boston College. http://crr.bc.edu/images/stories/Briefs/ib_9-3.pdf

Mottola, Gary R. and Stephan P. Utkus (2008*a*). 'The Retirement Income Landscape.' *Vanguard Center for Retirement Research* Volume 34. Valley Forge, PA: The Vanguard Group, Inc.

————(2008*b*). 'Spending the Nest Egg: Retirement Income Decisions Among Older Investors,' *Vanguard Center for Retirement Research* Volume 35. Valley Forge, PA: The Vanguard Group, Inc.

Olsen, Anya and Kevin Whitman (2007). 'Effective Retirement Savings Programs: Design Features and Financial Education,' *Social Security Bulletin* Vol. 67 No. 3. Washington, DC: Social Security Administration.

Pessin, Jaime L. (2008). 'Investing in Funds: A Monthly Analysis – Be Skeptical of the Hard Sell, Even If It's in the Workplace,' *The Wall Street Journal*, February 4.

Phoenix, Tim and Mark Dzierzak (2008). *401(k) Benchmarking Survey: 2008 Edition*. New York: Deloitte Consulting LLP, the International Foundation of Employee Benefit Plans, and the International Society of Certified Employee Benefit Specialists.http://www.deloitte.com/assets/Dcom-UnitedStates/Local%20Assets/Documents/us_consulting_401(k)BenchmarkingSurvey2008Edition160708.pdf

PlanSponsor.com (2008). *2008 PlanSponsor Recordkeeping Survey: Top 10 Recordkeepers*. Stamford, CT: PlanSponsor Institute.

Sirkin, Stuart A. and Sonja J. Coffin (2008). 'Would It Have Mattered? The Consequences of Favoring Short-Term Budget Goals Over Long-Term Retirement Policy,' *Benefits Quarterly*, First Quarter, n.p.

Smith, Leslie V. (2006). *Annual 401(k) Benchmarking Survey 2005/2006 Edition*. New York: Deloitte Consulting LLP, the International Foundation of Employee Benefit Plans, and the International Society of Certified Employee Benefit Specialists. http://www.ifebp.org/pdf/research/2005-06Annual401kSurvey.pdf

T. Rowe Price Group, Inc. (2009). *The T. Rowe Price Retirement Savings Guide: Plan, Save, and Enjoy Your Retirement*. Baltimore, MD: T. Rowe Price Group, Inc. https://individual.troweprice.com/Retail/Shared/PDFs/retPlanGuide.pdf

The Federal Retirement Thrift Investment Board (2009). *2008 TSP Participant Survey Results*. Washington, DC: The Federal Retirement Thrift Investment Board.

Tyson, Wendy and Mike Palumbo (2008). 'Congressional Support for Advice Programs in the PPA,' *Vanguard Regulatory Brief 2008-07*. Valley Forge, PA: The Vanguard Group, Inc.

Ungurean, Scarlett (2004). '401(k) Plans: Are Employers Taking on More Risk by Providing Investment Advice to Participants?,' White Paper. New York: Mercer Investment Consulting, Inc.

United States Department of Labor Bureau of Labor Statistics (USDOL) (2008). *Employee Tenure in 2008*. Washington, DC: United States Department of Labor Bureau of Labor Statistics.

United States Department of Labor Employee Benefits Security Administration (USDOL) (2007). *Field Assistance Bulletin No. 2007-01*. Washington, DC: United States Department of Labor Employee Benefits Security Administration.

——(2009). *Investment Advice – Participants and Beneficiaries; Final Rule*. Washington, DC: United States Department of Labor Employee Benefits Security Administration.

United States Department of Labor Pension and Welfare Benefits Administration (USDOL) (1996). *Interpretive Bulletin 96-1; Participant Investment Education; Final Rule*. Washington, DC: United States Department of Labor Pension and Welfare Benefits Administration.

United States Department of Labor Pension and Welfare Benefits Administration Office of Regulations and Interpretations (USDOL) (2001). *Advisory Opinion 2001-09A ERISA Sec. 406(b)*. Washington, DC: United States Department of Labor Pension and Welfare Benefits Administration Office of Regulations and Interpretations.

Vanguard (2008). *How Financial Literacy and Trust in Financial Institutions Affect 401 (k) Savings Behavior*. Valley Forge, PA: The Vanguard Group, Inc. https://institutional.vanguard.com/VGApp/iip/site/institutional/researchcommentary/article?File=FinancialLiteracyTrust

Warshawsky, Mark J. (2007). 'The New Pension Law and Defined Benefit Plans: A Surprisingly Good Match,' Working Paper No. 2007-06. Philadelphia, PA: The Pension Research Council of the Wharton School, University of Pennsylvania.

Part II
The Environment for Retirement Plan Redesign

Chapter 6

The Effect of Uncertain Labor Income and Social Security on Life-Cycle Portfolios

Raimond Maurer, Olivia S. Mitchell, and Ralph Rogalla

Risky labor income and pension payouts are key determinants of retirement well-being and investment behavior over the life cycle. In the past, defined benefit (DB) pension plans and social security benefits provided a substantial and relatively stable component of retirement wealth, whereas more recently, labor market flexibility has grown, along with defined contribution (DC) plans. As a result, households will be required to take on increased responsibility for retirement accumulation and decumulation in a more uncertain world. This chapter examines how consumers can optimally allocate their saving among two major asset classes, namely, equity and bonds, and two types of retirement assets, namely, liquid saving and illiquid annuities. We illustrate how incorporating labor income risk as well as social security benefits influences optimal asset allocation, in a realistically calibrated dynamic life-cycle model.

Our study extends prior literature by taking into account life annuities that pay a defined stream of benefits over the remaining lifetime (e.g., Cocco, Gomes, and Maenhout 2005). This work evaluates the impact of alternative empirical labor income trajectories, allowing for an observed inverted-U-shaped age-related pay profile as well as volatility around that profile. We use this approach to assess how differences in earnings profiles and shocks may drive life-cycle investment behavior and the demand for annuities. We also build on our own prior work (Horneff et al. 2009, 2010) that shows that households can benefit substantially from holding annuities as well as capital market assets. As demonstrated there, the particular appeal of annuities is that they offer consumers not only an investment return from the underlying assets but also the survival credit generated from pooling mortality risk.[1] These papers provide insight into how a reasonable investor would optimally save and invest her wealth across bonds, stocks, and annuities, taking into account various levels of social security replacement rates.

In what follows, we model the effect of uncertain labor income and social security benefit replacement ratios on life-cycle portfolios. After outlining the empirical framework employed, we present results on optimal expected consumption, saving, asset allocation, and annuity purchases for representative households. We show that higher labor income risk and lower social security replacement rates will induce higher demand for stable income – not only in retirement but also earlier in life. In other words, individuals exposed to labor earnings risk can, to some extent, 'roll their own' personal DB scheme by resorting to the private annuity market. We also show that a declining equity glide path with age is appropriate for both low- and middle-income risk workers, while, for the high-income risk worker, equity exposure rises until retirement.

Empirical strategy

To illustrate how different levels of labor income uncertainty and social security retirement benefits affect outcomes of interest, we examine the case of an individual who is assumed to work from the age of 20 until retirement at age 65, after which she expects to rely on social security benefits, withdrawals from liquid saving, and privately purchased life annuity income.[2] The maximum assumed survival age is 100. She can invest her liquid saving in riskless bonds or risky stocks, and she may also purchase immediate real fixed payout annuities, both before and after retirement. The individual anticipates surviving from period t to $t+1$ with probability p_t^s, which is her subjective probability. She derives constant relative risk aversion (CRRA) utility from consumption of a single nondurable good C. The value function is maximized over the arguments C_t, π_t, and a_t according to $V_t = \frac{C_t^{1-\rho}}{1-\rho} + \beta p_t^s E_t[V_{t+1}]$, where ρ is the coefficient of relative risk aversion, β is a time discount factor, π_t is the share of liquid assets held in equities, and a_t refers to annuity purchases each period.[3] The individual is precluded from borrowing against future labor income and from short-selling bonds, stocks, and life annuities.

A topic of considerable recent interest is how to model labor income uncertainty.[4] We posit that each period's labor income Y_t is given by $Y_t = exp(f(t))P_t U_t$ with $P_t = P_{t-1}N_t$, where $f(t)$ represents a hump-shaped income profile over the life cycle often used in empirical research (Cocco, Gomes, and Maenhout 2005). Here, P_t represents the permanent human capital component and N_t allows for stochastic changes; U_t is a transitory shock; σ_u is the volatility of the transitory shock, and σ_n of the permanent shock.[5] In retirement ($t > K$), we assume (for simplicity) that the individual receives constant and real social security benefits with a constant benefit replacement ratio (ζ) with respect to final salary, expressed as $Y_t = \zeta exp\left(f(K)\right)P_K$, where K is the final year of work.

Our benchmark case for an illustrative consumer sets preference parameters to standard values found in the life-cycle literature: the relative risk aversion coefficient is $\rho = 5$, and the discount factor $\beta = 0.96$ (e.g., Gomes and Michaelides 2005). Representing subjective survival probabilities, we apply nonlinear least squares to fit the Gompertz force of mortality to the 2000 population basic mortality table for US females. To calculate the actuarial premium of a life payout annuity, we use annuitant mortality tables and include expense loading λ of 7.2 percent, consistent with Mitchell et al. (1999). The household can directly invest in two financial assets: riskless bonds and risky stocks. The riskless real bond gross return is 2 percent, while the real risky stock return is log-normally distributed with an expected return of 6 percent and a volatility of 18 percent as in much of the literature. The deterministic age-dependent labor income function for an individual with only a high-school education is taken from Cocco, Gomes, and Maenhout (2005). The assumed base case social security replacement rate ζ of 68 percent is currently typical of low-wage retirees in the United States (Mitchell and Phillips 2006). In an alternative scenario, we also show how outcomes would change with a lower replacement rate of 50 percent; this figure is consistent with replacement ratios for low-wage earners in Japan (OECD 2009: 39). These two alternatives are of interest given that Japan's current demographic situation and social security shortfalls may well presage the future for the United States.

The labor income volatility parameters for the base case are $\sigma_n = 0.05$ and $\sigma_u = 0.075$, representing a labor income profile with relatively low risk; here correlations between the stock returns and the permanent (transitory) income shocks are set to $\phi_n = 0(\phi_u = 0)$. In the alternative scenario, we evaluate results using a much higher labor income risk volatility of four times the base level as well as $\phi_n = 0.25$. In sensitivity analysis, we also show results for lower ($\rho = 3$) and higher ($\rho = 8$) levels of risk aversion.[6] Table 6.1 summarizes model parameters.

TABLE 6.1 Behavioral and market parameters employed in empirical analysis

	σ_n	σ_u	ϕ_n	ζ	ρ
Low	0.05	0.075	0.00	0.50	3
Medium	0.10	0.200	0.00	0.60	5
High	0.20	0.300	0.25	0.68	8

Notes: σ_n and σ_u refer, respectively, to the volatility of the permanent and transitory income shocks, ϕ_n is the correlation of labor income risk with stock returns, ζ is the social security replacement rate, and ρ is the relative risk aversion coefficient; see text.

Source: Authors' calculations; see text.

Life-cycle patterns of investment, saving, and consumption

The base case investor is one with low labor income risk, high social security replacement rate, and medium risk aversion, who faces incomplete private markets for immediate annuities with high loadings. Results appear in Figure 6.1, which displays the expected development of labor income, consumption, liquid saving, annuity purchases, and annuity income from age 20 to 100. To generate a smooth lifetime consumption path, the worker saves from her 30s to her mid-50s so as to pay for later consumption. By her late 50s, liquid assets – outside of annuities – rise to a maximum of almost

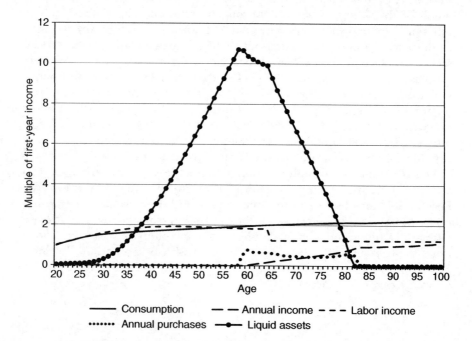

Figure 6.1 Life-cycle asset allocation patterns: low labor income risk and high social security replacement rate. *Notes*: The Figure embodies a retirement age of 65, replacement rate of 68%, annuity loading of 7.2%, moderate risk aversion ($\rho = 5$), volatility of transitory income shock = 7.5%, volatility of permanent income shock = 5%, and correlation of permanent labor income shock with equity returns = 0 (see text). Labor income, consumption, liquid assets, annuity purchases, and annuity payouts are expressed as a multiple of first-year labor income. *Source*: Authors' calculations; see text.

11 times her starting or initial labor income. After that, the investor gradually starts drawing down assets to compensate for declining labor income; after about age 60, liquid assets are deployed to buy private annuities. From retirement at age 65, liquid assets are depleted rapidly permitting the retiree to maintain preretirement consumption; as well, she relies increasingly on income flowing from private annuities, which she continues to buy even well beyond retirement age. In her early 80s, her liquid assets are fully exhausted because she has no bequest motive; after that point, the annuity payout stream is considerable, helping maintain a smooth consumption path throughout her remaining lifetime.

Figure 6.2 indicates how liquid assets, as a multiple of first-year labor income, and saving rates are expected to change with age. The saving rate is defined as $SRate_t = 1 - C_t/Income_t$ and $Income$ refers to the flow of labor income and annuity benefits.[7] The base case is represented by the solid line, for the low labor income risk/high social security replacement rate scenario. In this safer world, the individual has little need to save early in life: the saving rate is low at young ages and only from the mid-20s does saving rise, with a peak in the mid-40s of 10 percent per year, and it becomes negative (-5%) in the mid-50s. After retirement, saving rates drop precipitously and reach -40 percent so as to smooth consumption; the elderly, older than about age 85, have a saving rate of zero. Liquid assets grow slowly early in life, rising to around 10 times first-year labor income at their peak.

In the riskier scenario, the social security replacement rate is reduced to 50 percent, and labor income risk is four times the base level and correlated with the stock market. Here, the young adult will engage in substantially higher saving to build a buffer against high labor income volatility – over 40 percent per annum. Assets rise to 40 times first-year income by the late 50s. Next, the saving rate falls, crossing the zero mark around the early 60s; thereafter it rises again briefly just before retirement to offset low social security benefits. As we shall show next, the money is used mainly to purchase annuities that provide a secondary stable income stream in retirement. Nevertheless, this individual's liquid saving continues to rise through the mid-50s, due to returns on investment. After retirement, at 65, when the social security benefit begins, assets are consumed, and the saving rate trajectory follows the one described earlier.

Turning to Figure 6.3, the three Panels illustrate how the individual will optimally allocate her total financial wealth by age across equities, bonds, and private annuities; here, total financial wealth is defined to include both liquid assets and the present value of future private annuity income claims. On average, as is indicated in Panel A, the base case individual (solid line) will optimally hold only equities from youth to about age 50 (apart from a few bonds early on, shown in Panel B). This is a common result in many

(A)

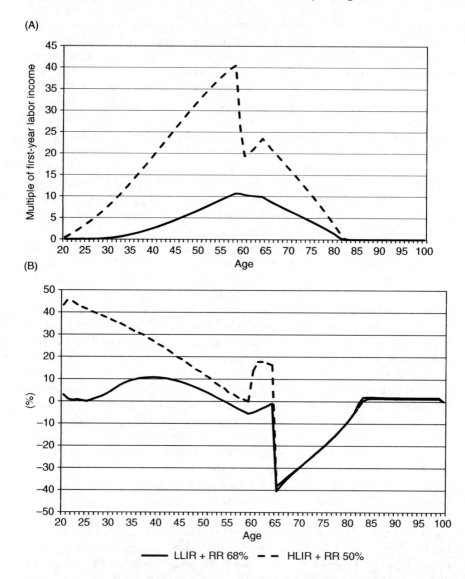

(B)

Figure 6.2 Liquid assets and saving rates for low versus high labor income risk levels and high versus low social security replacement rates. Panel A: Liquid assets. Panel B: Saving rates. *Notes*: Liquid assets (held in stocks and bonds) are expressed as a multiple of first-year labor income; saving rates are the percent of labor plus annuity income saved. LLIR + RR 68% stands for low labor income risk, high (68%) social security replacement rate; HLIR + RR 50% stands for high labor income risk, low (50%) social security replacement rate. *Source*: Authors' calculations; see text.

life-cycle studies and occurs because, early in life, the individual's main asset is human capital that has bond-like payout characteristics. This is especially true with low labor income uncertainty, where her relatively safe labor income is also protected in retirement with a relatively high social security benefit. She will optimally diversify her complete portfolio, which includes both the present value of her human capital (labor income plus social security benefits) as well as financial assets, by holding little to nothing in bonds and instead invests entirely in equities. Beginning about age 55, her asset allocation begins to include more bonds as her remaining work years dwindle.

The optimal pattern for privately purchased annuities is illustrated in Panel C; these play no role in the investor's portfolio prior to the age of 59, as they are relatively unattractive *vis-à-vis* bonds due to high loading and the use of annuitant survival tables in pricing. At older ages, however, the annuity survival credit rises above the bond rate; as a result, annuities crowd out bonds. In retirement, liquid assets are depleted to support consumption and buy annuities, which provide a secure private income stream (assuming no bequests). Beginning in her early 80s, the retiree is fully annuitized.

These results should be contrasted to those generated by the alternative scenario with high labor income uncertainty and low social security replacement rates.[8] In general, we would expect that this consumer will need to save more, and hold more safe assets. This is borne out in Panels A–C (dashed line), where the equity fraction starts at zero and even in middle age remains below 30 percent; by contrast the bond fraction starts out at 100 percent and falls as the worker nears retirement. This is because labor income no longer produces a bond-like stream of payments that previously pushed the young investor into equities. This investor also demands more annuities, beginning around age 45, to help offset variable work earnings. The annuitized fraction then rises quickly around retirement, to help offset the now-low social security replacement rates. Around age 60, the rising survival credit dominates the annuity pricing offsets due to loads and the use of annuitant mortality tables. In all cases the transition to annuities is accomplished by a substantial movement out of bonds: her allocation to bonds drops from 65 to about 15 percent. As in the base case, the individual is fully annuitized from age 83 onward. It is also worth noting that, around age 65 when she becomes entitled to social security benefits, she is no longer exposed to labor income risk. Accordingly, the stabile private annuity income plus the social security payments permits the investor to hold more equities. Thus, equity exposure rises to over 40 percent, and then it gradually declines in favor of annuities, until liquid savings are exhausted at age 83.[9]

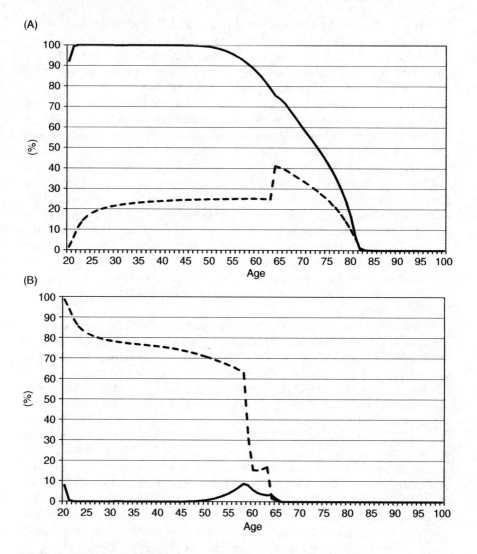

Figure 6.3 Life-cycle asset allocation for low versus high labor income risk levels and high versus low social security replacement rates. Panel A: Equity weights. Panel B: Bond weights. Panel C: Annuity weights. *Notes*: Asset weights expressed as a percentage of total wealth (liquid assets + present value of annuity claims). LLIR + RR 68% stands for low labor income risk, high (68%) social security replacement rate; HLIR + RR 50% stands for high labor income risk, low (50%) social security replacement rate. *Source*: Authors' calculations; see text.

(C)

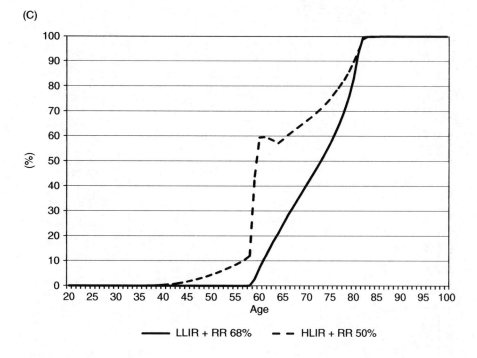

        LLIR + RR 68%   – – HLIR + RR 50%

Sensitivity analysis

Next we review how results change across six combinations of labor income risk levels and social security replacement rates; comparative results appear in Table 6.2. Panel 1 focuses on the high social security replacement rate scenario and reports liquid assets, saving rates, and asset allocation fractions, for three workers: the *low* income volatility case (the base case from earlier), a *high* volatility case (the alternative scenario defined earlier), and a *middle* risk case (defined as $\sigma_n = 0.10$, $\sigma_u = 0.20$, and $\phi_n = 0$). Panel 2 indicates the same results for a lower social security benefit replacement rate of 50 percent. We report patterns for 5 decades of life from age 45 to 85.

Comparing Panels 1 and 2 for all three levels of labor income risk, it is evident that the Panel 2 individual (with lower old-age benefits) accumulates more liquid assets (row 6 versus row 1) by saving more early in life (row 7 versus row 2) but she draws down her assets more quickly after retirement, so as to preserve her consumption stream. Now, moving horizontally across the table, irrespective of social security benefit levels, as labor income risk rises, so too do liquid assets. For example, even by age 45, the high labor income risk individual has amassed assets five times more due to a much higher saving rate (17.4 percent versus 8.5 percent).[10]

TABLE 6.2 Life-cycle saving rates and portfolio mixes for alternative labor income risk levels and social security replacement rates

		Low labor income risk					Medium labor income risk					High labor income risk				
		Age					Age					Age				
		45	55	65	75	85	45	55	65	75	85	45	55	65	75	85
		(1)	(2)	(3)	(4)	(5)	(6)	(7)	(8)	(9)	(10)	(11)	(12)	(13)	(14)	(15)
Panel 1: High social security replacement rate (68%)																
Liquid assets	(1)	4.6	9.3	9.3	4.1	0.0	11.1	17.9	12.9	5.7	0.0	25.7	36.3	23.6	11.1	0.0
Saving rate (%)	(2)	8.5	−1.2	−40.4	−19.8	1.9	5.9	−11.0	−41.5	−20.0	1.8	17.4	−0.1	−35.8	−19.7	1.8
Equities (%)	(3)	100.0	95.8	74.0	43.1	0.0	92.8	75.6	59.3	34.9	0.0	24.4	24.8	47.3	29.6	0.0
Bonds (%)	(4)	0.0	4.2	1.3	0.0	0.0	7.2	24.3	1.3	0.0	0.0	74.0	67.3	0.8	0.0	0.0
Annuities (%)	(5)	0.0	0.0	24.7	56.9	100.0	0.0	0.1	39.4	65.1	100.0	1.6	7.9	51.9	70.4	100.0
Panel 2: Low social security replacement rate (50%)																
Liquid assets	(6)	6.0	12.3	9.2	4.0	0.0	12.4	20.4	12.2	5.3	0.0	26.3	38.0	22.3	10.2	0.0
Saving rate (%)	(7)	11.4	2.3	−42.9	−20.1	1.4	8.4	−6.6	−42.6	−20.1	1.4	18.9	3.8	−38.3	−19.9	1.3
Equities (%)	(8)	99.8	86.5	52.9	31.0	0.0	88.9	66.3	46.3	27.5	0.0	24.5	25.0	40.5	25.0	0.0
Bonds (%)	(9)	0.2	13.5	1.3	0.0	0.0	11.1	33.6	1.2	0.0	0.0	73.8	66.6	0.8	0.0	0.0
Annuities (%)	(10)	0.0	0.0	45.8	69.0	100.0	0.0	0.1	52.5	72.5	100.0	1.7	8.4	58.7	75.0	100.0

Notes: Model assumes a retirement age of 65, annuity loading of 7.2%, moderate risk aversion ($\gamma = 5$). For the case of low labor income risk, the volatility of transitory income shock is 7.5%, the volatility of the permanent income shock is 5%, and the correlation of the permanent income shock with equity returns is 0. For the medium labor income risk case, the volatility of transitory income shock is 15%, the volatility of the permanent income shock is 10%, and the correlation of the permanent shock with equity returns is 0. For the high labor income risk case, the volatility of transitory income shock is 30%, the volatility of the permanent income shock is 20%, and the correlation of the permanent shock with equity returns is 0.25. Investment weights are computed as a fraction of total wealth (liquid assets + present value of annuity claims); liquid assets are computed as a multiple of initial labor income; saving rates are the percent of labor plus annuity income saved.

Source: Authors' calculations; see text.

TABLE 6.3 Life-cycle saving rates and portfolio mixes for alternative levels of risk-aversion and social security replacement rates

		Low risk aversion (γ = 3)					Medium risk aversion (γ = 5)					High risk aversion (γ = 8)				
				Age					Age					Age			
		45	55	65	75	85	45	55	65	75	85	45	55	65	75	85
		(1)	(2)	(3)	(4)	(5)	(6)	(7)	(8)	(9)	(10)	(11)	(12)	(13)	(14)	(15)

Panel 1: High social security replacement rate (68%)

Liquid assets	(1)	6.5	11.4	14.3	7.2	0.8	11.1	17.9	12.9	5.7	0.0	15.6	22.0	8.4	3.8	0.0
Saving rate (%)	(2)	5.7	−7.4	−69.8	−48.3	−15.6	5.9	−11.0	−41.5	−20.0	1.8	7.8	−10.9	−17.8	−6.0	6.2
Equities (%)	(3)	100.0	99.3	94.7	74.5	29.3	92.8	75.6	59.3	34.9	0.0	49.3	39.2	32.6	19.3	0.0
Bonds (%)	(4)	0.0	0.6	0.4	0.0	0.0	7.2	24.3	1.3	0.0	0.0	50.7	60.7	0.5	0.0	0.0
Annuities (%)	(5)	0.0	0.0	4.9	25.5	70.7	0.0	0.1	39.4	65.1	100.0	0.0	0.1	66.9	80.7	100.0

Panel 2: Low social security replacement rate (50%)

Liquid assets	(6)	7.6	14.2	16.9	7.6	0.8	12.4	20.4	12.2	5.3	0.0	16.4	23.8	7.9	3.5	0.0
Saving rate (%)	(7)	8.0	−4.0	−98.2	−54.1	−16.2	8.4	−6.6	−42.6	−20.1	1.4	10.2	−6.2	−18.2	−6.0	6.3
Equities (%)	(8)	100.0	98.1	84.5	56.7	15.0	88.9	66.3	46.3	27.5	0.0	46.4	35.1	26.9	16.1	0.0
Bonds (%)	(9)	0.0	1.9	1.0	0.0	0.0	11.1	33.6	1.2	0.0	0.0	53.6	64.8	0.3	0.0	0.0
Annuities (%)	(10)	0.0	0.1	14.6	43.3	85.0	0.0	0.1	52.5	72.5	100.0	0.0	0.1	72.8	83.9	100.0

Notes: Results are computed for the medium labor income risk case where the volatility of transitory income shock is 15%, the volatility of permanent income shock is 10%, and the correlation of the permanent shock with equity returns is 0. For other definitions, see Table 6.2.

Source: Authors' calculations; see text.

Moving horizontally across the table, it is clear that more labor income risk reduces the demand for equities (rows 3 and 8), irrespective of the social security replacement rate. Similarly, higher income risk makes annuities more attractive at younger ages, in all cases (rows 5 and 10). As seen earlier, a declining equity glide path with age is appropriate for both low- and middle-income risk workers, while, for the high-income risk worker, equity exposure optimally rises until retirement. Moving down the table, we note that lower replacement rates prompt lower equity holdings for both low- and middle-income risk workers, while bonds and annuities become more desirable. For those facing high labor income risk, asset allocation patterns are less sensitive to old-age benefit levels, though the direction is similar.

Next we investigate the sensitivity of our results with respect to the investor's level of risk aversion. In addition to the base case risk parameter ($\gamma = 5$) analyzed earlier, Table 6.3 tabulates results for low ($\gamma = 3$) and high ($\gamma = 8$) relative risk aversion levels, assuming the worker has a medium labor income volatility (so she is exposed to risk other than through the capital market). As before, Panel 1 presents patterns of liquid saving and saving rates, as well as allocations to equities, bonds, and annuities for the high social security replacement rate; Panel 2 provides results for the lower value.

Here, as risk aversion rises (moving horizontally across the table), liquid assets and expected saving rates again rise (rows 1, 2, 6, and 7), irrespective of the social security replacement rate; that is, higher risk aversion enhances the appeal of saving. Moving down the table, when social security benefits are reduced at a given level of labor uncertainty, higher saving rates and liquid assets are observed at younger, but not at older, ages. Also, as we move to the right in the table, as risk aversion rises, it is evident and unsurprising that the fraction in equities falls in favor of bonds and annuities. Going down a column, when the replacement rate drops, again the equity fraction falls – though it is interesting that at age 85, the least risk-averse consumer still holds 15 percent of her portfolio in equities. In all three cases, bonds dominate at younger ages, while annuities crowd out bonds at older ages.

Conclusion

Retirement risk management is likely to become increasingly important with global demographic aging, a phenomenon already requiring social security benefit cuts in some developed nations such as Japan. This chapter illustrates how increasing labor income risk and reductions in social security replacement rates would be predicted to influence saving, life-cycle portfolio asset demand, and purchases of payout annuities. Our model shows that higher labor income risk and lower social security replacement rates boost saving rates early in life and liquid assets accumulated for precautionary purposes. A more uncertain and less generous environment also induces greater demand for protection in the form of stable income – early in life and in retirement. The enhanced need for safety is met not only with bonds, but also with payout annuities whereas the demand for equities falls. Also, individuals who are more risk averse save more early in life, and hold fewer equities.

Our analysis offers several useful implications. For instance, financial advisers must be aware of possible future social security benefit cuts as they design optimal lifetime asset accumulation paths and portfolio allocations for younger clients. Also, the financial services industry and pension sponsors must take careful account of labor income risk when formulating recommendations for client portfolios. Thus, we show that low- and middle-income risk workers will favor an equity glide path that declines with age, but for those facing high income risk, equity exposure should be low early in life and rise until retirement. Moreover, for those with uncertain labor income, it is desirable to purchase immediate payout annuities early in life so as to build up a second more stable stream of income. Our work underscores the need for workers to have a way to create their own 'DB plan equivalents' with privately purchased payout annuities.

Acknowledgments

This research was conducted with support from the Pension Research Council at The Wharton School of the University of Pennsylvania. We are grateful for useful comments from Jason Scott and Ramu Thiagarajan. This is part of the NBER's program on the Economics of Aging.

Notes

[1] For additional references to the rapidly growing literature on realistically calibrated discrete dynamic portfolio choice models, see Horneff et al. (2009, 2010) and Wachter and Yogo (2009).

[2] For a more detailed description of the modeling approach see Horneff et al. (2009, 2010); flexible hours and endogenous retirement ages are considered in Chai et al. (2009).

[3] For this analysis, we assume that the household derives no utility from bequests. Hurd (1989) suggests that most bequests are accidental.

[4] Notable prior studies on asset allocation that consider uninsurable labor income risk include Campbell and Viceira (2002), Heaton and Lucas (1997), Viceira (2001), Bodie et al. (2004), and Polkovnichenko (2007).

[5] The logarithms of both N_t and U_t are normally distributed with means 0 and with volatilities σ_n and σ_u, respectively. The shocks are assumed to be uncorrelated.

[6] We solve the optimization problem by backward induction in a three-dimensional state space, whereby for each grid point we evaluate the policy and value functions using Gaussian quadrature integration and cubic spline interpolation. For technical details, we refer the interested reader to Horneff, Maurer, and Stamos (2008) and Horneff et al. (2009, 2010).

[7] Here, we report the saving rate as $\text{SRate}_t = 1 - E(C_t)/E(\text{Income}_t)$; in unreported results, we have also computed $\text{SRate}_t = 1 - E(C_t/\text{Income}_t)$ which is substantially lower in the high risk/low replacement rate scenario.

[8] These are partial equilibrium computations, in that lower social security benefit are not offset by social security tax cuts.

[9] This is because of the increasing survival credit at older ages, which raises expected annuity payouts *vis-à-vis* equities (Horneff et al. 2009, 2010).

[10] In the medium-income labor case, the saving rate is always lower than for the low-income risk case, though liquid assets are higher in all cases. This is due to the fact that this medium-income risk individual saves from a younger age, and at a higher rate (in results available on request).

References

Bodie, Zvi, Jérôme B. Detemple, Susanne Otruba, and Stephan Walter (2004). 'Optimal Consumption–Portfolio Choices and Retirement Planning,' *Journal of Economic Dynamics and Control*, 28: 1115–48.

Campbell, John and Luis Viceira (2002). *Strategic Asset Allocation: Portfolio Choice for Long-Term Investors*. Clarendon Lectures in Economics. Oxford, UK: Oxford University Press.

Chai, Jingjing, Wolfram Horneff, Raimond Maurer, and Olivia S. Mitchell (2009). 'Extending Life Cycle Models of Optimal Portfolio Choice: Integrating Flexible Work, Endogenous Retirement, and Investment Decisions with Lifetime Payouts,' NBER WP 15079. Cambridge, MA: National Bureau of Economic Research.

Cocco, João, Francisco Gomes, and Pascal Maenhout (2005). 'Consumption and Portfolio Choice over the Life Cycle,' *Review of Financial Studies*, 18: 491–533.

Gomes, Francisco and Alexander Michaelides (2005). 'Optimal Life-Cycle Asset Allocation: Understanding the Empirical Evidence,' *Journal of Finance*, 60: 869–904.

Heaton, John and Deborah Lucas (1997). 'Market Frictions, Savings and Portfolio Choice,' *Macroeconomic Dynamics*, 1: 76–101.

Horneff, Wolfram, Raimond Maurer, and Michael Stamos (2008). 'Life-Cycle Asset Allocation with Annuity Markets,' *Journal of Economic Dynamics and Control*, 32: 3590–612.

————— Olivia S. Mitchell, and Michael Stamos (2009). 'Asset Allocation and Location over the Life Cycle with Survival Contingent Payouts,' *Journal of Banking and Finance*, 33: 1688–99.

————————(2010). 'Variable Payout Annuities and Dynamic Portfolio Choice in Retirement,' *Journal of Pension Economics and Finance*, 9: 163–83.

Hurd, Michael (1989). 'Mortality Risk and Bequests,' *Econometrica*, 57: 779–813.

Mitchell, Olivia S. and John Phillips (2006). 'Social Security Replacement Rates for Alternative Earnings Benchmarks,' *Benefits Quarterly*, 4th Q: 37–47.

—— James Poterba, Mark Warshawsky, and Jeffrey Brown (1999). 'New Evidence on the Money Worth of Individual Annuities,' *American Economic Review*, 89: 1299–318.

OECD (2009). *Pensions at a Glance: 2009, Retirement Income Systems in OECD Countries.* Paris, France: OECD.

Polkovnichenko, Valery (2007). 'Life-Cycle Portfolio Choice with Additive Habit Formation Preferences and Uninsurable Labor Income Risk,' *Review of Financial Studies*, 20: 83–124.

Viceira, Luis (2001). 'Optimal Portfolio Choice for Long-Horizon Investors with Non-tradable Labor Income,' *Journal of Finance*, 56: 433–70.

Wachter, Jessica and Motohiro Yogo (2009). 'Why Do Household Portfolio Shares Rise in Wealth?' AFA 2008 New Orleans Meetings Working Paper. Philadelphia, PA: The Wharton School of the University of Pennsylvania.

Chapter 7

The Declining Role of Private Defined Benefit Pension Plans: Who Is Affected, and How

Craig Copeland and Jack VanDerhei

The policy debate over retirement security has focused in part on whether retirees will have sufficient pension income. As defined benefit (DB) pension sponsors continue to freeze accruals for new and/or current employees, they often substitute either new or enhanced defined contribution (DC) plans in their place. The question is whether the total *expected* retirement income from the combination of the frozen DB and any new/ additional 401(k) balances will equal or exceed what employees had anticipated receiving from the original DB plan, had it continued without modifications.

What it might take to indemnify an employee for such a freeze is the subject of this chapter. Because workers affected by a DB pension freeze vary according to age, salary, and job tenure, as well as the DB and DC plan provisions and formulas and the economic assumptions used to estimate the effects of a pension freeze, there is no simple answer. Prior studies have indicated how patterns might vary by age and job tenure: older, longer-tenured workers tend to be affected by a pension freeze from the *current* plan sponsor more than younger workers, because they have less time remaining in their working careers in a 401(k) plan to offset the accrual loss from the pension freeze (VanDerhei 2006).

In what follows, we first discuss data on the fraction of Americans aged 65 and older receiving annuity income flows from an employer pension. We also mention how pension income flows vary across various demographic characteristics and characteristics of the employers providing the plans. Next we build on newly available information to examine the financial impact of pension freezes upon the employee population. Of key relevance is the need for information on what improvements, if any, tend to be made to DC plans when DB plans are frozen. We draw on VanDerhei (2007) for this data and the Employee Benefits Research Institution/Education and Research Fund (EBRI/ERF) Retirement Security Project Model to assess the impact of pension freezes on future private DB plan accruals.

To summarize findings, we show that benefits as.a fraction of preretirement pay would decline by an annual 0.5–2.1 percentage points, depending on the retiree's age and sex. Yet some employees, almost one-third of those under age 35, could do better at retirement due to enhanced DC contributions.

Trends in pension benefits for Americans aged 65 and older

DB pensions have traditionally paid retirees periodic lifetime incomes, or annuities.[1] In the US Census Bureau's Current Population Survey, the percentage of Americans aged 65 and older that reported having a pension and/or annuity income was 24 percent in 1974, and it rose to almost 38 percent in 1992 (Figure 7.1).[2] The fraction subsequently fell to 34 percent by 2007. In other words, less than 40 percent of Americans aged 65 and older have ever received pension and/or annuity income. Even among those with income in the top two quintiles, no more than 62 percent receive pension incomes in the most recent years of the data (2006–7). Furthermore, the peak year appears to have been already reached almost 15 years ago.

A similar question is asked in the Census Bureau's Survey of Income and Program Participation (SIPP), where we see that 35 percent of Americans aged 65 and older had pension and/or annuity income from their former employers in 2006 (Table 7.1). If we also include this income from spouse's former employers, the fraction rises to 44 percent. These fractions have fallen below prior surveys (36 and 44 percent in 1998 while 38 and 46 percent in 2003). Younger retirees (aged 65–69) were less likely to have this type of income with 32 percent in 2006, versus 36 percent or more for those aged 70 and older. Men and the better educated were also more likely to have pension income, while White and Black Americans aged 65 and older were also more likely to have pension income than Hispanic Americans. For those with pension and/or annuity income, the median amount was about $9,700 in 2006, up from $9,100 in 2003 (all in 2006 dollars). For those aged 65–69 receiving pension income, the median annual benefit was about $12,100, higher than $10,300 for those aged 70–74 and $9,600 for those aged 75–79. Those with a college or postgraduate degree received pensions worth significantly more, $17,300 and $21,600, respectively.

A unique feature of the SIPP data is that it asks retirees questions about characteristics of the employers from which they retired along with their earnings prior to retirement, so that some conclusions can be drawn about the likelihood of receiving pension income from specific types of employers. For those aged 65 and older who had worked for pay for at least 5 years

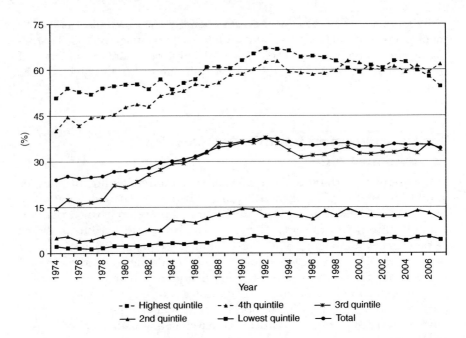

Figure 7.1 Percentage of Americans aged 65 or older with pension and annuity income, by income quintile; 1974–2007. *Source*: EBRI (2009).

before retiring, 52 percent received pension and/or annuity income in 2006 (Table 7.2), down from 55 percent in 2003. Those who had worked for larger firms, were covered by a union and were in the public sector, had longer job tenure, and earned more were more likely to have pension income. For instance, a retiree aged 65 and older who had worked at a larger firm (100 or more employees) had a median annual amount of $10,700 versus $7,000 or less for retirees from smaller firms. Public-sector retirees had significantly higher pension incomes ($15,600 versus $6,800) than those retiring from private-sector jobs. It must be noted that in some cases, public-sector retirees received no Social Security income, whereas private-sector retirees did.

The lesson, then, is for the last 30 years in America, at most 40 percent of the elderly received pension and/or annuity income from an employer. Even those who retired from a job after 20 or more years with an employer, fewer than two-thirds, had pension income in 2006. Furthermore, the median pension income received by former private-sector workers was relatively low, under $7,000 per year in 2006. While this benefit was valuable to those receiving it, it was unlikely to free older Americans of financial concern.

TABLE 7.1 Characteristics of Americans aged 65 or older with pension income by demographic characteristics: 1998, 2003, and 2006

	1998				2003				2006			
	Pension income from				Pension income from				Pension income from			
	Number (M)	Own former employer (%)	Own/ spouse's former employer (%)	Median yearly pension income amount[a] ($)	Number (M)	Own former employer (%)	Own/ spouse's former employer (%)	Median yearly pension income amount[a] ($)	Number (M)	Own former employer (%)	Own/ spouse's former employer (%)	Median yearly pension income amount[a] ($)
Total	32.2	36.0	44.3	7,167	34.1	37.6	45.6	9,073	35.4	35.4	43.5	9,696
Age												
65–69	9.4	35.3	41.7	8,120	9.6	37.7	42.7	11,044	10.2	32.1	37.0	12,144
70–74	8.6	38.3	45.5	7,833	8.5	39.0	45.5	9,138	8.4	36.6	43.7	10,320
75–79	6.9	36.8	47.6	6,997	7.4	36.2	46.3	8,172	7.2	37.9	47.0	9,600
80 or older	7.3	33.6	42.9	5,052	8.7	37.2	48.2	7,180	9.6	36.0	47.6	7,200
Sex												
Male	13.6	53.2	56.0	9,138	14.4	54.0	57.0	11,397	15.1	48.4	52.7	12,000
Female	18.6	23.5	35.7	4,517	19.6	25.5	37.3	5,940	20.3	25.7	36.6	6,384
Race/ethnicity												
White	27.0	37.8	46.6	7,311	28.2	39.3	47.9	9,138	28.7	36.6	45.3	9,804
Black	2.6	33.5	39.5	6,619	2.7	34.4	41.2	7,572	2.9	35.4	41.2	8,004
Hispanic	1.6	22.0	25.5	4,896	2.0	24.4	28.6	7,154	2.2	23.6	29.3	7,800
Other	0.9	17.5	22.0	5,431	1.1	25.9	28.9	9,138	1.5	29.6	33.9	12,000
Education												
No high school	11.0	27.9	35.3	5,209	9.3	26.5	34.5	5,287	5.5	21.8	28.4	4,908

(continued)

TABLE 7.1 (*Continued*)

| | 1998 | | | | 2003 | | | | 2006 | | | |
| | Pension income from | | | | Pension income from | | | | Pension income from | | | |
	Number (M)	Own former employer (%)	Own/ spouse's former employer (%)	Median yearly pension income amount[a] ($)	Number (M)	Own former employer (%)	Own/ spouse's former employer (%)	Median yearly pension income amount[a] ($)	Number (M)	Own former employer (%)	Own/ spouse's former employer (%)	Median yearly pension income amount[a] ($)
High school degree	10.7	35.2	44.3	6,136	11.4	35.5	45.2	7,389	13.9	31.9	40.9	7,056
Some college	6.1	39.8	48.9	8,420	7.5	40.4	48.7	9,489	9.5	39.0	47.6	9,720
College degree	2.6	47.4	54.9	11,097	3.6	51.2	55.1	13,055	3.8	44.9	52.3	17,268
Postgraduate degree	1.8	62.2	67.8	15,666	2.3	62.3	67.6	18,329	2.7	55.1	61.2	21,600
Marital Status												
Married	17.2	40.7	44.0	7,833	19.4	42.3	45.5	10,183	19.2	38.4	42.2	11,592
Widowed	10.9	28.4	46.2	5,222	10.8	28.5	46.7	7,102	11.1	31.0	48.4	7,128
Divorced/ separated	2.6	35.3	39.0	8,003	2.9	37.2	41.7	8,159	3.7	32.5	36.7	9,612
Never married	1.5	39.3	41.9	7,833	1.1	43.8	47.4	7,833	1.5	36.0	39.8	8,700

[a] All pension amounts in 2006 dollars.

Source: Derived from Employee Benefit Research Institute estimates of the 1996, 2001, and 2004 Survey of Income and Program Participation (SIPP) Topical Module 7; see text.

TABLE 7.2 Characteristics of Americans age 65 or older who have worked for pay with pension income and median pension income amounts, by individual's former employer characteristics: 2003 and 2006

	2003			2006		
	Number (M)	Pension income from own former employer (%)	Median yearly pension income amount[a] ($)	Number (M)	Pension income from own former employer (%)	Median yearly pension income amount[a] ($)
Total	23.2	55.2	9,073	24.0	52.2	9,696
Employer size						
<10	3.4	20.1	6,319	3.8	18.6	6,564
10–24	1.4	31.5	6,841	1.5	27.7	7,020
25–49	1.3	38.2	6,501	1.1	35.0	6,840
50–99	1.0	38.3	6,319	1.2	43.5	6,000
≥100	16.1	67.0	9,295	16.4	64.0	10,680
Union status						
Covered	6.2	77.1	8,747	6.3	75.7	10,584
Nonunion	17.0	52.8	9,138	17.7	43.9	9,360
Class of worker						
Private	15.7	50.4	6,984	16.2	47.1	6,840
Self-employed	1.6	21.8	7,180	1.7	14.0	8,952
Public	5.9	79.0	13,055	6.1	76.6	15,600
Tenure on last job (years)						
<5	1.0	22.4	5,104	1.1	19.0	6,600
5–9	2.8	28.5	4,974	2.5	25.5	3,960
10–19	5.7	46.5	5,209	6.0	45.5	5,160
≥20	13.7	66.9	10,666	14.4	62.2	12,000
Earnings prior to retirement (2006 $)						
<10,000	2.8	27.8	4,543	3.2	29.9	5,160
10,000–19,999	3.4	43.4	5,483	2.9	35.0	5,352
20,000–29,999	3.3	50.2	5,222	3.3	45.9	6,048
30,000–49,999	5.7	61.3	8,668	5.1	56.5	8,652
≥50,000	8.0	67.8	13,054	9.6	64.6	12,600

[a] All pension amounts in 2006 dollars.

Source: Derived from Employee Benefit Research Institute estimates of the 2001 and 2004 Survey of Income and Program Participation (SIPP) Topical Module 7; see text.

Pension freezes and DB accruals

The news media has recently focused on the supposedly 'new' phenomenon of pension freezes among private DB plan sponsors for current or new workers. In fact, however, this practice has been around for some time, part of the long-term decline of 'traditional' DB pension plans in the United States. What is unusual, of late, is the fact that many large employers have recently announced pension freezes.

Naturally, pension plan freezes will affect some workers negatively, but it is not obvious which workers are most affected nor to what degree they are affected. This is because of the unique characteristics and terms of each pension plan and each freeze, as well as the age and characteristics of the affected workers.[3] The literature documenting the evolution from DB to DC retirement plans in the last 20 years is replete with studies analyzing the change in the relative composition of plans and participants;[4] however, very few have focused on the sizeable number of large plan sponsors that have had *both* DB and DC plans in place, at least since the advent of the 401(k) plan in the early 1980s.[5] For these sponsors, the primary decision in many cases is not whether to retain *both* forms of retirement plan, but how to manage the liabilities of each in terms of future accruals or contributions. Recognizing certain legal[6] and/or financial constraints, including the inability to terminate an underfunded pension plan (with the exception of certain sponsors satisfying the bankruptcy conditions necessary to trigger pension insurance coverage by the Pension Benefit Guaranty Corporation) and the imposition of a 20 or 50 percent excise tax on the recoupment of excess assets in the case of a reversion (VanDerhei 1989), the best choice for many firms may be to gradually reduce the relative value of the DB plan in the future by the imposition of a pension freeze.

Retirement program changes after the Pension Protection Act

After the enactment of the Pension Protection Act (PPA) of 2006 (VanDerhei 2007), the Employee Benefit Research Institute (EBRI) and Mercer fielded a survey designed to elicit information on retirement program changes. Employers that sponsored DB pension plans were asked to complete the survey. This survey was distributed in 2007 making it likely that plan sponsors would have time and information to do a cost/benefit analysis of possible plan modifications and/or investment changes. Survey respondents were asked to indicate what changes they had made, or expected to make, to their DC plans. One-third of the DB sponsors expected to make an increase in employer matching contributions, and 21 percent expected to make an increase in nonmatching employer contributions. A total of 43 percent of the DB sponsors indicated that they would increase employer contributions.

Focusing on DB sponsors planning to increase employer contributions to a DC plan, we also asked whether they had closed their DB plan to new hires in the last 2 years. A majority (78 percent) of these sponsors indicated that they would increase employer contributions to the DC plan or planned to do so in the next 2 years (81 percent). Slightly smaller percentages were associated with DB sponsors freezing their plans to all members. Of those that had frozen (would freeze) in the last (next) 2 years, 62 percent (76 percent) indicated they would increase employer DC contributions. This makes it very clear that any serious attempt to model retirement income adequacy for future cohorts of retirees must control for this widespread phenomenon of employers providing new or additional employer contributions to a DC plan. The reason is that many firms seek to at least partially compensate employees for lower DB accruals that they may have expected if the original DB plan had not been closed or frozen.

In the aftermath of PPA, 401(k) plan sponsors must also decide whether to introduce automatic enrollment features. An extensive literature discussed the potential benefits of automatic enrollment on participation rates, especially for young employees and those with low incomes (DiCenzo 2007). But these programs also have a tendency to anchor participants' contribution rates and asset allocation to the defaults chosen by the sponsor (Choi et al. 2005, 2006), and the overall increase in expected account balances from adopting these plans will be a function of employee relative wage levels and employer default decisions (Holden and VanDerhei 2005).

The PPA provided a significant incentive for employers that had not already adopted automatic enrollment to reconsider their decisions.[7] It is interesting that prior surveys of likely adoption rates in the post-PPA environment have not linked this behavior with sponsor decisions to close or freeze their DB plans. Yet it has been noted that a shift from DB to DC plans (especially 401(k) plans) may increase the variability of retirement income for future cohorts (Samwick and Skinner 2004). At least among the DB pension sponsors that have closed their plan to new hires in the last 2 years or are planning to do so in the next 2 years, VanDerhei (2007) found that a relatively large percentage had already adopted automatic enrollment in their 401(k) plans (and many who had not are considering doing so). Of those that already closed their DB plans to new hires, 59 percent had adopted automatic enrollment features in the 401(k) plan, as opposed to 42 percent of those that had not. Plan sponsors indicating that they will close the DB plan to new hires in the next 2 years have also moved to adopt automatic DC enrollment features (61 percent of the time) versus only 39 percent for those that do not intend to close the plan in the next 2 years.[8]

Impact of freezing new employee DB plan accruals

Next we turn to an analysis of the likely impact of continued trends with respect to DB plan freezes. Building on the work of VanDerhei (2007) and VanDerhei and Copeland (2008) using the EBRI/ERF Retirement Security Projection Model[9] we simulate the impacts of freezing new employee DB plan accruals. Accordingly, we assume that no current employees are impacted by a DB plan freeze; that is, all DB freezes are assumed to affect new employees only. Each time an employee is simulated to have a job change, the probability that he would be covered by a DB plan is computed based on the assumption that DB plans have not been frozen. The cumulative value of all DB accruals for *new* jobs is determined for each employee under the assumption that no terminated vested benefits are commuted to lump-sum distributions prior to retirement age (which is currently assumed to be age 65 for all employees).[10]

We also assume that all private DB plans will be immediately amended so that any new employees will accrue no pension benefits, and any employee selected by the model to otherwise have been eligible for a DB plan (in the absence of a freeze) is assigned a nonelective enhanced[11] employer contribution to a DC plan based on the EBRI/Mercer survey described previously. The enhanced employer contributions are accumulated based on age-specific asset allocations derived from year-end 2006 Employee Benefit Research Institute/Investment Company Institute (EBRI/ICI) data (Van-Derhei et al. 2008). All simulation results use annual returns data from Ibbotson Associates (2009).[12] At age 65, all accumulated account balances attributed to the enhanced contributions are converted to nominal annuities (for consistency with the DB accruals) using sex-specific annuity purchase prices. Unlike previous applications of the EBRI/ERF model, in this case the module used to simulate cash-out versus rollover behavior for DC balances at job change is effectively turned off for any new jobs. This is likely to overstate the eventual balances attributed to the enhanced contributions, but it allows a consistent comparison to the DB accruals that would have resulted but for the new pension freeze scenario.[13]

The expected reduction in nominal replacement rates if all private DB plans were to freeze accruals for NEW employees immediately appear in Figure 7.2, displayed by sex and age. The average reduction is below 1 percent for young (under age 25) and old (55 and older or 60 and older, depending on sex) employees, and the values peak at slightly over 2 percent for males aged 30–34, and 1.75 percent for females aged 30–34.

While these numbers may seem small, they are computed over a large segment of the population not expected to have a DB accrual from future jobs (this is particularly true of the older employees). Therefore, in Figure 7.3 we display the expected conditional reduction in nominal

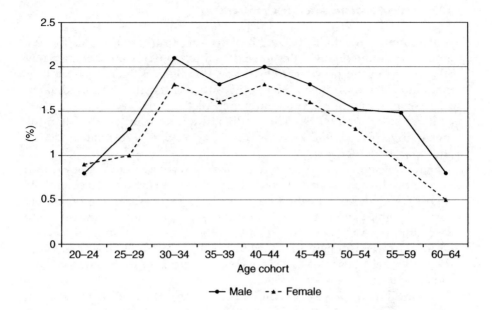

Figure 7.2 Expected reduction in nominal replacement ratios if all private defined benefit (DB) plans were to freeze accruals for new employees immediately, by sex and age. *Source*: Authors' calculations; see text.

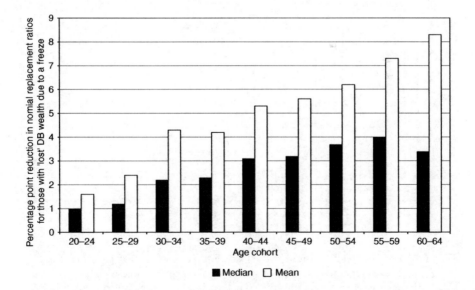

Figure 7.3 Expected conditional reduction in nominal replacement ratios if all private DB plans were to freeze accruals for new employees immediately, by sex and age. *Source*: Authors' calculations; see text.

replacement rates if all private DB plans were to freeze accruals for new employees immediately. In essence, this filters out anyone lacking a new DB plan from the previous figure. Now the mean reduction in replacement rates is monotonically increasing with age, starting at approximately 1.5 percent for employees currently aged 20–24, and increasing to 8.3 percent for those aged 60–64. The medians are significantly lower than the means, as expected, and increase until they reach 4 percent at age 55–59 and then drop slightly.

Figure 7.4 shows the percentage of those with DB wealth foregone due to the freeze who are expected to have a larger total nominal replacement rate from DC enhanced contributions (if any). As expected, young employees have the highest percentage, with nearly 40 percent of those between 20 and 24 ending up with more retirement wealth from the annuitized account balances from the enhanced contributions than they would have had under the additional DB accruals. This percentage drops to 6 percent for those aged 55–59.

Finally, Figure 7.5 shows the median percentage of compensation required as financial indemnification, in the form of an enhanced contribution, for future years covered by a DC plan in lieu of a frozen DB plan. The majority of employees under age 30 can be financially indemnified with an employer contribution of 6 percent of compensation; by contrast, the number increases to nearly 16 percent for those over 60.

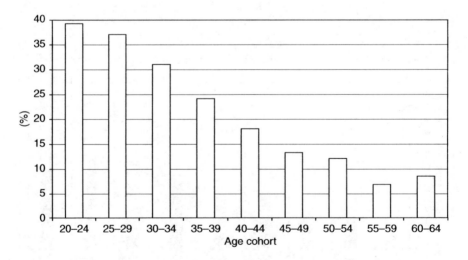

Figure 7.4 Percentage of those with 'lost' defined benefit (DB) wealth due to a pension freeze expected to have a larger total nominal replacement rate from the enhanced defined contributions (DC) (if any). *Source*: Authors' calculations; see text.

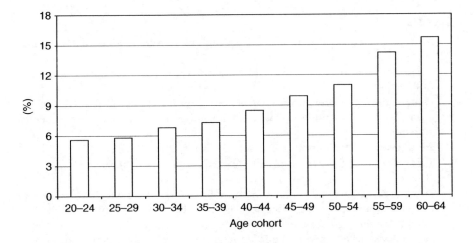

Figure 7.5 Median percentage of compensation required as an enhanced employer contribution for future years covered by a defined contribution (DC) plan in lieu of a frozen defined benefit (DB) plan for financial indemnification. *Source*: Authors' calculations; see text.

Conclusion

This chapter investigated how the role of private DB pension plans has declined since the advent of the Employee Retirement Income Security Act in 1974, by focusing on the falling percentages of Americans aged 65 and older with pension or annuity income. Even including public-sector retirees, Americans with DB plan income never attained 40 percent of the retiree population, and the fraction has receded several percentage points from its highest levels in the early 1990s.

Of course, these historical figures do not reflect the considerable recent activity in DB freezes for new (and sometimes existing) employees since 2006. We have simulated the impact of such freezes on expected future pension wealth for new employees. Looking at this portion of pension wealth provides one estimate of the impact on overall retirement wealth but it is incomplete, since many sponsors either increase employer DC contributions or set up new DC plans. Factoring in these enhanced DC contributions (if any), we estimate the net loss that future employees may experience is small overall, amounting to a 0.5–2 percentage point reduction in replacement rates. Some employees, as many as 30 percent of those aged 35 or younger, may be better off in retirement due to the enhanced contributions.

Notes

[1] Nevertheless, even DB plans have increasingly given retirees access to lump sums over time.

[2] This excludes distributions from DC plans or individual retirement accounts; see EBRI (2009).

[3] VanDerhei (2006) provides a detailed analysis of how pension freezes are likely to impact existing employees as a function of plan type and employee demographics.

[4] For a review of this literature, see Gale, Papke, and VanDerhei (2005).

[5] For an analysis that looks at the cash flow implications, see Olsen and VanDerhei (1997).

[6] Another constraint that may be operative for some sponsors is the legal uncertainty surrounding a conversion to a cash balance plan; see VanDerhei (1999).

[7] The PPA preempts state laws that might affect plans adopting automatic enrollment provisions and provides additional nondiscrimination safe harbor protections for them.

[8] Sponsors that already closed their plans in the last 2 years are excluded from the analysis of those in the 'next 2 years' group. An analysis of DB sponsors freezing the plan for all members is less straightforward. While 57 percent of those who froze the DB plan in the last 2 years indicated they had already adopted 401(k) automatic enrollment features, compared with 45 percent of those who had not, the phenomenon is reversed for those planning to freeze the plan in the next 2 years. In that case, only 33 percent of those that plan to freeze their pension have adopted 401(k) automatic enrollment, as opposed to 46 percent of those that do not plan to freeze the plan in the next 2 years. However, 42 percent of those planning to freeze their pension in the next 2 years are currently considering 401(k) automatic enrollment features.

[9] See VanDerhei and Copeland (2003), for a detailed description of the EBRI/ERF Retirement Security Projection Model.

[10] Butrica et al. (2009) uses the Model of Income in the Near Term (MINT) to simulate the impact of an accelerated transition from DB to DC pensions on the distribution of retirement income among boomers in a scenario in which employers freeze all remaining private-sector DB plans and a third of all state and local plans over the next 5 years.

[11] The term 'enhanced' includes those with no additional employer contributions to the DC plan (approximately 21 percent of the DB plan sponsors in the survey were in this category—in other words, approximately four out of five plans sponsors in the survey who had frozen or were planning to freeze their DB plans had either increased employer contributions to an existing DC plan or initiated a new one).

[12] Time series returns for the years 1926 through 2008 were used for large cap stocks and long-term corporate bonds to simulate the portfolios of all 401(k) participants. Simulated rates of return used a modified version of the method of overlapping periods (Cooley, Hubbard, and Walz 2003; Schleef and Eisinger 2007).

[13] Two additional assumptions are used for this analysis: (*a*) all DB plans are currently treated as though they were final average pay plans and (*b*) only private-sector workers are modeled (and if a worker is currently in the private sector, it was assumed he or she would remain there until age 65). The first assumption reflects an upper bound on the expected reductions in future retirement wealth for most cohorts of DB participants (see VanDerhei (2006) for a detailed analysis of the various DB plan types). The second assumption is required as a result of the survey population used to collect the enhanced contribution information in the EBRI/Mercer survey.

References

Butrica, Barbara A., Howard M. Iams, Karen E. Smith, and Eric J. Toder (2009). 'The Disappearing Defined Benefit Pension and Its Potential Impact on the Retirement Incomes of Boomers,' Center for Retirement Research at Boston College Working Paper No. 2009-02. Chestnut Hill, MA: Center for Retirement Research at Boston College.

Choi, James J., David Laibson, Brigette C. Madrian, and Andrew Metrick (2005). 'Optimal Defaults and Active Decisions,' NBER Working Paper No. 11074. Cambridge, MA: National Bureau of Economic Research.

—— —— —— ——(2006). 'Saving for Retirement on the Path of Least Resistance,' in E. McCaffrey and J. Slemrod, eds., *Behavioral Public Finance: Toward a New Agenda*. New York: Russell Sage Foundation, pp. 304–51.

Cooley, Phillip L., Hubbard, Carl M., and Walz, Daniel T. (2003). 'A Comparative Analysis of Retirement Portfolio Success Rates: Simulation Versus Overlapping Periods,' *Financial Services Review*, 12: 15–128.

DiCenzo, Jodi (2007). 'Behavioral Finance and Retirement Plan Contributions: How Participants Behave, and Prescriptive Solutions,' *EBRI Issue Brief 301*. Washington, DC: Employee Benefit Research Institute.

Employee Benefit Research Institute (EBRI) (2009). *Chapter 8 – Retirement Annuity and Employment-Based Pension Income. EBRI Databook on Employee Benefits.* Washington, DC: Employee Benefit Research Institute. http://www.ebri.org/pdf/publications/books/databook/DB.Chapter%2008.pdf

Gale, William G., Leslie E. Papke, and Jack VanDerhei (2005). 'The Shifting Structure of Private Pension Plans,' in J.B. Shoven, M.J. Warshawsky, and W.G. Gale, eds., *The Evolving Pension System*. Washington, DC: Brookings Institution Press.

Holden, Sarah and Jack VanDerhei (2005). 'The Influence of Automatic Enrollment, Catch-Up, and IRA Contributions on 401(k) Accumulations at Retirement,' *EBRI Issue Brief 283*. Washington, DC: Employee Benefit Research Institute.

Ibbotson Associates (2009). *Stocks, Bonds, Bills & Inflation (SBBI) Yearbook.* Chicago, IL: Ibbotson Associates.

Olsen, Kelly and Jack VanDerhei (1997). 'Defined Contribution Dominance Grows Across Sectors and Employer Sizes, While Mega Defined Benefit Plans Remain Strong: Where Are We and Where Are We Going?,' in D. Salisbury, ed., *Retirement*

Prospects in a Defined Contribution World. Washington, DC: Employee Benefit Research Institute, pp. 55–92.

Samwick, Andrew A. and Jonathan Skinner (2004). 'How Will 401(k) Pension Plans Affect Retirement Income?,' *American Economic Review,* 94(1): 329–43.

Schleef, Harold J. and Robert M. Eisinger (2007). 'Hitting or Missing the Retirement Target: Comparing Contribution and Asset Allocation Schemes of Simulated Portfolios,' *Financial Services Review,* 16: 229–43.

VanDerhei, Jack (1989). 'Pension Plan Surplus: Revert, Transfer, or Hold?' *EBRI Issue Brief 88.* Washington, DC: Employee Benefit Research Institute.

——(1999). 'The Controversy of Traditional vs. Cash Balance Plans,' *ACA Journal,* 8(4): 7–16.

—— (2006). 'Defined Benefit Plan Freezes: Who's Affected, How Much, and Replacing Lost Accruals,' *EBRI Issue Brief 291.* Washington, DC: Employee Benefit Research Institute.

——(2007). 'Retirement Income Adequacy After PPA and FAS 158: Part One – Plan Sponsors' Reactions,' *EBRI Issue Brief 307.* Washington, DC: Employee Benefit Research Institute.

——and Craig Copeland (2003). 'Can America Afford Tomorrow's Retirees: Results from the EBRI-ERF Retirement Security Projection Model,' *EBRI Issue Brief 263.* Washington, DC: Employee Benefit Research Institute.

————(2008). 'The Impact of PPA on Retirement Savings for 401(k) Participants,' *EBRI Issue Brief 318.* Washington, DC: Employee Benefit Research Institute.

——Sarah Holden, Craig Copeland, and Luis Alonso (2008). '401(k) Plan Asset Allocation, Account Balances, and Loan Activity in 2007,' *EBRI Issue Brief 324.* Washington, DC: Employee Benefit Research Institute.

Chapter 8

Rebuilding Workers' Retirement Security: A Labor Perspective on Private Pension Reform

Damon Silvers

This chapter looks at issues of risk, funding, and benefit design in the US private pension system, with particular attention to the labor movement's interest in obtaining retirement security for America's working families. The chapter seeks to address the question of how to best develop public policies that would encourage broad-based retirement provisions sufficient to provide most Americans with a comfortable retirement.

The labor movement created retirement in the United States. Prior to the rise of the labor movement in the 1930s and 1940s, old age meant poverty or economic dependence for most Americans (Epstein 1922; Altman 2005).[1] A privileged few received company or government pensions (Seburn 1991). A pension was seen as a special reward for loyal service, and was associated with the top echelon of white-collar workers. The wealthy lived in comfort in retirement off of their accumulated wealth, that is, their savings. Of course, the world of the early twentieth century was demographically different in two key ways – people died earlier and more people lived on farms.[2] Prior to the development of social insurance, workers often formed unions to directly provide health care, pensions, and life insurance (Ghilarducci 2008). Direct collective insurance rather than bargaining with employers was the primary function of many unions, making unions often hard to distinguish from insurance companies and mutual aid societies.[3]

Post-New Deal America was a world of large public and private sector employers, with rising living standards and relatively high levels of unionization.[4] Collective bargaining set the pattern for labor markets not only for the workers directly covered by union contracts, but also for large employers as a whole (Freeman and Medoff 1984). This period was characterized by rapidly rising wages and productivity, rising life expectancy, and shrinking farm employment (Price and Spriggs 2005; BLS 2009a). These were the years that produced the concept of retirement being founded on a three-legged stool – Social Security, a pension, and personal saving (Chao 2007).

Since 1980, the United States has become a different kind of economy, with different demographics. Industrial employment has declined dramatically, as have traditional employment relationships generally (Estreicher 1993).[5] While workers still tend to have longer job tenure in middle age, there has been an increase in job changes over a career since 1980 (Munnell, Haverstick, and Sanzenbacher 2006). Life expectancy has grown dramatically, as have health-care costs (Fronstin and Salisbury 2003; Feldstein 2008). And most importantly, from the perspective of retirement policy, the labor movement has weakened dramatically, particularly in the private sector.[6] While all of these developments have contributed to the fraying of the post-World War II retirement fabric, it is the decline of the labor movement that has ensured that, instead of responding to economic and demographic change, our retirement systems have crumbled. What remains – tax-favored saving accounts in the form of 401(k)s and the like – have proven to be poor substitutes for pensions because they lack key social insurance functions that the traditional pension provided.

The challenge we now face as a society is whether we want to perpetuate retirement as part of the life experience of most Americans, or instead return to a twenty-first century version of the state of affairs that existed at the beginning of the twentieth century. Unfortunately, we face this choice in the context of daunting circumstances. Our demographic history is with us in the form of the baby boomers. Even before the collapse of the capital markets in the fall of 2008, early baby boomers appeared to be the last cohort to enjoy better retirement prospects than their parents (Butrica and Uccello 2005). The fall in the equities markets and the residential real estate markets has likely made this situation far worse in recent times.

The implications for the US economy in the coming years are very serious. Low incomes for older Americans will mean less aggregate demand. They will also mean higher workforce participation, but often in less demanding and thus less productive jobs. Already, youth employment experts are pointing to the unusual persistence of baby boomers in the workforce in entry-level jobs, effectively diminishing entry-level opportunities for younger workers (Sum, Khatiwada, and Palma 2005).

While it is possible to envision ways of rebuilding America's private sector retirement system, it will be extraordinarily difficult to design and provide meaningful solutions for baby boomers in their 50s, simply because there is not enough time.

In this context, the labor movement faces the choice of whether to focus on defending what remains of the traditional retirement system, or to look to the creation of a more broad-based sustainable system of retirement provision. This choice is tied up with broader choices that all labor movements face at all times, between a narrow focus on improving the lives of current union members and broad efforts to improve the lives of all workers.

In the aftermath of World War II, when the labor movement was strong and growing, a similar choice emerged around retirement security. Some advocated increasing Social Security to the point where it could function as a stand-alone retirement security system, but ultimately the labor movement focused on winning pensions through collective bargaining in organized workplaces (Lowenstein 2008). This strategy appeared, for a time, to have almost produced universal pension coverage in large workplaces – pension coverage peaked around 50 percent in the 1970s when private sector union density was less than 30 percent (Freeman 1997: 60–1). But this success did not endure. Now, a much weakened labor movement faces similar choices, as it concurrently confronts decisions about how much of its remaining resources to expend on policy relating to the right to organize and health care.

The remainder of this chapter will look at broad-based approaches to retirement security, designed both to address the disintegration of traditional pension plans, and the failure of corporate pseudo-individualism represented by the 401(k) plan. The discussion will sketch how the individualistic promise of the 401(k) plan – you determine whether to fund your plan, you determine how to invest your plan, and you can withdraw funds for other needs – all turn out to have perverse consequences. Ironically, these results are now known and acknowledged even by 401(k) advocates. The consequence is that companies and consultants now propose new plan designs consciously intended to counteract the flaws in the 401(k) model – with default contribution provisions, service providers offering customers customized guidance on how to invest their accounts, and employers seeking to persuade employees not to withdraw funds prematurely from their accounts.

Conversations about these issues take on a peculiar quality, as successively each supposed advantage of saving accounts is renounced by their advocates, along with the logic supporting them. In the end, the listener is left wondering: if employees are unable to make investment decisions on their own and, if purely voluntary contributions are ineffective, why do we not return to real (traditional) pensions?

Problems in retirement security

Money

The retirement security crisis is a problem of money. While there are inferior and superior ways of managing retirement assets, there is no way to provide retirement security without adequate funding. The history of retirement provision in the private sector since 1980 is the history of employers replacing defined benefit (DB) pension plans, which were funded on average by employer contributions worth 8 percent of payroll, with voluntary saving plans such as 401(k)s, where average employer contributions are less than 3 percent of payroll (Munnell and Sundén 2006; Munnell, Aubry, and Muldoon 2008).

Of course, workers generally have the choice of putting more money in their 401(k) plans. Even before the recent steep increases in contribution limits, all but the highest-income workers could set aside 10 percent of their income on a pretax basis to their 401(k) plans. But in practice only a very few workers do so. The result is that median 401(k) account balances before the financial crisis were $19,000, while median account balances for the typical household approaching retirement age were $50,500 in a combination of 401(k) and individual retirement accounts (IRAs) in 2007 (VanDerhei et al. 2007; Munnell, Golub-Sass, and Muldoon 2009). The General Accounting Office has predicted that 401(k), IRA, and other retirement saving accounts will replace only 22 percent of annualized career earnings and 37 percent of workers will retire with a zero balance (USGAO 2007). By comparison, it costs about $250,000 to buy a fixed life annuity sufficient to replace 40 percent of the median family income of $48,000.[7]

This employer retreat from funding pensions was contagious. Once one employer in an industry had cut pension costs by moving to a 401(k), others followed suit. In industries where multiemployer pensions were predominant, the rise of non-pension providing employers was even more destructive, as it directly reduced the funding base of multiemployer plans (Traffic World 2007; Millonzi 2008;UPS 2009).

The lesson of this experience is that, like health care, pension coverage is sustainable when it is universal and involves a minimum percentage of payroll. There are really only two ways of achieving this goal – the reinvigoration of the collective bargaining process or a government mandate.

There are a number of international models for this type of approach, including, prominently, Australia, the Netherlands, and Switzerland (Harris 2000; Rix 2005; Ponds and van Riel 2007; Clare 2008). In each case, government mandated pension coverage and pension funding has emerged against the backdrop of strong labor movements.

Effective retirement systems aiming at income replacement ranges in the area of 30–40 percent need to be funded at no less than 8 percent of payroll.[8] Voluntary schemes relying on employee contributions will not reach these levels, nor have they done so historically or on a comparative international basis. Because of the regressive distribution of voluntary contributions – that is, high-income individuals voluntarily contribute not just higher dollar amounts, but much higher percentages of salary – tax-favored treatment of voluntary saving structures ends up being one of the most regressive and least effective tax expenditures (Ghilarducci 2008: 20–1).

Naturally, the precise institutional form of mandatory pensions varies from country to country, and in some countries individual saving accounts are similar to elements of US 401(k) plan structures (Rix 2005; Ponds and van Riel 2007; Clare 2008). Adequate funding does not make the flaws of the 401(k) model go away, but it removes the most serious flaw – too little money.

Investment management

Investment management is about expertise and bargaining power. In a DB plan or a pooled investment plan, the pension beneficiary has expertise and some level of market power as a result of pooling the resources of many beneficiaries. Plans with individual accounts, unless modified, provide the beneficiary with neither expertise nor bargaining power. The result is substantially higher cost of money management and lower risk-adjusted returns across plan participants (Buck Consultants 2000; Levitz 2008).

The management of retirement assets is about two separate tasks: asset allocation and the management of funds within the allocation. With the exception of some individual IRAs, virtually all US retirement funds are professionally managed within a given asset allocation – in the case of 401(k) plans, by mutual fund managers. The issue in the area of picking individual investment assets is not whether the money is managed professionally, but how the fees and other terms are negotiated. Here we have a stark contrast between the bargaining power of collective trusts and that of individual employees. The combination of weak bargaining power and additional administrative costs of individual accounts leads the cost structure of money management for defined contribution (DC) plans to generally be far greater than the costs of DB plans.

In the area of asset allocation, however, the change from professional management to self-directed investment represents a loss of expertise in the management of retirement assets. Furthermore, as discussed later, the full exposure of individuals to market risk leads rational employees to make more conservative asset allocation decisions, because of a rational fear of exposure to volatility that a pooled approach to retirement security has a better ability to withstand.

Market risk

Of course, all funded plans are exposed to market risk. Like banks and other financial intermediaries, both DB and DC plans seek to receive compensation for taking investment risk. However, there is a fundamental difference between the nature of the exposure to market risk taken by DB and DC plans. In DB plans, the obligation to pay benefits is pooled among beneficiaries through time. The obligation to pay benefits is fixed, and the fund holds, or should hold, enough assets to meet current obligations and invest to fund future obligations. By contrast, in DC plans with individual accounts, each person's account is a kind of mini-fund, with one set of payment obligations to one person during one fixed time frame.

Exposure to market risk creates the real possibility of DC participants reaching retirement age at a time when capital markets are depressed, particularly equity markets. This issue of market timing can expose DC participants to the risk of unacceptable losses, losses which can severely impact their standard of living in retirement (Weller 2005). Though this risk can be lessened by slowly converting equity holdings to debt holdings, prolonged bear markets limit the effectiveness of this strategy. The only way within the DC structure to address this problem is to maintain high fixed-income allocations – which some DC participants do – much to the dismay of academic and policy commentators who note the cost of this strategy in terms of returns (Mitchell and Utkus 2004; Munnell and Sundén 2004; Benartzi and Thaler 2007).

Ironically, there is an entire academic literature devoted to the proposition that DB plans should be invested entirely in bonds, while DC participants are underinvested in equities (JAAA/SA 2006). The opposite is true, assuming the DC participants' plans are their major retirement asset after Social Security, and assuming the DB plan is demographically healthy.

This issue of market timing is embedded within the larger issue of exposure to market losses. DB plans provide what their name suggests: a fixed benefit. At one level, this means no direct exposure to market risk. But DB plans still have to fund those obligations, which expose participants indirectly to market risk. Here, the risk is not that of short-term volatility, but rather of long-term secular decline in the capital markets of the kind that has not occurred in the developed world in modern times.

Nonetheless, regulatory and accounting regimes can undo much of the value of DB plans, as an absorber of market volatility, by requiring plans to behave as if they were facing liquidation at all times, or by punishing plan sponsors for market volatility that the plan can in fact absorb. The recent direction of both generally accepted accounting principles (GAAP) accounting and more importantly of Employee Retirement Income Security Act (ERISA) regulation has had this effect (United States Congress 2006a; FASB 2009).

Employer credit risk

The other side of the coin of market timing risk is employer credit risk, perhaps the most serious issue for US DB plans. This occurs because the single employer plan system allows solvent employers to withdraw from providing retirement security to their employees by freezing or terminating pension plans. The result for employees in terms of final average salary calculations and benefit accruals can be disastrous. In multiemployer plans, the failure of individual employers to honor commitments made to the fund, or their desire to withdraw from a fund, can destabilize the finances of the fund as a whole, affecting the benefits of employees of other firms. The Pension Benefit Guaranty Corporation (PBGC) has offered effective partial insurance against employer credit risk for a generation. However, there is no question that, as employers withdraw from providing retirement security for their employees, the number of private sector DB pension plans will shrink and the PBGC's insurance pool will become destabilized.

Employer credit risk in the context of employee benefits, more generally, has been a major issue in the auto industry crisis. Nevertheless, the real issue in this area has been unfunded retiree health benefit obligations, whose value was being driven by projections of infinitely increasing health-care costs. These retiree health benefit obligations ultimately led to the creation and funding of voluntary employee beneficiary associations (VEBAs; Eisenbrey 2009). In the recent GM and Chrysler bankruptcies, the VEBAs have ended up as large shareholders of both firms as a result of converting a large portion of those companies' obligations to their respective VEBAs into equity (Eisenbrey 2009). GM and Chrysler's pension plans, on the other hand, were funded and have continued through the bankruptcy of both companies (Gettelfinger, Holiefield, and Payne 2009; Gettelfinger, Rapson, and Payne 2009). While there is certainly continued employer credit risk through those plans, as with all single employer plans, neither of those plans has failed.

The case of Delphi, the auto parts maker spun off from GM, shows both the salience of funding issues in the context of employer credit risk and the dangers beneficiaries face when employers seek to escape benefit obligations. In contrast with GM's relatively well-funded plan, Delphi began cutting back on pension contributions almost from the moment of its spin-off from GM, leaving its plan unable to weather the market volatility of this decade (Walsh 2009). In July 2009, the PBGC took over the Delphi plan, causing its beneficiaries to have their benefits drop to PBGC guaranteed levels (Walsh 2009). The United Auto Workers (UAW) protected its members against this possibility by having GM guarantee pension benefits of Delphi employees represented by the UAW (Walsh 2009). Management participants in Delphi's plan were not thus protected.

Employer credit risk is also significant for DC plans in two ways, both of which could easily be fixed. It is a minor, if widespread, problem when financially weak employers refuse to pass on employee or employer contributions to employee accounts (Burton 2005). On a much larger, and at times, catastrophic scale, employer credit risk presents itself when DC plans are invested in employer stock (Altman 2002; Feder 2002; Lim 2008). Employer stock is, of course, both volatile and junior in the capital structure to employer fixed obligations to DB plans. Ironically, ERISA limits the amount of employer stock that can be held in DB plans, where funding losses create a senior employer obligation, but are not limited in DC plans, where there is no further employer backup to employee losses (United States Congress 1974).

Employer credit risk in both its DB form and its DC form is the logical consequence of trying to design a system of retirement security that simultaneously seeks to be a finance tool for firms and an employee retention incentive. While any retirement plan can be a way for employers to attract and retain employees, non-portable plans with cliff vesting have a special retaining power. But along with that power comes an unavoidable exposure to employer credit risk. In DC plans, employer stock is an inexpensive way to finance retirement and provide capital to a firm. Of course, along with these financing advantages to the firm comes the firm-specific risk for the employee.

Longevity risk

A DB plan, like any other basic annuity, is a form of insurance against the possibility of outliving one's saving. A traditional pension promises a stream of payments for the remainder of the participant's life. By contrast, a retirement saving account like a 401(k) is simply that – an account which, when it is depleted, is no more.

The shift from DB to DC plans has eliminated the longevity insurance aspect of employee benefit plans. In the DB world, the increased popularity of cash balance plans and cash payout options has a similar effect, though, of course, employees still have the options in these circumstances to leave their money in their pension plans and participate in the longevity insurance feature of such plans.

DC plan participants always have the option of annuitizing their plan balances at retirement through private providers of annuity contracts. Such an option involves taking on the credit risk of annuity providers, although until recently it was easy to contract with a highly rated insurer, and annuities are further backed by state insurance guarantee funds. A greater problem has long been the opacity of annuity structures and the high transaction costs associated with annuitizing retirement accounts with private parties, compared to the costs implicit in pension funds, particularly large pension funds.

In recent decades, advances in medical care and consequent increases in life expectancy have made the issue of longevity risk of greater concern to participants, plan sponsors, and insurers. One of the troubling aspects of longevity risk may well be that one of the main reasons for low levels of annuitization among 401(k) participants is that annuitization results in payment streams much lower than that expected by plan participants. Sadly, the annuity terms, while in part reflecting a high fee margin for the annuity company, may largely be driven by the realities of longevity risk and the amount of money that must be set aside to provide for it.

Portability and early withdrawals

Portability is the great success of the DC plan revolution. Although portability within industries and geographical areas had always been a feature of multiemployer pension plans, there was no full portability in the multiemployer sector, and generally no portability between firms in the single employer pension sector. 401(k) plans brought with them portability throughout the entire economy, and the ability to enter and leave the workforce without having any disproportionate impact on retirement saving.

Full portability should have contributed to a much more effective level of lifetime retirement provision. This is because mobile younger workers could have accumulated retirement saving starting from the beginning of their workforce participation, rather than waiting until they had found long-term jobs a decade or more into their working lives. Although we lack a full time series to evaluate, initial indications are that full portability in the context of the typical 401(k) plans has not led to a more effective level of lifetime retirement provision.

Furthermore, along with portability came the right to withdraw money from retirement accounts. Even though the tax code imposes a 10 percent surcharge on any such preretirement withdrawal, this surcharge appears to be relatively ineffective in encouraging younger workers to roll over 401(k) plans, rather than cash them out when they change jobs (Munnell and Sundén 2004; Weller 2008).

In periods of stagnant wages or tight credit, workers have particularly strong incentives to use their retirement accounts as sources of consumer finance or as rainy-day funds. A particularly tragic form of this is the instinct to draw down on retirement savings during unemployment or financial crisis. Although the heyday of DB plans was also a period of economic cycles that brought with it industrial unemployment, in those days, it was impossible for workers in the postwar era to tap their pension funds.

While preretirement withdrawals from retirement plans can be harmful to participants' retirement security, withdrawals in times of economic hardship may be particularly problematic; unless they are financed from sources outside the workers' accounts, withdrawals necessarily involve selling assets at depressed prices, locking in what would otherwise be paper losses.

In this respect, accessing almost any other source of emergency funds may be preferred to facilitating emergency withdrawals from benefit plans. Such other sources could include extended unemployment benefits, eased consumer bankruptcy provisions, universal health care, more direct aid for college students, and the like. As an aside, personal financial crises of the sort that lead to a temptation to withdraw money from retirement accounts usually turn out to be health-care cost related (Himmelstein et al. 2005).

Regulation

It has long been observed by plan sponsors that the regulatory environment surrounding DB plans has contributed to their decline, particularly compared to the relatively light regulatory environment for DC plans. The passage of the Pension Protection Act and its implementation in the context of the financial crisis that began in 2007 have only added to these complaints (Manning 2008; ERIC 2009).

There are several ironies to this situation. The first irony is that DB pensions that are backed up by the full credit of employers are more heavily regulated than plans where employees' money is fully at risk. Of course, there are historical and analytical reasons for this paradox, most importantly the long-standing combination of concerns that plan sponsors would either underfund plans or overfund them for the purposes of tax evasion, in the context of a regulatory regime where plan termination and fund recapture were possible. Nonetheless, one clear benefit of moving away from pension fund dependence on individual employer credit risk and employer management of pension capital would be to lessen the need for such detailed regulatory oversight of pension-funding issues. On the other hand, there is a clear and immediate need to strengthen the regulation of DC plans around issues like employer stock, mutual fund fees, and conflicts of interest in areas like investment advice where the Pension Protection Act actually radically weakened participant protections against conflicts of interest (United States Congress 2006b; Bullard 2009).

A pension agenda that works for all

In 2006, the AFL-CIO Executive Council (2006) passed a resolution laying out principles for broad-based pension reform. In the 3 years since, the

AFL-CIO has worked with the Pension Rights Center (PRC) to formulate a pension reform agenda based on principles adopted in 2006, and now involving a broad coalition of pension and retiree advocates (PRC 2007). In pursuing these agendas, the labor movement has operated in an intellectual landscape defined on the right by proposals for universal voluntary saving accounts coming from the Brookings Institution, and on the left by proposals for national DB programs such as that put forward by Teresa Ghilarducci under the auspices of the Economic Policy Institute (Ghilarducci 2008: 237–90).

The thoughts that follow are not the official position of the AFL-CIO; rather they represent an effort to outline a possible program for addressing the problems outlined earlier, in the context of a national retirement policy consistent with the AFL-CIO's goals.

Mandatory retirement contributions

Any serious discussion of solving America's retirement security crisis must mandate a level playing field on contribution levels, and part of that mandate must be an employer contribution. In Australia, the mandatory contribution level is 9 percent of salary (Rix 2005); Teresa Ghilarducci suggests 5 percent for the United States (Ghilarducci 2007). Of course, there is a trade-off between comprehensiveness and percentage amounts. If the contribution is applied to all income (e.g., all payments recorded on Form 1099 and Schedule C of the Tax Code as well as on wages), then the percentage of payroll required could be lower.

There is also the issue of who technically makes the contributions. While economic theory tells us it should make no difference, the experience of the last 30 years suggests that both workers and employers perceive a difference in who pays. Employers are often unable to pass on the entire impact of mandatory employer contributions to their employees, and employees perceive deductions from their paycheck as a net loss of income compared to employers having to make contributions to a fund. The choice is whether society wants to encourage an overall higher level of wages, in which case we would tilt toward making the mandatory contributions come from the employer, or whether we wish to compete internationally on the basis of low labor costs, in which case we would seek to have retirement plans funded with direct employee contributions.

Portability and withdrawal issues

Any practical system of universal pension coverage conceptually requires benefit portability. Portability is often treated as somehow at odds with providing a DB pension, though in the United States, Social Security is a giant, portable DB pension scheme. On a more limited scale, for generations, multiemployer plans have provided portable DB coverage to employees within particular industries.

What portability requires is either a standard accounting framework that can be applied across plans, or a scheme in which workers can participate in as they move from one employer to another. There are two options here, which would be most effective if combined. The first option is plans that people can participate in as they move from employer to employer – much as Social Security allows one to move from one company to the next. The second option is a common currency and set of benefit transfer rules for all tax-exempt plans, with the logical administrator of such a system being a government entity.

Mandatory portability must limit withdrawals from funds. One possibility would be a complete ban on preretirement withdrawals, perhaps with some sort of extraordinary administrative procedure for hardship situations such as terminal illnesses. In some respect, this achieves better outcomes than higher excise taxes – there is some reason to believe younger workers would still take the withdrawals and incur much higher taxes, which defeats the policy objectives. Historically, DB plans offered no ability to cash out early in life, and in the United States, Social Security offers no such option. An additional factor to consider here is that midlife withdrawals from 401(k) plans often occur in the context of health-care expenditure emergencies; a universal health-care system would remove this need.

Asset management

Collective professional management of retirement assets is clearly more cost-effective than individual amateur management of those assets. When 401(k) advocates talk about the need for investment advice, they are conceding this point. Encouraging cost-effective retirement asset management means channeling retirement assets into collective management vehicles. Similarly, it is advantageous for retirement plans to provide not just a vehicle for saving, but also insurance against investment and longevity risk. There are real costs to providing this type of insurance, just as there is a real risk-return trade-off around investment allocation.

Nevertheless, telling workers with existing 401(k) accounts that they must give up those accounts and their existing account balances is neither politically realistic nor necessarily good policy. A wiser approach would be to foster the creation of large investment management pools with clear government-monitored investment characteristics and low fees.

Social insurance and the fate of the 401(k)

Our model might resemble Australian superannuation funds or existing large US public pension funds, and it would involve several possible options: a traditional DB plan, a low risk (largely fixed income) DC plan, and a higher risk plan (mixed equity and debt). Such large multi-industry funds should be able to attract the bulk of both employers and participants because they would offer low fees, professional management, and relieve employers of the administrative burden of managing their own benefit plans. On the other hand, employers who wanted to offer particularly generous benefits or customized structures to attract or retain employees would be free to do so. Under such a policy, participants in existing DC and DB plans would be allowed to continue to participate in those plans if they chose – assuming these existing plans conformed to the minimum contribution and withdrawal regulation requirements. This would allow for plans that exceeded the minimum contribution requirements, and it would allow for workers to have the benefit of past accruals in DB plans, and for DC participants to remain with their existing plan options if they wished.

Finally, any serious effort at universal retirement income security would likely require compulsory annuitization at retirement. Hence, this approach ends up requiring insurance against longevity risk, but not against market timing risk. There is an issue with annuitization involving pooling the differing life expectancies of different occupational groups and income levels. One big national annuity pool could have the unintended consequence of a regressive subsidy toward higher income, higher life expectancy white-collar workers, and from lower income and lower life expectancy blue-collar workers. The alternative of mandating that all participate in a DB structure would be the only way to effectively require insurance against market timing risk. For reasons discussed earlier, this does not seem to be a realistic option.

An alternative choice in the context of economic crisis: expanding Social Security

The policy program described earlier is likely to involve a dramatic increase in the level of saving in the United States. But this could have a negative impact on consumer spending and aggregate demand, unless accompanied by the immediate deployment of the saving in job-creating activities such as infrastructure projects or large-scale responses to challenges in areas like energy and auto manufacturing. Even given large-scale investment of the saving, the net impact on economic activity could be negative in the near term. Should our economy remain weak enough such that this is a valid consideration, policymakers might learn from the experience of New Deal policymakers in a similar situation. Rather than increasing saving, those policymakers created Social Security, a retirement program where the tax dollars raised by the program were immediately deployed in the economy in the form of benefits.

This logic would suggest dealing with dwindling retirement security by enacting measures to boost the income that Social Security provides its recipients. Such an increase in benefits would be funded entirely on a pass-through basis by current increases in tax revenues, separate and apart from the management of the Social Security Trust Fund. It would be difficult to make the transition from an expanded Social Security to a funded universal pension plan, for some of the same reasons that bedeviled the Bush Administration's effort to privatize Social Security.

Conclusion

Post-World War II economic growth offered a middle class standard of living to the majority of Americans. Part of the American Dream was the promise of retirement in dignity, and collective bargaining was the primary vehicle for the realization of that promise. Since the 1950s, the labor movement has weakened and life expectancies have dramatically increased, as has the economy's exposure to foreign competition. But at the same time, the nation has grown dramatically more wealthy. As DB pension coverage shrinks and 401(k) balances remain low, there is reason to worry that retirement once again will become a privilege of the affluent. But this trend is the outcome of choices made in the recent past. If these trends continue, it will be because we chose not to make retirement a priority: because policymakers decided our wealth was better spent in other ways than in keeping the American Dream alive in our old age. The labor movement takes the position that, along with health care and the right to have workers' voices heard in the workplace and the public arena, the right to a comfortable retirement defines a civilized society, and we need to act to revive that right as a living aspect of how our society functions.

Acknowledgments

The author wishes to express gratitude to colleagues and friends Joseph Canovas, Karin Feldman, and Beth Almeida for their assistance with this chapter.

Notes

[1] 'Surveys by Wisconsin and New York, published in 1925 and 1929 respectively, found that over half of the population aged 65 and older had "insufficient subsistence income"' (Altman 2005: 8).

[2] In the United States in 1900, life expectancy at birth was 47.3 years; by 2005, life expectancy at birth was 77.8 years (NCHS 2007). In 1930, 43.9 percent of the population lived in rural areas; in 2008, only 16.5 percent of the population lived in rural areas (USCB 1993; USDA 2009).

[3] In the 1880s, unions and mutual aid societies were often indistinguishable. In the 1920s, the American Federation of Labor founded its own insurance company, the Union Labor Life Insurance Company, and in 1929, the International Brotherhood of Electrical Workers established the first multiemployer benefit plan (Ullico 2005; Ghilarducci 2008: 240–1). By 1930, union pension plans covered 20 percent of all union members, while corporate pension plans covered only 15 percent of the private sector workforce (Latimer 1932; Ghilarducci 1992: 30).

[4] Union density was greater than 30 percent from 1943 until 1960 (Freeman 1997: 59–60).

[5] For a discussion on the increasing use of temporary employment arrangements, contract arrangements, and the misclassification of employees as independent contractors, see Ruckelshaus (2008).

[6] Only 7.6 percent of the private sector workforce is unionized (BLS 2009*b*).

[7] Annuity prices are widely available on the Internet. As of the drafting of this chapter, the calculator cited showed that a lifetime annuity paying $1,600 per month would cost $250,000 (NewRetirement, LLC 2009).

[8] By comparison, Social Security provides a benefit in the range of 30–40 percent of preretirement income of the median worker at a cost of 12.4 percent of payroll. An extremely efficiently managed funded plan could achieve 30 percent replacement rates for around 8 percent. The typical DC plan, however, is likely to be less inefficient due to small size.

References

AFL-CIO Executive Council (2006). *Ensuring Retirement Security for America's Workers.* Washington, DC: AFL CIO. http://www.aflcio.org/aboutus/thisistheaflcio/ecouncil/ec08082006a.cfm/aboutus/thisistheaflcio/ecouncil/ec08082006a.cfm

Altman, Daniel (2002). 'Enron's Collapse: Pensions; Experts Say Diversify, but Many Plans Rely Heavily on Company Stock,' *New York Times,* January 20: 26.

Altman, Nancy J. (2005). *The Battle for Social Security: From FDR's Vision to Bush's Gamble.* Hoboken, NJ: John Wiley & Sons, Inc., p. 8.

Benartzi, Shlomo and Richard H. Thaler (2007). 'Heuristics and Biases in Retirement Savings Behavior,' *Journal of Economic Perspectives,* 21(3): 81–104.

Buck Consultants (2000). *Benefit Review Study of the Nebraska Retirement Systems.* Denver, CO: Buck Consultants. http://www.pebc.ca.gov/images/files/Benefit%20Review%20Study%20of%20the%20Nebraska%20Retirement%20Systems.pdf

Bullard, Mercer E. (2009). 'Testimony of Mercer E. Bullard Before the Subcommittee on Health, Employment, Labor, and Pensions, Committee on Education and Labor, US House of Representatives,' Washington, DC, April 22.

Bureau of Labor Statistics (BLS) (2009*a*). 'Major Sector Productivity and Costs Index, Business and Nonfarm Business Sectors,' Series Id PRS84006043 and PRS85006043. Washington, DC: United States Department of Labor. http://www.bls.gov/lpc/#data

——— (2009*b*). *Union Members Summary.* Washington, DC: United States Department of Labor. http://www.bls.gov/news.release/union2.nr0.htm

Burton, Jonathan (2005). 'Skimming the 401(k): Delayed Deposits Costing US Workers Millions,' MarketWatch. http://www.marketwatch.com/News/Story/Story.aspx?guid={55D4E190-F43D-4919-851A-D3160C113D9D}&siteid=netscape&dist=netscape

Butrica, Barbara A. and Cori E. Uccello (2005). *Older Americans' Economic Security.* Washington, DC: Urban Institute Retirement Project. http://www.urban.org/UploadedPDF/311431_Annuities_Spending.pdf

Chao, Elaine L. (2007). 'Remarks Prepared for Delivery By US Secretary of Labor Elaine L. Chao, SOAFO 16th Annual Dinner and Scholarship Awards Night,' Flushing, New York, May 18. https://www.dol.gov/_sec/media/speeches/20070518_SOAFO.htm

Clare, Ross (2008). *The Age Pension, Superannuation and Australian Retirement Incomes.* Sydney, Australia: The Association of Superannuation Funds of Australia Research and Resource Centre. http://www.professionalplanner.com.au/attachments/3522_ASFA%20-%20Retirement%20incomes%20paper.pdf

Eisenbrey, Ross (2009). 'Setting the Record Straight on GM,' Economic Policy Institute. http://www.epi.org/analysis_and_opinion/entry/setting_the_record_straight_on_gm/

Epstein, Abraham (1922). *Facing Old Age: A Study of Old Age Dependency in the United States and Old Age Pensions.* New York: Alfred A. Knopf, Inc., pp. 20–1.

The ERISA Industry Committee (ERIC) (2009). 'Major Consulting Firms Write Congressional Leadership on Need for Additional Pension Funding Relief.' The ERISA Industry Committee. http://www.eric.org/forms/documents/DocumentFormPublic/view?id=17F3B000001B3

Estreicher, Samuel (1993). 'Labor Law Reform in a World of Competitive Product Markets,' *Chicago Kent Law Review,* 69: 6.

Feder, Barnaby J. (2002). 'Technology Briefing/Telecommunications: WorldCom Sued By Employees,' *New York Times,* March 21: C4.

Feldstein, Martin S. (2008). 'Did Wages Reflect Growth in Productivity?,' *Journal of Policy Modeling,* 30(4): 591.

Financial Accounting Standards Board (FASB) (2009). *Phase II: Postretirement Benefit Obligations, Including Pensions.* Norwalk, CT: FASB. http://www.fasb.org/project/postretirement_benefits_phase2.shtml

Freeman, Richard B. (1997). 'Spurts in Union Growth: Defining Moments and Social Processes,' NBER Working Paper No. 6012. Cambridge, MA: National Bureau of Economic Research.

——and James L. Medoff (1984). *What Do Unions Do?* New York: Basic Books.

Fronstin, Paul and Dallas Salisbury (2003). 'Retiree Health Benefits: Savings Needed to Fund Healthcare in Retirement,' *EBRI Issue Brief 254*. Washington, DC: Employee Benefit Research Institute.

Gettelfinger, Ron, General Holiefield, and Bill Payne (2009). *A Message to UAW Chrysler Retirees*. Detroit, MI: United Automobile, Aerospace & Agricultural Implement Workers of America International Union.

——Cal Rapson, and Bill Payne (2009). *A Message to UAW GM Retirees*. Detroit, MI: United Automobile, Aerospace & Agricultural Implement Workers of America International Union.

Ghilarducci, Teresa (1992). *Labor's Capital: The Economics and Politics of Private Pensions*. Cambridge, MA: The MIT Press, p. 30.

——(2007). 'Guaranteed Retirement Accounts: Toward Retirement Income Security,' Economic Policy Institute. http://www.sharedprosperity.org/bp204.html

——(2008). *When I'm Sixty-Four: The Plot Against Pensions and the Plan to Save Them*. Princeton, NJ: Princeton University Press.

Harris, David O. (2000). 'Switzerland's National Retirement Approach,' Heritage Lecture #672. Washington, DC: The Heritage Foundation.

Himmelstein, David U., Elizabeth Warren, Deborah Thorne, and Steffie Woolhandler (2005). 'MarketWatch: Illness and Injury as Contributors to Bankruptcy,' Health Affairs. http://content.healthaffairs.org/cgi/content/full/hlthaff.w5.63/DC1

Joint American Academy of Actuaries/Society of Actuaries Task Force on Financial Economics and the Pension Actuarial Model (JAAA/SA) (2006). Pension Actuary's Guide to Financial Economics. Washington, DC. http://www.actuary.org/pdf/pension/finguide.pdf

Latimer, Murray Web (1932). *Industrial Pensions, vol. 1*. New York: Industrial Relations Counselors, Inc.

Levitz, Jennifer (2008). 'When 401(k) Investing Goes Bad,' *The Wall Street Journal*, August 4: R1.

Lim, Paul J. (2008). 'Don't Paint Nest Eggs in Company Colors,' *New York Times*, March 30.

Lowenstein, Roger (2008). *While America Aged: How Pension Debts Ruined General Motors, Stopped the NYC Subways, Bankrupted San Diego, and Loom as the Next Financial Crisis*. New York: The Penguin Press.

Manning, Stephen (2008). 'Companies Push Congress for Pension Relief,' *USA Today*, November 12.

Millonzi, Tom (2008). 'Teamsters Refute Misinformation in Press by Waste Management; Official Statement of Teamsters Local 200 Secretary-Treasurer Tom Millonzi,' Milwaukee, WI, August 31.

Mitchell, Olivia and Stephen Utkus (2004). *Pension Design and Structure: New Lessons from Behavioral Finance*. Oxford, UK: Oxford University Press.

Munnell, Alicia H. and Annika Sundén (2004). *Coming up Short: The Challenge of 401(k) Plans*. Washington, DC: The Brookings Institution.

Munnell, Alicia H. and Annika Sundén (2006). '401(k) Plans are Still Coming Up Short,' *Issue Brief 43*. Chestnut Hill, MA: Center for Retirement Research at Boston College. http://crr.bc.edu/images/stories/Briefs/ib_43.pdf?phpMyAdmin =43ac483c4de9t51d9eb41

——Kelly Haverstick, and Geoffrey Sanzenbacher (2006). 'Job Tenure and Pension Coverage,' CRR Working Paper 2006-18. Chestnut Hill, MA: Center for Retirement Research at Boston College.

——Jean-Pierre Aubry, and Dan Muldoon (2008). 'The Financial Crisis and Private Defined Benefit Plans,' *Issue Brief 8-18*. Chestnut Hill, MA: Center for Retirement Research at Boston College. http://crr.bc.edu/images/stories/Briefs/ib_8-18. pdf.

——Francesca Golub-Sass, and Dan Muldoon (2009). 'An Update on 401(k) Plans: Insights from the 2007 SCF,' *Issue Brief 9-5*. Chestnut Hill, MA: Center for Retirement Research at Boston College. http://crr.bc.edu/images/stories/ Briefs/ib_9_5.pdf

National Center for Health Statistics (NCHS) (2007). *Health, United States, 2007: With Chartbook on Trends in the Health of Americans*. Washington, DC: GPO, p. 175.

NewRetirement, LLC (2009). 'Calculator Results, Lifetime Annuity.' http://www. newretirement.com/Services/Annuity_Calculator_Results.aspx?AnnuityCalcula torTab.DateOfBirth=4/10/1944&AnnuityCalculatorTab.Gender=True&Annuity CalculatorTab.HasJointAnnuitant=True&AnnuityCalculatorTab.SpouseDateOf Birth=4/23/1944&AnnuityCalculatorTab.DesiredSurvivorBenefit=75&Annuity CalculatorTab.AnnuityStartDate=9/30/2009&AnnuityCalculatorTab.Address State=MD&AnnuityCalculatorTab.DesiredMonthlyBenefit=1600&AnnuityCal culatorTab.LumpSum=-1

Pension Rights Center (PRC) (2007). *Covering the Uncovered: Final Report of the Conversation on Coverage*. Washington, DC: The Pension Rights Center. http:// www.conversationoncoverage.org/about/final-report/covering-the-uncovered.pdf

Ponds, Eduard H.M. and Bart van Riel (2007). 'Sharing Risk: The Netherlands New Approach to Pensions,' *Issue Brief 7–5*. Chestnut Hill, MA: Center for Retirement Research at Boston College. http://crr.bc.edu/images/stories/Briefs/ib_7-5.pdf? phpMyAdmin=43ac483c4de9t51d9eb41

Price, Lee and William E. Spriggs (2005). 'Productivity Growth and Social Security's Future,' *EPI Issue Brief 208*. Washington, DC: Economic Policy Institute. http:// www.epi.org/publications/entry/ib208/

Rix, Sara E. (2005). *Old-Age Income Security in Australia*. Washington, DC: American Association of Retired People. http://assets.aarp.org/rgcenter/econ/fs108_ss_aus. pdf

Ruckelshaus, Catherine K. (2008). 'Labor's Wage War,' *Fordham Urban Law Journal*, 35: 373.

Seburn, Patrick W. (1991). 'Evolution of Employer-provided Defined Benefit Pensions,' *Monthly Labor Review*, 114(12): 16.

Sum, Andrew, Ishwar Khatiwada, and Sheila Palma (2005). *The Age Twist in Employment Rates in the US, 2000–2004: The Steep Tilt Against Young Workers in the Nation's Labor Markets*. Washington, DC: American Youth Policy Forum. http://www.aypf. org/publications/EmploymentRatesofyoungworkers.pdf

Traffic World (2007). *Pension Freedom for ABF? UPS Withdrawal from Central States Could Be Good Omen for Others Hoping to Follow the Same Path.* Washington, DC: Traffic World.

Ullico, Inc. (2005). *About Us.* Washington, DC: Ullico, Inc. http://www.ullico.com/about-ullico

United Parcel Service of America, Inc. (UPS) (2009). *UPS Reports Results for 4th Quarter, Full Year.* Atlanta, GA, February 3. http://www.pressroom.ups.com/Press+Releases/Archive/2009/Q1/UPS+Reports+Results+for+4th+Quarter,+Full+Year

United States Census Bureau (USCB) (1993). *Populations, 1790 to 1990, United States Urban and Rural.* Washington, DC: United States Census Bureau. http://www.census.gov/population/censusdata/table-4.pdf

United States Congress (1974). 'Employee Retirement Income Security Act of 1974,' Public Law 93-406 § 407(a), codified at 29 U.S.C. § 1107(a). Washington, DC: GPO.

——(2006*a*). 'Pension Protection Act of 2006,' Public Law 109–280, codified at 29 U.S.C. §§ 1001, et. seq. Washington, DC: GPO.

——(2006*b*). 'Pension Protection Act of 2006,' Public Law 109–280, § 602(2), codified at 29 U.S.C. § 1108(g)(2)(A)(ii). Washington, DC: GPO.

United States Department of Agriculture (USDA) (2009). *United States Fact Sheet.* Washington, DC: Economic Research Service. http://www.ers.usda.gov/StateFacts/US.htm

United States Government Accountability Office (USGAO) (2007). 'Private Pensions: Low Defined Contribution Plan Savings May Pose Challenges to Retirement Security, Especially for Many Low-Income Workers,' *GAO-08-8.* Washington, DC: GPO.

VanDerhei, Jack, Sarah Holden, Luis Alonso, and Craig Copeland (2007). '401(k) Plan Asset Allocation, Account Balances, and Loan Activity in 2007,' *EBRI Issue Brief 324.* Washington, DC: Employee Benefit Research Institute.

Walsh, Mary Williams (2009). 'Government Takes over Delphi's Pensions,' *New York Times,* July 23: B1.

Weller, Christian E. (2005). *Social Security Privatization, with Social Security Privatization, Timing Matters – for Some More than for Others.* Washington, DC: Center for American Progress. http://www.americanprogress.org/issues/2005/07/b900925.html

——(2008). *401(k) Financial Planning.* Washington, DC: Center for American Progress. http://www.americanprogress.org/issues/2008/07/401k.html

Chapter 9

Longevity Risk and Annuities in Singapore

Joelle H.Y. Fong, Olivia S. Mitchell, and Benedict S.K. Koh

A central concern in the debate over pension reform in defined contribution (DC) systems is how plan participants should draw down their accumulated asset balances during retirement. Annuitization is often recommended as a means to help plan participants manage their longevity risk, since otherwise they may outlive their assets in retirement. Some form of annuitization in the payout phase helps ensure that plan participants have a dependable flow of income beyond the retirement date all the way to death. For instance, in the United Kingdom, retirees have been required to use at least part of the lump-sum available at retirement to purchase an annuity (Finkelstein and Poterba 2002, 2004); in Chile, the DC retirement systems give plan members the choice of taking scheduled withdrawals or buying life annuities upon retirement (Mitchell and Ruiz 2009).

This chapter reviews the nature of longevity risk and annuities in Singapore in order to draw some implications about the prospects for future annuitization under one of the world's largest DC schemes, the Central Provident Fund (CPF) of Singapore. In particular, we examine how the current life annuity market appears to be operating and assess the likely attractiveness of compulsory annuitization under proposed reforms.[1]

In what follows, we first describe the way in which the retirement system works in Singapore. Next we assess the value for money of existing annuity products. We conclude with a brief discussion of the issues that arise when discussing the options for a mandatory annuity model such as those recently suggested in the Singaporean context.

The retirement framework in Singapore

Singapore's CPF is one of Asia's oldest retirement programs, as it was established in 1955. Built around individual accounts, the scheme is mandatory and employment-linked. The current contribution rate under the DC plan is divided between employers and employees; currently the total stands at 34.5 percent (though it has been as high as 40 percent in the past).[1]

Since inception, participants have been able to leave their contributions with the CPF to earn a guaranteed risk-free interest rate (currently at least 2.5 percent [CPF 2009*a*]). The system has also been reformed several times with the goal of enhancing the system's asset *accumulation* by stimulating more saving for retirement, housing, and health-care needs. The CPF Investment Scheme, introduced in 1986 and broadened in 1993, allowed pension contributions to be invested in mutual funds and alternative asset classes including gold. In 1993 and again in 1996, CPF members were permitted to buy shares of Singapore Telecom at a discount with their CPF contributions.

The CPF Board, responsible for managing the system, has undertaken a set of reforms focused on the asset *decumulation* process, responding in part to the rapid aging of the CPF membership base. In the last 2 decades, the proportion of members aged 55 and older experienced a fourfold increase from 5.5 percent in 1985 to 22.9 percent in 2005; at the same time, the proportion of those younger than 24 years fell from 25.1 percent to 9.2 percent (CPF 2007*a*). This trend occurred, in part, because Singapore has one of the world's lowest fertility rates (1.29 per female) and longest life expectancies (80.6 years at birth).[2] These facts imply that retirement expenses are projected to rise, as people live longer and have fewer children on which to rely.

The CPF regulates how retirees can access their money via the so-called Minimum Sum Scheme (MSS). This includes three main components: the value of the Minimum Sum (MS), the age at which drawdown can start, and the form of payouts. This scheme was introduced in 1987 to ensure that CPF members could anticipate at least a basic standard of living in retirement. At present, system participants at age 55 must set aside the MS in their Retirement Account from their total accumulations;[3] this amount is then preserved and may be paid out only as of the official drawdown age. In July 2007, for instance, the required MS was set at S$99,600 and the official drawdown age at 62. The MS is not a threshold easily met; for instance, only 36.4 percent of active members could set aside the required MS in 2006 (CPF 2007*b*).

In response to the rapid aging of the CPF membership base and the need to save more for retirement, the components have been fine-tuned. Table 9.1 summarizes the evolution of the MSS and projected changes to 2013. Here we see that the stipulated MS rises progressively until it reaches S$120,000 by 2013.[4] Concurrently, the drawdown age is rising gradually from 62 to 65 by 2018.

Retirees can currently take their payouts in the form of phased withdrawals, though as of 2013, the government has announced there will be a transition to a compulsory deferred annuitization format, which we discuss later. Under the present rules, most retirees take drawdowns from their MS

TABLE 9.1 Singapore's Minimum Sum Scheme (MSS) schedule: 2003–13

Period	Required minimum sum (2003 S$)	Required minimum sum (real S$)	Drawdown age	MSS payout structure
2003	80,000	80,000	62	• Default: phased withdrawal (administered by CPF).
2004	84,000	84,500	62	• Alternative: voluntary purchase of annuities
2005	88,000	90,000	63	(choose from MSS annuities offered by private insurers. Starting from 2009, participants may also choose from LIFE annuities).
2006	92,000	94,600	63	
2007	96,000	99,600	64	
2008	100,000	106,000	64	
2009	104,000	–	65	
2010	108,000	–	65	
2011	112,000	–	65	
2012	116,000	–	65	
2013	120,000	–	65	• Default: compulsory annuitization (choose from MSS annuities offered by private insurers or LIFE annuities offered by CPF). • Alternative: nil.

Notes: As of 2003, the Minimum Sum (MS) will be raised from S$80,000 to S$120,000 by 2013 (in 2003 dollars) and adjusted for inflation. The drawdown age refers to the official age at which the member may start drawing down the MS plus interest. For example, a member who turns 55 on July 1, 2007 must set aside S$99,600 as the MS in his/her Retirement Account at age 55 and may start draw down only when he/she reaches age 64. If he/she dies before drawdown starts, the balance in the Retirement Account will be fully refunded to his/her beneficiary. From 2003 to 2012, CPF is operating a voluntary annuity purchase scheme; life annuities may be purchased with the MS voluntarily from qualifying annuities offered by private insurers. Starting from 2009, participants may also choose from life annuities offered by CPF. From 2013, CPF will operate a mandatory annuitization scheme with compulsory purchase of life annuities using the MS; annuities will be offered by CPF-LIFE and private insurers.

Source: Authors' calculations; see text.

over about 20 years, or until the balance is exhausted. An alternative to this phased withdrawal approach is a life annuity sold by private insurers. In 2007, nine MSS annuities were offered; these involve a life annuity where the lump-sum premium is the stipulated MS.[5] These private insurers tend to be well known in Singapore and international insurance markets

TABLE 9.2 Monthly nominal payouts for life annuities purchased at the Minimum Sum (MS) of S$99,600 (2007; S$ per month)

Company and product	Monthly annuity payout for entry age of 55		Guaranteed amount upon death
	Male (S$)	Female (S$)	
Nonparticipating Annuities			
Asia Life Assurance	505.47	454.47	Premium − total annuity payments
Prudential Assurance	518.44	449.87	Premium − total annuity payments
American International Assurance (AIA)	530.87	513.94	Premium − total annuity payments
Great Eastern Life (GE Life I)	535.35	484.30	Premium + interest accumulated at 0.75% p.a. to age 62 − total annuity payments
Overseas Assurance Corporation (OAC)	535.35	494.26	Premium + interest accumulated at 0.75% p.a. to age 62 − total annuity payments
Aviva	559.00	507.00	Premium + accrued interest compounded at 1% p.a. to annuity commencement date − total annuity payments
Great Eastern Life (GE Life II) (Note: This product includes long-term care benefit.)	494.26	440.73	Premium + interest accumulated at 0.5% p.a. to age 62 − total annuity payments
Subaverage	525.53	477.80	
Participating Annuities			
NTUC Income Co-op	523.50 (591.08[a])	490.25 (557.83[a])	Premium + interest accumulated at 2.5% p.a. and bonuses to age 62 − total annuity payments
HSBC Insurance	474.00 (541.58[a])	458.00 (525.58[a])	Premium + interest accumulated at 2% p.a. to age 62 − total annuity payments
Subaverage	498.75	474.13	
Average without bonus adjustment	519.58	476.98	
Average with bonus adjustment	534.60	492.00	

[a] Bonus rates depend on company performance; NTUC Income's annual bonus rates were 1–3.5 percent historically; a 2 percent bonus is used in NTUC Income benefit illustrations. Original payouts without bonus expressed without parentheses; figures in parentheses incorporate bonus component assuming an annual projected bonus rate of 2 percent and a projected annual investment rate of return of 5 percent.

Notes: Monthly payouts for a nominal deferred annuity purchased at age 55 with payments starting at age 62. The lump-sum premium is the MS of S$99,600 for members age 55 (July 07–June 08). Annuities under the MSS currently guarantee a given *amount* in the event of annuitant's death; the positive difference of the guaranteed amount less annuity payments made would be paid to nominated beneficiaries. Previously (in 2000), most MS annuities were guaranteed for a certain *period* so if death occurred during the guaranteed period, remaining annuity payments would be converted into a lump sum paid to beneficiaries.

Source: Authors' calculations; derived from CPF (2008a).

including American International Assurance (AIA), Prudential, and HSBC Insurance, as well as some local insurance providers.

Table 9.2 summarizes attributes of the nine qualifying MS annuities offered in 2007 by private insurers. There are some differences in provisions, but the products offered are similar in that they are all single-premium, deferred, life annuities. The lump-sum premium is the entire MS amount of S$99,600 to be paid at age 55, in exchange for annuity payments beginning at exactly age 62. All have fixed (level nominal) payouts, with two annuities having an additional participating bonus feature; these latter are not guaranteed and depend on the profits of the insurer each year. Nonparticipating annuities payouts average S$526 per month for males and S$478 for females, while participating payouts (minus the bonus) average S$499 for males and S$474 for females. Participating payouts are slightly lower since the consumer may receive bonus payouts on top of the specified base rate. Overall, Table 9.2 shows that women receive lower payouts for the same premium given their longer life expectancies; it is also noteworthy that the annuity payouts are sex-specific, resulting in females obtaining a lower annual payout than males for a given premium (by contrast, the annual payouts under phased withdrawal are sex-neutral). It is also worth noting that all MS annuities on offer include a 'guaranteed amount' feature. Thus, at the annuitant's death, his/her beneficiary receives at least the premium paid (at least a premium of S$99,600)[6] less annuity payouts already made. In effect, this means that the protection has an element of capital-protection on the premium remaining.

Despite the assortment of annuities available on the market, most CPF retirees to date have elected phased withdrawal rather than life annuities. While only 4–5 percent of the retiring cohorts in recent years have voluntarily purchased MS annuities, this small percentage must be evaluated in the proper perspective. For one thing, about a quarter of the retiring cohort was exempted due to medical grounds, small balances, or other reasons. For another, almost half (48 percent) of the retirees were ineligible to buy this annuity because they had not set aside the full MS in cash; this group is, by default, channeled into the phased withdrawal payout option. In other words, of the remaining 27 percent who had a choice between phased withdrawals versus lifetime annuity payouts, a relatively high proportion – one out of six – opted for annuitization.[7]

This relatively high annuitization rate among the eligible compares to much lower annuitization rates in other countries, where it has been suggested that people may fail to annuitize because of crowd-out from public defined benefit (DB) pensions, a desire to leave bequests, the need for liquidity, and adverse selection, among other reasons (Mitchell et al. 1999). In the Singaporean context, however, we can rule out the crowd-out by a public DB pension as there is none. The bequest motive is unlikely to be a deterrent since existing rules permit bequests via refunds to beneficiaries. More plausible is a desire for liquidity, since the phased withdrawal approach yields monthly payouts of S$790, compared to the average annuity payout of about S$520.[8] It is plausible that myopic participants as well as those expecting to live a shorter period will opt for phased withdrawal. Another factor may be inertia: pension plan participants are often found to accept whatever is the default option, which in this case is a phased withdrawal (Koh et al. 2008). The possibility of adverse selection may also be a consideration in the Singaporean annuity market, though the issue has not yet been fully evaluated. We turn to an examination of this issue next.

Money's worth valuation for Singaporean annuities

To examine the extent of adverse selection in the Singaporean voluntary annuity market, it is necessary to compare the money's worth of the life annuity benefit using population survival versus annuitant tables. Specifically, we note that a life annuity is a contract that pays the buyer a benefit as long as he/she lives, which insures the annuitant against the risk of outliving accumulated resources, in exchange for a premium. By so doing, the purchaser transfers his/her longevity risk to the insurer, who pools the survival experience of multiple buyers. Following Mitchell et al. (1999), the money's worth ratio (MWR) is therefore the ratio of the expected present discounted value (EPDV) of annuity payouts divided by the initial premium (K):

$$MWR = [EPDV(benefits)]/K \qquad (9.1)$$

In the Singaporean context, K reflects the S$99,600 lump-sum premium (the MS in 2007). The age of entry is age 55 when the annuity is purchased. The general expression for the EPDV is as follows:

$$EPDV = \sum_{t=1}^{\infty} \frac{_tp_a \cdot A_a}{(1 + i_t)^t} \qquad (9.2)$$

where a is the age at which the annuity is purchased, t represents the number of months beyond annuity starting date, A_a refers to the (level or fixed) monthly nominal annuity payout for the individual purchasing annuity at age a, i_t is the nominal interest rate at month t, and $_tp_a$ is the probability of an individual of age a still surviving after t months. The expression runs over the maximum life span in a given mortality table; for a deferred annuity, payments A_a are zero during the deferred period.

Assuming no commercial costs (loads), actuarial fairness requires that the discounted value of the annuity stream will equal the premium paid; accordingly, the MWR for an actuarially fair annuity is unity. In practice, two factors make annuities actuarially unfair for the average person. First, insurers must charge enough to cover administrative costs and earn a profit. Second, those who buy annuities tend to live longer than those who do not. Accordingly, in a market where people buy annuities voluntarily, this adverse selection raises prices for those who buy. As demonstrated by Mitchell et al. (1999), one can separately value these two sources of actuarial unfairness by comparing the difference in the MWR using the population versus the annuitant survival tables. An appeal of the MWR concept is that it is readily quantifiable and facilitates comparisons across products and countries. Nevertheless, these calculations are necessarily sensitive to underlying mortality and interest rate assumptions.

Prior studies on the Singaporean annuity market

Two studies have previously evaluated the money's worth of MSS annuities offered under the Singaporean system; both use data available in the year 2000.[9] Fong (2002) investigates nine annuity products using a fixed interest rate he proxies with the 10-year government bond yield. He reports a mean MWR of 0.997 for the male population so his implied cost of adverse selection is about 0.011. Doyle, Mitchell, and Piggott (2004) use five flat-rate annuities and employ a term structure of interest rates that more accurately discounts future cash flows. That analysis generates a slightly lower MWR of 0.947 for the male population and a much lower cost of adverse selection, 0.0026.

Both of these studies attribute the small degree of adverse selection detected to the fact that the lack of a public DB pension system makes the CPF annuitization scheme close to a 'captive market.' Yet there is reason to worry that these money's worth values could be overstated and the degree of adverse selection biased down, due to the lack of good mortality data. For instance, Doyle, Mitchell, and Piggott (2004) uses abridged life tables from the World Health Organization,[10] and Fong (2002) extrapolates mortality patterns estimated from 1960 period life tables. In addition, both studies assume a constant force of mortality for fractional ages within a year without justifying why this might be appropriate in the Singapore context.[11] Another data limitation in past studies is that their mortality tables have different limiting ages for the population and the annuitant group. For instance, Fong (2002) assumed a maximum life span of 99 years for the population but 109 years for the annuitant group; this naturally leads to higher MWRs for the annuitants. In what follows, we seek to improve on these shortcomings.

Two other drawbacks of prior studies are worth noting. First, they use low interest rates (long-duration T-bonds were not available at that time) that may overstate the MWR results. The emergence of longer-duration bonds offers us the opportunity to improve on this issue. And second, both studies do not model the specific characteristics of the MSS annuities currently offered. Specifically, they ignore the guarantee effective during the 7-year deferral period and the lump-sum nature of the guarantee payments. That is, they assume that CPF life annuities have two terms, where the first term applies to the 15-year guarantee period, and the second term to the life payout period thereafter:

$$\text{EPDV} = \sum_{t=1}^{15\times12} \frac{A_a}{(1+i_t)^t} + \sum_{t=181}^{\infty} \frac{{}_tp_a \cdot A_a}{(1+i_t)^t} \tag{9.3}$$

But Equation (9.3) does not capture the value of the refund if death occurs prior to age 62,[12] so it will understate the MWR. It also does not correctly capture the fact that if death occurs during the 15-year guarantee period, the refund is a lump-sum payment to the beneficiary minus payouts.

Our MWR equation extends the approach used in the past in four key ways. First, we match the limiting age of the population group with that of the annuitant group. Second, we include all the annuities currently on offer under the CPF scheme, as opposed to selecting a subsample; we also incorporate expected bonus payouts for participating annuities using historical rates to reflect the participation upside on such products. Third, we account for the guaranteed amount inherent in the 2007 MSS annuities when undertaking the valuation analysis. Fourth, we apply a uniform distribution of deaths assumption to better reflect the pattern of mortality in Singapore.[13]

Adapting the valuation model for the joint-and-contingent annuity, and using actuarial techniques to incorporate product-specific characteristics, the following formula is then suitable for valuing a MS nominal annuity with guaranteed amount refund:

$$\text{EPDV} = \sum_{t=1}^{83} \frac{{}_{(t-1)}p_a \cdot q_{a+(t-1)} \cdot G_t}{(1+i_t)^t}$$

$$+ \sum_{t=84}^{\infty} \frac{{}_tp_a \cdot A_a + {}_{(t-1)}p_a \cdot q_{a+(t-1)} \cdot \max\left[0, G_t - \sum_{s=0}^{t-84} A_{a,s}\right]}{(1+i_t)^t} \tag{9.4}$$

Here a, t, A_a, i_t, and $_t p_a$ are defined as before, G_t is the guaranteed amount (premium plus accrued interest) at time t, s is a counter for the number of annuity payments made to annuitant before death, $_{(t-1)}p_a$ is the probability of an annuitant age a being alive after $(t-1)$ months, $q_{a+(t-1)}$ is the probability of the annuitant age $a + (t-1)$ months dying within the following 1 month. Taken together, $_{(t-1)}p_a \cdot q_{a+(t-1)}$ is the probability of an annuitant aged a surviving to $(t-1)$ months and then dying between month $(t-1)$ and month t. Thus, this model extends Fong (2002) and Doyle, Mitchell, and Piggott (2004) by explicitly including the refund upon death before age 62 to represent expected benefits due to the annuitant and his/her beneficiaries.[14]

In implementing this valuation, we are also fortunate to have access to new population mortality tables recently published by Singapore Statistics (SDOS 2008b) with a limiting age of 100. Building on this base, we then must cohortize the population tables, as cohort mortality tables are not available in Singapore to date. To derive birth cohort tables using period life tables using the year 2007 period life table, we compute:

$$\hat{q}_x(2007 + t) = q_x(2007) \times (1 - \alpha_x)^t \qquad (9.5)$$

where q_x (2007) is the annual mortality rate for age x in year 2007, $\hat{q}_x(2007 + t)$ is the estimated annual mortality rate for age x in year $(2007 + t)$, and a_x represents the estimated annual mortality improvements for an individual aged x extrapolated from mortality changes between 1990 and 2005. As in previous studies, mortality improvement rates are projected from the abridged period population tables for Singapore published by the World Health Organization. In addition, we match the limiting age of the population group with that of the annuitant group by extrapolating population mortality estimates to the common maximum age of 117 to properly capture the longevity tail risk in the population group; this is particularly important for females.

Little information is currently publicly available on the annuitant mortality experience in Singapore. Standard insurance industry practice and previous research (Fong 2002) adopted the UK annuitant mortality experience with adjustments for local conditions, similar to what is done in Australia. Moreover, the Monetary Authority of Singapore (MAS), in its capacity as insurance regulator, requires firms to employ the UK a(1990) Ultimate Tables rated down 5 years for reserves and liability valuations pertaining to annuities sold (MAS 2008a).[15] Accordingly, we use the a (1990) tables with a 5-year setback to estimate the annuitant experience for our valuation year, and then we cohortize the resulting annuitant tables.[16]

(A)

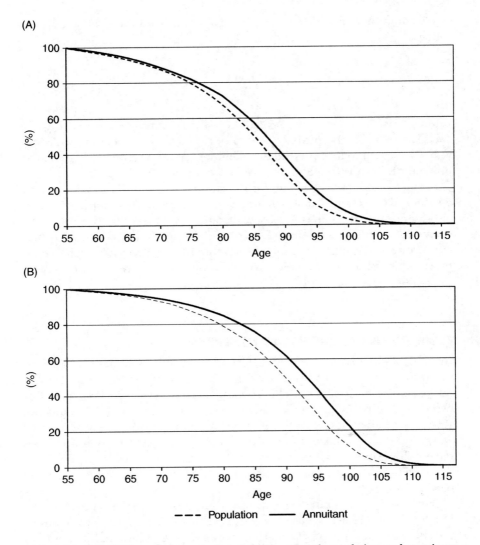

(B)

Figure 9.1 Cumulative cohort survival probability: general population and annuitant groups (conditional on attaining age 55 and limiting age of 117, 2007). Panel A: Singaporean males. Panel B: Singaporean females. *Source*: Authors' calculation; see text.

We compute cumulative survival probabilities from the cohort tables as follows:

$$_tp_a = \prod_{j=0}^{t-1} (1 - q_{a+j}) \tag{9.6}$$

where $_tp_a$ is the cumulative probability of a person aged a surviving for t years, and q_{a+j} is the probability of a person age $(a + j)$ dying within the year. These cumulative survival probabilities are sex-specific and calculated on a monthly basis to match the frequency of the annuity payouts.

Figure 9.1 plots our estimates for the cumulative survival probabilities for 55-year-old males and females in Singapore, for the general population and also for annuitants. The key takeaway from the figure is that the annuitant survival curves lie above that of the general population, confirming that cumulative survival probabilities for annuitants are generally higher than those of the general population (or conversely, mortality for annuitants is lower since they live longer).

Annuity quotes and interest rates

In 2007, eight private insurers offered life annuities under the MSS to CPF members; they provided a total of nine qualifying annuities for the MS premium of S$99,600 (CPF 2008a). All annuities paid level benefits; two were also participating annuities (see Table 9.2). The NTUC Income (2009) participating annuity offers an annual projected bonus rate of about 2 percent; incorporating this rate for both participating annuities means the average payout across all 2007 MSS annuities averages about S$535 per month for a male participant and S$492 per month for a female participant.

Data on interest rates are drawn from market information. As in Mitchell et al. (1999), we use a term structure of interest rates to discount the stream of annuity payments to the present. We judge the Singaporean Treasury bond rates as appropriate here since the MSS annuities are viewed as capital-protected and thus riskless. Relying on the prices and yields of the Singapore Government Securities Treasury bonds at end 2007, we compute the riskless spot rates to proxy the yields on hypothetical zero coupon bonds.[17] Table 9.3 summarizes the key inputs and compares them to assumptions used in prior studies on Singaporean annuities.

TABLE 9.3 Money's worth ratios (MWRs) computed for Minimum Sum Scheme (MSS) life annuities

Study	Valuation date and sample	Mortality assumption		Interest rate assumption	MWR for 55-year-old male		Adverse selection
		Annuitant	Population		Ann.	Pop.	(%)
W.M. Fong (2002)	2000; subset of eight nonparticipating annuities and one participating annuity	a(90) with 2-year setback Limiting age used is 109	Derived from 1960 and 1990 ordinary male and female lives tables (Singstat) Limiting age of 99	Flat interest rate (proxy by the 10-year Government bond yield of 4.6%)	0.997	0.986	1.1
Doyle, Mitchell, and Piggott (2004)	2000; subset of five nonparticipating annuities with a 15-year guarantee period or similar	a(90) with 2-year setback Limiting age used is 109	Abridged life tables for Singapore (World Health Organization) Limiting age of 100	Term structure (yield curve with long-term rate assumption of 4.76%)	0.947	0.945	0.26
Present study (2009)	2007; all MSS annuities: seven nonparticipating and two participating annuities	a(90) with 5-year setback Limiting age used is 117	Complete life tables for Singapore resident population 2007 (Singstat), plus extrapolate from age 100 to 117 Limiting age of 117	Term structure (yield curve with long-term rate assumption of 3.44%)	0.947	0.910	3.69

Notes: A total of 13 MSS life annuities were offered in July 2000 of which 9 were flat-rate annuities, 2 were participating annuities, and 2 were increasing annuities. The increasing annuities offered by AIA were dropped after that year (*Source:* Personal communication from CPF Board). The a(90) table refers to the United Kingdom a(1990) period life table for annuitants. It is based on UK annuitants' experience from 1967 to 1970, with mortality improvements projected to 1990. Because of lack of annuitant experience in Singapore, previous studies used the a(90) and with a 2-year setback to account for lower mortality among annuitants. A 2-year setback means that a 65-year-old is treated as having the same mortality rate as a 63-year-old has in the initial table.

Source: Authors' calculations; see text.

MWRs for MSS annuities

We next provide money's worth results using population mortality tables, focusing on MSS life annuities offered by private insurers in the voluntary annuity purchase scheme in 2007. Results in Table 9.4 show that, on average, S$1 of premium spent on a nominal MS annuity by a 55-year-old male drawn from the general population would generate nearly S$0.910 in expected annuity income (in net present value terms). Likewise, a female in the general population could anticipate receiving S$0.906. Though the monthly payouts are lower for females than males, the MWR values converge for both sexes, once life expectancy is taken in account. We also note that NTUC Income annuity offered the highest money's worth to retirees in Singapore. The MWR of 1.006 (males) and 1.024 (females) exceeded the average MWR by almost 10.5 percent and 13.1 percent, respectively.

TABLE 9.4 Money's worth ratios (MWRs) and adverse selection cost of Minimum Sum Scheme (MSS) annuities (nominal life annuities offered by private insurers under Central Provident Fund (CPF) plan; 2007)

Company and product	Male			Female		
	Population MWR	Annuitant MWR	Adverse selection (%)	Population MWR	Annuitant MWR	Adverse selection (%)
Nonparticipating annuity						
Asia Life Assurance	0.861	0.896	3.47	0.840	0.885	4.44
Prudential Assurance	0.879	0.915	3.62	0.833	0.876	4.37
AIA	0.907	0.943	3.62	0.943	0.995	5.20
GE Life I	0.910	0.947	3.71	0.893	0.941	4.78
OAC	0.907	0.945	3.74	0.908	0.957	4.98
Aviva	0.943	0.982	3.98	0.930	0.981	5.14
GE Life II	0.846	0.879	3.34	0.818	0.860	4.22
Participating annuity						
NTUC Income Co-op	1.006	1.047	4.09	1.024	1.081	5.61
HSBC Insurance	0.933	0.969	3.59	0.969	1.021	5.20
Mean	0.910	0.947	3.69	0.906	0.955	4.88

Notes: MWRs are in decimals. Adverse selection costs are in percentage points. Computations pertain to a CPF participant who purchases the MSS annuity at entry age 55 for a premium of S$99,600, and starts receiving payouts at age 62.

Source: Authors' calculations; see text.

This could be explained by the fact that NTUC Income operates as a cooperative company with a mission to give back 98 percent of profits to policyholders in bonuses. Further, its monthly annuity payouts are the highest among the MSS annuities (having factored in the estimated bonus).[18] Perhaps not surprisingly, this firm has the largest market share of annuities in Singapore.

The MWR values may be used to estimate total loadings, which average about 9.2 percent. These estimates are lower than those for UK nominal annuities of about 14 percent (Finkelstein and Poterba 2002), and for US annuities where the loads amount to about 15–20 percent (Mitchell et al. 1999). But the Singaporean results for 2007 are much higher than those reported in previous studies on CPF-linked annuities using pricing from earlier years and less precise mortality tables. That is, Fong (2002) reports an average loading of only 1.4 percent for males and a negative loading for females (MWR exceeded 1), while Doyle, Mitchell, and Piggott (2004) found loadings of about 5.5 percent for both sexes. Such small loadings make sense, given their very high MWR figures (0.945–1.009 using population mortality). A possible explanation for the difference, as acknowledged by the authors, is that their MWRs might be overstated due to the lack of long duration Treasury bonds at the time. Their loading figures seem implausibly low inasmuch as the products are mainly offered by private insurers who could not survive for long if they paid such high benefits.

Our main explanations for the differences in the results are as follows:

- Different products evaluated: We value the MSS annuities offered in 2007, which include a guaranteed *amount* refund; earlier studies valued the annuities with a 15-year guaranteed *period*.
- Different mortality assumptions: Prior studies employ a constant force of mortality assumption for fractional ages within a year; by contrast, we apply a uniform distribution of deaths assumption to better reflect the pattern of mortality in Singapore.
- Higher premium and lower annuity payouts: Annuity quotes in the year 2000 were based on a lower premium (S$65,000) and paid out higher average monthly benefits (about S$555 for males; Doyle, Mitchell, and Piggott 2004). By 2007, the premium had risen to S $99,600 but the average annuity payouts were lower (S$520 for males).

Next we turn to a discussion of the cost of adverse selection. We compute this by taking the difference between a given annuity's MWR using annuitant mortality, versus the same product's MW calculated using population mortality. Table 9.4 shows that, on average, adverse selection costs are 3.69 percentage points for males and 4.88 percentage points for females. These results are comparable to empirical findings in the United Kingdom where adverse selection costs amount to about 4.6 percentage points (Finkelstein and Poterba 2002) and below the 6 percentage points reported for Australian annuities (Doyle, Mitchell, and Piggott 2004). They are much lower than the 10 percentage points reported for the United States (Mitchell et al. 1999).

Overall, our findings suggest that a retiree in Singapore's CPF having cash of at least the MS would have been able to purchase longevity protection on competitive terms, without much concern for adverse selection. Total loads might be further reduced, of course, if annuitization were mandatory, a topic to which we turn next.

Policy proposals for mandatory annuitization

Though the existing default phased withdrawal with voluntary annuitization may have worked well in the past in Singapore, there is now concern that future retirees may be at risk of running out of money. In 1990, for instance, the average male and female life expectancy at birth was 73 and 77, respectively; by 2007, life expectancies at birth had risen to 78.2 and 82.9, respectively. And, of those aged 65 in 2007, two-thirds would expect to still be alive at 80, and 48 percent at 85 (CPF 2007a). This means that about half of all aged 65 CPF members alive today might outlive their CPF savings under the 20-year phased withdrawal program (CPF 2009c). A related concern is that the entire age structure of members has aged substantially, while membership growth has tapered off. These factors are, quite sensibly, turning policymaker's attention to the role of longevity protection.

To this end, the Singapore Government has recently announced plans to implement a mandatory annuitization scheme, slated to pay out benefits for the first time in 2013. This program, dubbed the CPF-LIFE program, is being integrated with the existing CPF MSS. At the time the plan was announced in 2007, a National Longevity Insurance Committee (NLIC) was formed to help design the program's elements (SPMO 2007). This group released a report in 2008 outlining preliminary details and the design continues to be refined. Accordingly, as of this writing, since only the broad outlines of the new mandatory annuitization scheme are available, we do not offer MWR computations; these must await more information of the product and pricing structure of products to be offered. Nevertheless, the key elements of the new proposal are usefully summarized.

The new scheme will automatically enroll members aged 51 and younger from 2009 forward, who have at least S$40,000 cash saving in the Retirement Account at age 55. The entity that supervises the current system, the CPF Board, is to administer the scheme drawing on the advice of independent actuarial consultants to determine premium and payout levels. Members may purchase their annuities either from a government-administered entity, or from qualifying private insurers.

Key changes to be implemented under the LIFE scheme are later payouts and a different default payout structure. Specifically, at age 55, a participant must set aside a MS; in 2013, this is expected to be about S $134,000 (CPF 2008$b$). Instead of having payouts begin at age 62, as now, the MS is to be partially annuitized by default at age 65, so there is a 10-year deferral period from age 55 to 65. The MS will be split into a term component and an annuity component, with the split depending on which plan the participant chooses. The term investment amount (T) plus interest earned on T is intended to finance payouts from age 65 to some older age (Y), where Y may be elected by the participant within some bounds (e.g., Y might be either age 65, 75, or 85). The annuity component (N) is intended to finance payouts from age Y to death. In any case, however, the requirement is that the member must receive a fixed dollar payout every month from age 65 to death as long as he/she lives; they can also bequeath the term amount plus interest minus payouts. One other decision to be made is whether the participant wishes to have his/her remaining annuity premium (N minus payouts) provided to his/her heirs on their death, which is called the 'refund portion.' For example, the R80 plan starts the annuity payout at age 80, and the annuity would have a refund element; the NR65 plan starts the annuity payment at age 65 and has no death benefit.

The rationale for making the system compulsory is to prevent adverse selection, and it is logical to assume that making the program mandatory will mitigate this problem. On the other hand, while the rules permit members to elect either the CPF-managed annuity or a private annuity provider, it is unclear whether private firms will be able to compete. There is already some suggestion of a market response: in 2008, for instance, only two MSS annuities were offered by private insurers, compared to nine the previous year. The shrinkage of private annuity offerings could indicate that private insurers are scrambling to reprice their products more competitively, but it could also indicate that they have been crowded out more permanently.

In the future, private annuity providers might instead refocus their business outside the CPF scheme for those seeking to annuitize non-pension wealth. There is a cap to the amount in the Retirement Account that CPF members can annuitize, namely, the stipulated MS that will rise over time. Very wealthy individuals seeking a higher monthly annuity payout would still turn to commercial annuities. It is also worth nothing that the plan will exempt CPF members who hold alternative lifelong pensions or receive annuities from the government-run annuity scheme.

Conclusion

This chapter offers new evidence on the annuity market in Singapore focusing on products offered by private insurers, and it discusses the possible impact of imposing mandatory annuitization through the national CPF system. We show that an average 55-year-old male could purchase annuities providing a MWR value of about 0.910, using population tables; this is similar to figures in other countries. But the costs of adverse selection in Singapore are smaller than elsewhere, on the order of 0.3–5 percentage points. Adverse selection accounts for 47 percent of total loadings; Brown et al. (2001) by comparison found that roughly half of the cost of purchasing a voluntary annuity in the US annuity market could be attributed to adverse selection. What this means is that – given the best available data – annuitization costs in Singapore are equally influenced by insurance company loadings and adverse selection.

For these reasons, we would expect that requiring mandatory annuitization in Singapore is likely to have little impact on the money's worth valuations of lifetime annuity payouts due to the elimination of adverse selection. Instead, what will enhance the value for money of annuity payouts is the fact that the government will provide them, presumably without the need to make a profit. To the extent that taking the CPF-provided annuity is the default, this will likely hold down advertising, marketing, and distribution costs as well. Accordingly, the entry of the CPF Board into the market is expected to narrow the traditional gap between premiums and anticipated benefits, and it will likely make the new payout products quite attractive.

Acknowledgments

The authors acknowledge research support from the Wharton–SMU Research Center at Singapore Management University and the Pension Research Council/Boettner Center at The Wharton School of the University of Pennsylvania. They also acknowledge helpful assistance and advice from Desmond Chew, Lee Ee Jia, Jean Lemaire, and Libby Sang.

Notes

[1] For workers aged 50 and younger, the government has set the long-term target CPF contribution rates at 30–36 percent, with an employee contribution of 20 percent and an employer contribution varying between 10 and 16 percent. For those older than age 50 and up to 55, the long-term target range is set at

24–30 percent, with the employee contribution at 18 percent and the employer contribution varying between 6 and 12 percent (SPMO 2003).

[2] Figures are from year-end 2007 and obtained from the Singapore Department of Statistics (SDOS 2008*a*).

[3] If a member's total balance is higher than the MS, any remaining balance can be withdrawn as a lump sum. If the total balance is less than the MS, the following withdrawal rules currently apply for members who reach 55 between January 1, 2009 and June 30, 2009: total balance ≤ S$5,000 (withdraw everything), S$5,000 < total balance ≤ S$12,500 (withdraw S$5,000 and set aside remainder in Retirement Account), and S$12,500 < total balance ≤ S$176,667 (withdraw 40 percent of total balance and set aside remainder in Retirement Account; see CPF 2009*b*).

[4] This change was announced in 2003. The other two changes on the drawdown age and payout structure were announced in 2007 in Prime Minister Lee's National Day Rally speech (SPMO 2007).

[5] It must be noted that the CPF Board does not endorse any specific life annuity product offered under the MSS nor does it screen private insurers (although any life insurer exhibiting poor conduct or unacceptable behavior may have its contract suspended).

[6] In some products, the guaranteed amount is the premium plus annual interest accrued from age 55 when the annuity is purchased up to age 62 when payouts start; see Table 9.2. The results in Table 9.4 account for the different specifications of guaranteed amount for each product.

[7] This is consistent with Doyle, Mitchell, and Piggott (2004).

[8] This is for the case of a member who has set aside the full MS of S$99,600 at age 55 as of 2007. Under phased withdrawal, he/she can draw down this amount plus interest via monthly payouts of S$790; of course, this will last for only about 20 years at which point the balance is likely to be exhausted.

[9] A total of 11 flat-rate (level) nonparticipating and participating annuities were offered in July 2000 (excludes two annuities with increasing payouts). Doyle, Mitchell, and Piggott (2004) sampled five nonparticipating annuities. Fong (2002) included all eight nonparticipating annuities plus one participating annuity but did not incorporate potential bonus payouts from the participation feature.

[10] The World Health Organization (various years) offers abridged life tables that provide mortality estimates in 5-year age intervals; they are less detailed than complete life tables providing mortality rates for every individual age.

[11] Three actuarial assumptions could be used for fractional ages within a year, namely, a uniform distribution of deaths assumption, a constant force of mortality assumption, and a hyperbolic assumption.

[12] In results not reported here, we find that 3–5 percent of EPDV is attributable to refunds to the beneficiary upon the annuitant's death (hence failure to capture this understates the MWR by 3–5 percent).

[13] The uniform distribution of deaths assumption for fractional ages within a year is appropriate given the lack of variation in Singapore's weather (so death rates are unlikely to vary seasonally).

[14] This formula is appropriate for money's worth values when the annuity has a guaranteed amount or 'capital-protection' feature. Previous studies using US data have focused on simpler products, mainly single-premium, immediate, nominal annuities, and they differentiate between the single-life versus joint-life annuities (see Mitchell et al. 1999; Brown et al. 2001). Studies on the UK compulsory and voluntary annuity markets (Finkelstein and Poterba 2002) have compared the money's worth of nominal, real, and escalating annuities, some with guarantee periods of 0, 5, and 10 years; these report that MWRs rise with the length of the guarantee period. Thorburn, Rocha, and Morales (2005) report that the MWRs of guaranteed annuities in Chile are smaller than those of non-guaranteed annuities, possibly due to the fact that long periods of guarantee tend to increase duration, thus reinvestment risk, forcing premiums up for a given value of benefits.

[15] The Sixth Schedule of the Insurance Regulations 2004 stipulates that insurers may employ the rates in the UK a(90) tables with a 5-year setback to value their annuity liabilities. Previously, the Insurance Regulations 1992 regulations required insurers to employ the a(1990) tables with a 2-year setback. These a(1990) tables are constructed based on UK annuitants' mortality experience from 1967 to 1970 with mortality improvements projected to 1990. By applying the 5-year setback, we effectively age the tables to year 2007 and then cohortize it for the MWRs.

[16] As a robustness check, we verify that our calculations yield a lower mortality for annuitant cohort than the population cohort; for instance, a 65-year-old male in the general population has a mortality of 0.01133 compared to 0.01027 for an annuitant, which seems reasonable.

[17] The first-year rate is derived from the 1-year Treasury bill (MAS 2008b). Thereafter, the 2-, 5-, 7-, 10-, 15- and 20-year Treasury bond rates as of 2007 are used to estimate the riskless spot rates. Our annual spot rate ranges from 1.4 to 3.44 percent. Since maximum duration available is only 20 years, we then extrapolate the last spot rate into the future, yielding a nominal riskless term structure of interest rates on Singapore's Treasury bonds.

[18] Historically, NTUC Income's average bonus participation rate has ranged between 1 and 3.5 percent, and a 2 percent future bonus rate is typically used to value its annuity (NTUC Income 2009).

References

Brown, Jeffrey, Olivia S. Mitchell, James Poterba, and Mark Warshawsky (2001). *The Role of Annuity Markets in Financing Retirement*. Cambridge, MA: MIT Press.

Central Provident Fund Board (CPF) (2007a). *CPF Trends: Changing Age Structure of CPF Members: Membership in Brief*. Singapore: Central Provident Fund Board. http://mycpf.cpf.gov.sg/NR/rdonlyres/1103E583-19A4-4B62-A38D-8D06B5C0 E071/0/ChangingAgeStructureofCPFMembers.pdf

——(2007b). *CPF Trends: Minimum Sum Scheme*. Singapore: Central Provident Fund Board. http://mycpf.cpf.gov.sg/NR/rdonlyres/27ACA8E5-7D0D-431F-B74B-D8D3A3E43463/0/CPFTrends_MSS.pdf

—— (2008a). *CPF Minimum Sum Scheme: Table of Monthly Payment Rates for the Minimum Sum of $99,600 Placed with a Participating Insurance Company*. Singapore: Central Provident Fund Board. http://mycpf.cpf.gov.sg/NR/rdonlyres/883DD6D3-D1EC-48DD-8B09-811C0D24ECE8/0/AnnuityComparison.pdf

—— (2008b). *Report by the National Longevity Insurance Committee (NLIC)*. Singapore: Central Provident Fund Board. http://mycpf.cpf.gov.sg/Members/Gen-Info/CPF_LIFE/NLIC.htm

—— (2009a). *Interest Earned by Members*. Singapore: Central Provident Fund Board. http://mycpf.cpf.gov.sg/Members/Gen-Info/Int-Rates/Int-Rates.htm

—— (2009b). *CPF Withdrawal Calculator*. Singapore: Central Provident Fund Board. https://www.cpf.gov.sg/cpf_trans/ssl/financial_model/wdl_assumption.asp

—— (2009c). *Frequently Asked Questions on CPF LIFE*. http://mycpf.cpf.gov.sg/Members/Gen-Info/CPF_LIFE/CPF_LIFE.htm

Doyle, Suzanne, Olivia S. Mitchell, and John Piggott (2004). 'Annuity Values in Defined Contribution Retirement Systems: Australia and Singapore Compared,' *Australian Economic Review*, 37(4): 402–16.

Finkelstein, Amy and James M. Poterba (2002). 'Selection Effects in the United Kingdom Individual Annuities Market,' *The Economic Journal*, 112(476): 28–50.

———— (2004). 'Adverse Selection in Insurance Markets: Policyholder Evidence from the U.K. Annuity Market,' *Journal of Political Economy*, 112(1): 183–208.

Fong, Wai M. (2002). 'On the Cost of Adverse Selection in Individual Annuity Markets: Evidence from Singapore,' *Journal of Risk and Insurance*, 69(2): 193–207.

Koh, Benedict S.K., Olivia S. Mitchell, Toto Tanuwidjaja, and Joelle H.Y. Fong (2008). 'Investment Patterns in Singapore's Central Provident Fund System,' *Journal of Pension Economics and Finance*, 7(1): 37–65.

Mitchell, Olivia S. and Jose Ruiz (2009). 'Pension Payments in Chile: Past, Present, and Future Prospects,' Pension Research Council Working Paper No. 2009-07. Philadelphia, PA: The Wharton School of the University of Pennsylvania.

——James Poterba, Mark Warshawsky, and Jeffrey Brown (1999). 'New Evidence on the Money's Worth of Individual Annuities,' *American Economic Review*, 89(5): 1299–318.

Monetary Authority of Singapore (MAS) (2008a). *Insurance (Valuation and Capital) Regulations 2004*. Singapore: Monetary Authority of Singapore. www.mas.gov.sg/resource/legislation_guidelines/insurance/sub_legislation/Insurance%20(Valuation%20and%20Capital)%20Regs%202004.pdf

—— (2008b). *Statistics Room: Daily SGS Prices*. Singapore: Monetary Authority of Singapore. www.mas.gov.sg/data_room/index.html

NTUC Income (2009). *Annuity Plans*. Singapore: NTUC Income. http://income.com.sg/insurance/annuity

Singapore Department of Statistics (SDOS) (2008a). *Statistics: Demography (Themes)*. Singapore: Singapore Department of Statistics. http://www.singstat.gov.sg/stats/themes/people/demo.html

—— (2008b). *Complete Life Tables for 2006–2007 for the Singapore Resident Population*. Singapore: Singapore Department of Statistics.

Singapore Prime Minister's Office (SPMO) (2003). 'Ministerial Statement by Prime Minister Goh Chok Tong in Parliament: Retuning the CPF,' Singapore, August 28.

——(2007). 'Transcript of Prime Minister Lee Hsien Loong's National Day Rally English Speech: City of Possibilities; Home for All,' Singapore, August 19.

Thorburn, Craig, Roberto Rocha, and Marco Morales (2005). 'An Analysis of Money's Worth Ratios in Chile,' *Journal of Pension Economics and Finance*, 6(03): 287–312.

World Health Organization (various years) *Life Tables for WHO Member States*. Geneva, Switzerland: World Health Organization. http://apps.who.int/whosis/database/life_tables/life_tables.cfm

Part III

Innovations in Retirement Risk Financing

Chapter 10

Outsourcing Pension Longevity Protection

Igor Balevich

Employer-provided defined benefit (DB) pension plans were a key component of the traditional 'three-legged stool' of retirement income in decades past, with the other two legs being Social Security and personal saving. Despite the steady decrease in the number of US participants covered by employer-sponsored DB plans over time and the sudden drop in value of retirement assets in 2008, $2 trillion of assets still remain in private DB plans and $3.5 trillion in government pension plans as of the end of 2008 (Investment Company Institute 2009). One of the valuable features of DB plans, when compared to the increasingly common defined contribution (DC) plan, is that the default form of benefit payment has been an annuity with payments continuing for at least the lifetime of the employee.

Managing a DB plan has proven to be a difficult task over the past 10 years. The early part of the decade was marked with significant funding declines (assets minus liabilities) and increases in the number of plan changes that either reduced or eliminated future benefit accruals. After many pensions worked their way back to a decent funded status by the end of 2007, capital market conditions in 2008 reversed all of the gains from the previous 5 years. Many corporate pension plans were in the process of deciding whether or how to implement liability-driven investing (LDI) strategies when the market turmoil struck. Ironically, such strategies could have helped protect against the volatile 2008 market conditions.

The last decade has also led to greater focus on the volatility of plan costs. In the United States, little attention has been devoted to mortality assumptions and their impact on costs. Yet this pattern is changing due to the 2006 Pension Protection Act (PPA) requirements to update mortality assumptions more frequently, as well as refinements in risk management strategies.

This chapter discusses mortality trends, the impact of longevity assumptions on pensions, and factors that drive plan sponsors' decisions on whether to outsource longevity exposure. We first review general population mortality improvement trends in the United States. Despite fairly steady improvement trends over most of the last century, opinions vary greatly on whether these trends will continue in the future. Although the mortality levels of people covered by pension plans tend to be lower than those of the general population, many of the methods and reasoning used to model general population mortality can be applied to pensions as well. Next we examine the impact of longevity assumptions and experience on pension plan liabilities. A comparison of the magnitude of this risk relative to the capital market risks can be informative in understanding whether and how pension plans sponsors may decide to outsource this risk. Finally, we discuss ways in which longevity exposures can be managed or out-sourced. These include plan design changes to shift longevity risk to employees, transferring the risk to insurance companies, and hedging without completely eliminating longevity risk.

Longevity trends and estimation

There is little dispute that life spans have increased significantly and fairly steadily over most of the last century. Nevertheless, there is considerable debate and disagreement over whether this trend will continue in the future, whether the mortality improvements will accelerate, or whether they will slow or even reverse for some generations. Similarly, although there are many ways of modeling future mortality rates, currently there is no single widely accepted best method for doing this. These varied views could be refined and converge as more people focus their attention on the impact of mortality on pensions.

Historic mortality trends

Life expectancy at birth in the United States has increased from 58.3 years in 1934 to 75.2 years in 2005 for males, and from 62.4 years in 1934 to 80.4 years in 2005 for females (Human Mortality Database 2008). On average, life expectancies increased by just under 0.24 years for males and just over 0.25 years for females, for each calendar year over this time period. Note that these are *period* life expectancies, indicating how long someone born in a given year would live if he or she experienced mortality rates equal to those calculated for each age in that year. This is generally not a true estimate of how long a person born in a given year is actually expected to live, since period life expectancy does not take into account the projected changes in mortality rates that a person would actually experience over their lifetime. Nonetheless, it is still a useful measure to illustrate trends in mortality rates over time (Figure 10.1).

Despite a relatively steady historic long-term increase in life expectancy at birth, there are vastly different views on whether this trend will continue

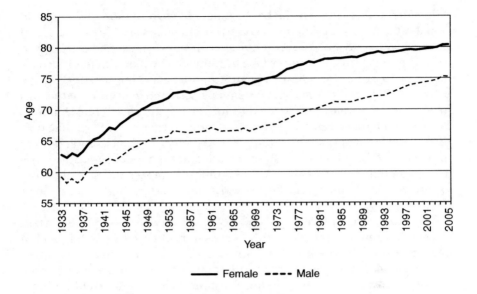

Figure 10.1 United States life expectancy at birth (period table). *Source*: Author's calculations derived from Human Mortality Database (2008).

in the future. At one end of the spectrum, some argue that there are biological limits to the increases in life spans (Carnes, Olshansky, and Grahn 2003), and that factors such as childhood obesity will even decrease life expectancy for younger generations (Olshansky et al. 2005). Opponents point to the lack of evidence of a limit to life expectancy (Oeppen and Vaupel 2002). One extreme point of view is that regenerative medicine could possibly halt the aging process and that the first person to live to 1,000 years old might be alive today (de Grey and Rae 2007). This broad range of opinions illustrates the challenges involved in accurately modeling future mortality rates.

Modeling future mortality

Projecting future mortality rates for a given population involves estimating four elements: current mortality rates for the population, long-term trends, short-term derivations from the trend, and infrequent onetime shocks. Stochastic mortality simulations can use separate distributions for each of the elements, or they may utilize a model with parameters that can estimate their impacts.

The difference between the best estimate of current mortality rates and actual rates for the population is referred to as the *basis*. Since the actual rates are generally not known in advance, even for fully medically under-written populations, it is important to estimate the magnitude of a confidence band around the best estimate to understand the basis risk of the projection. The long-term trend is generally assumed to capture reductions in the mortality rates over time due to medical advances. But as noted, there is much disagreement over how this long-term trend will change over time. Short-term deviations from the trend are typically small and random; they account for minor factors not included in the model explicitly. Infrequent onetime shocks can have a significant impact on mortality and examples include infectious diseases, natural disasters, and acts of war or terrorism.

There are many different types of projection models, and it is important to keep in mind the purpose of the projection when selecting a model in order to ensure the results are appropriate. Classes of models include those that extrapolate the trends of the calibrating past time horizon and those that rely heavily on expert opinion for inputs such as the likelihood of a disease being cured or the ultimate upper bound on life spans. Statistical extrapolation models are generally more appropriate for shorter projection periods; models that incorporate some degree of expert opinion (or range of expert opinions) seem more appropriate for long projections. Olshansky (1988) discusses various types of models and considerations for projecting mortality rates. Cairns et al. (2007) compare the results of eight statistical models for projecting mortality rates. In addition to selecting a model appropriate for its intended usage, careful attention should also be paid to the assumptions used for model calibration and the resulting model parameters. A given model can produce significantly different results when calibrated differently.

Mortality assumptions for pension plans

Long-term trends in mortality rates for employees covered by pension plans have been broadly similar to trends for the US general population. However, mortality rates for employees covered by pension plans are typically lower than for the general population. This relationship makes intuitive sense, since those covered by pensions sponsored by their employers usually also have some sort of employer-sponsored medical coverage. The period life expectancy at birth for 2000 is 74.3 years for males and 79.6 for females for the US population (Human Mortality Database 2008), while the period life expectancy at birth using the RP-2000 mortality table (commonly used for pension valuations) is 78.4 years for males and 81.6 years for females (see Figure 10.2).

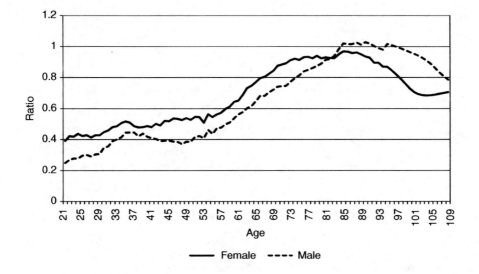

Figure 10.2 Ratio of RP-2000 combined healthy mortality rates to 2000 US population mortality rates. *Sources*: Author's calculations derived from Human Mortality
Database (2008) and Society of Actuaries (2000).

Mortality assumptions for pension liability valuations have historically
received little attention in the United States. Traditionally, the Internal
Revenue Service (IRS) has updated the required mortality table for pension current liability calculations approximately every decade. These tables
were static, where the same rates were used for all future years. It was fairly
rare for projected improvements to be explicitly calculated for future years
within a valuation or for future valuations after the table was initially
adopted. This approach then produced liability jumps whenever a new
table was adopted.

The PPA changed the way mortality assumptions are to be used for
pension plan purposes. Starting with 2008 valuations, there are generally
applicable mortality tables, based on the RP-2000 mortality tables as well as
guidance for the use of plan-specific mortality tables. Future mortality
improvements can be included in one of two ways: one uses static tables
with improvements projected for 7 years after the valuation date for
annuitants and projected for 15 years after the valuation date for non-
annuitants. Another uses projection Scale AA to calculate rates for each
future year. The plan-specific mortality tables can be used instead of
generally applicable mortality tables if certain conditions are met. These

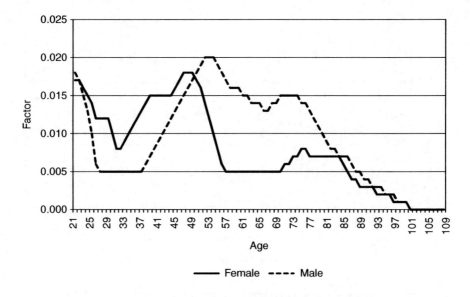

Figure 10.3 Annual mortality improvement factors using projection Scale AA. *Source*: Author's calculations derived from Society of Actuaries (2000).

changes will allow for more accurate and updated liability calculations (Figure 10.3).

It is interesting to note that the United Kingdom uses far more conservative mortality assumptions than the United States. It is estimated that pension liabilities in many countries would increase by 10–15 percent if assumptions similar to those in the United Kingdom were used (Hewitt Associates 2008).

Impact of longevity on pension plans

Next we analyze the impact of various mortality assumptions on life expectancies and pension liabilities. The assumptions are based on the 1983 GAM table, the RP-2000 table, projection Scale AA, as well as ad hoc adjustments to the underlying mortality table and improvement factors. The calculations are based on a sample plan consisting of retirees and terminated vested participants who have not yet commenced payments.

In Figure 10.4, we note that the impact of moving from the 1983 GAM table to the RP-2000 table is not as significant as one might expect. Life expectancy at birth increases 0.5 years, from 79.3 to 79.8. The life expectancy at age 65 is the same. Although the underlying data for the 1983 GAM

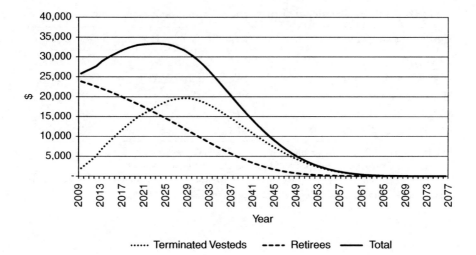

Figure 10.4 Sample pension plan benefit payments. *Source*: Author's calculations; see text.

table is from the 1960s, it was projected forward to 1983 and a 10 percent margin was applied for conservatism. The minimal impact shown is due to the fact that our mortality comparison uses a blend of 50 percent of the male and 50 percent of the female rates. The mortality rates of the RP-2000 table are lower for males and higher for females when compared to the 1983 GAM table.

The impact of using a projection scale has a significant impact on life expectancies as does applying an adjustment factor to the rates of an underlying table (Table 10.1). Life expectancy at birth increases from 79.8 to 85.1 years when Scale AA is applied to the RP-2000 table. Applying an adjustment factor of 75 percent to the RP-2000 table projected with Scale AA increases the life expectancy at birth by 2.6 to 87.7 years.

The liabilities increase by 2.6 percent when applying Scale AA to the RP-2000 table. The increase in liabilities of applying projection Scale AA is 3 percent when the benefit payments are increased by 1.5 percent after retirement (Table 10.2). Postretirement benefit increases enhance the impact on liabilities of changes in mortality assumptions. They are more common among pension plans in the United Kingdom and government pension plans in the United States, than among US corporate plans. The liabilities increase by 6.4 percent when reducing the Scale AA projected RP-2000 rates by 25 percent. This increase illustrates the potential basis risk of the underlying mortality assumption and the importance of trying to

TABLE 10.1 Life expectancy at birth and age 65 using various mortality assumptions

Mortality assumption[a]	Life expectancy at birth	Life expectancy at age 65
1983 GAM	79.3	18.7
RP-2000 combined healthy	79.8	18.7
RP-2000, projected Scale AA	85.1	19.5
RP-2000 × 75%, Scale AA[b]	87.7	21.9
RP-2000, Scale AA + 1%[c]	91.7	20.7

[a] All mortality assumptions use blended rates (50% male, 50% female).
[b] Mortality adjustment factor applied to mortality rates below terminal age (120).
[c] Scale AA improvement factors plus 1% applied to mortality rates at all ages below age 101.
Source: Author's calculations; derived from Society of Actuaries (2002).

TABLE 10.2 Liability values using various mortality assumptions[a]

Mortality assumption[b]	No postretirement benefit increases			1.5% postretirement benefit increases		
	TVs[c]	Retirees	Total	TVs[c]	Retirees	Total
1983 GAM	263,043	178,957	442,000	299,680	202,256	501,936
RP-2000 combined healthy	264,011	180,535	444,546	300,786	204,018	504,803
RP-2000, projected Scale AA	268,746	187,150	455,896	307,411	212,671	520,081
RP-2000 × 75%, Scale AA[d]	284,724	200,434	485,158	328,659	230,074	558,733
RP-2000, Scale AA + 1%[e]	275,553	195,701	471,254	317,349	224,532	541,881

[a] Liability calculations use 6% discount rate.
[b] All mortality assumptions use blended rates (50% male, 50% female).
[c] Terminated vested participants (TVs).
[d] Mortality adjustment factor applied to mortality rates below terminal age (120).
[e] Scale AA improvement factors plus 1% applied to mortality rates at all ages below age 101.
Source: Author's calculations; derived from Society of Actuaries (2002).

estimate mortality rates as closely as possible. As an example of the potential difference in mortality rates for different employee groups, it is estimated that workers in the primary metal industries have mortality rates
over 30 percent higher, and workers in the petroleum industry have mortality rates over 20 percent lower than those in the RP-2000 table for ages 60
through 80 (Society of Actuaries 2000).

Magnitude of longevity risk relative to other risks

It is instructive to calculate the size of mortality-related risks, compared to a few of the main financial market risks on the funded status of our sample pension plan. Of the factors included, equities have the largest impact with one standard deviation event over a 1-year period leading to an 8.6 percent change in funded status. Interest rate risk is the next largest factor, having a 6.6 percent impact on funded status. The basis risk of estimating the true mortality of the underlying population has a 6.4 percent impact while the risk of the longevity improvement trend has a 3.4 percent impact. The mortality-related factors are nearly 20 percent larger for a plan where the benefits increase with inflation after retirement.

Our funded status risk calculations make many simplifying assumptions. We assumed that the sample plan was 80 percent funded with an asset allocation of 60 percent equities and 40 percent medium duration fixed income. The risk impacts shown are the stand-alone risks for that factor. With the exception of offsetting the interest rate risk to the liabilities with the fixed income asset allocation, we incorporate no reductions for risk diversification. For simplicity, we do not illustrate the impact of credit spreads on the funded status risk, though these were one of the main drivers of funded status changes on an accounting basis for plans in 2008. One problem that arises when illustrating the magnitude of the mortality-related risks is that it is difficult to calibrate the likelihood of a particular change. It may be possible to show the likelihood of a change in the long-term improvement trend, but it is quite difficult to estimate the likelihood of an estimate of the underlying mortality basis risk for a pension population. For these reasons, the mortality-related risks we included apply a 75 percent factor to the mortality rates to illustrate the basis risk, while the improvement trend is estimated by adding 1 percent per year to the Scale AA improvement rates.

Deciding whether to outsource longevity

Plan sponsors have many factors to consider when deciding whether to outsource the longevity exposure in their DB plans. One factor is the magnitude of the risk individually, and compared to other risks. Others include which alternatives are available to manage the risk as well as whether it should be managed on its own or in combination with other risk exposures. A cost/benefit analysis can be performed to compare the effectiveness of managing the longevity risk compared to other risks. As an example, it may not make sense for a plan sponsor to spend more time and money managing plan longevity risk alone, if it is cheaper and results in greater overall funded status risk reduction to focus on the interest rate or equity investment exposures.

The global financial crisis has prompted pension sponsors to focus more than ever on ways to reduce the funded status volatility of their plans (see Figure 10.5). After recovering approximately half of the over 47 percent

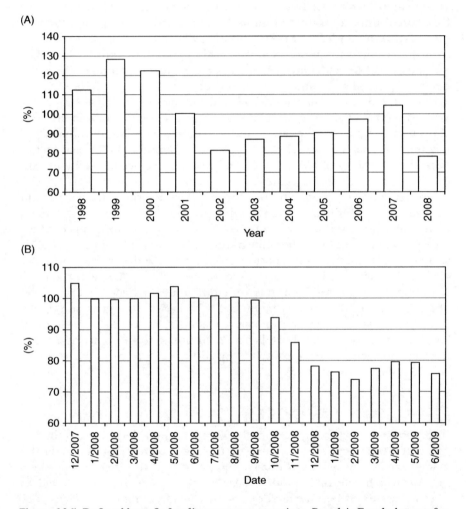

Figure 10.5 Defined benefit funding patterns over time. Panel A: Funded status for pensions sponsored by Standard & Poor's 500 companies. Panel B: Funded status for 100 largest corporate pension plans in the United States. *Sources*: Panel A derived from Silverblatt and Guarino (2009). Panel B derived from Milliman (2009*b*).

decrease in funded status experienced from the end of 1999 through the end of 2002, the funded status for the largest US plans fell over 30 percent between the end of 2007 and the end of February 2009 (Silverblatt and Guarino 2009; Milliman 2009*a*, *b*). Even companies that had focused almost entirely on asset-only measurement metrics are now seeking to better match their liabilities. Since exposures to financial market movements were the main drivers of the decrease in funding during 2008, and these comprise the largest portion of funded status risk, most of the risk reduction effort is focused on the financial risks. More plan sponsors are adopting LDI strategies to limit their exposure to financial market risks due to equity and other return-seeking investments, as well as the impact of interest rates and credit spreads on liability discounting. In the process, the risk due to mortality-related factors will become a larger proportion of the funded status risk. As the proportion of longevity-related funded status risk increases, the underlying mortality assumptions are updated more frequently, and strategies for managing longevity are refined, it seems inevitable that more plan sponsors take action.

Alternatives for longevity management

Plan sponsors have several alternatives to manage longevity exposure, and more are being developed. These include plan design changes, contracts with insurance companies that eliminate the longevity risk and typically other risks as well, and newer strategies that isolate the longevity risk and look like contracts typically used for financial market exposures. The alternatives differ by complexity, amount of risk transferred, and the period of time for which they are in effect.

Plan Design

Many DB pension plans have been at least partially replaced with DC plans (including 401(k)s) over the last decade. This change in plan design shifts the longevity risk as well as investment risk from plan sponsors to participants. To protect against outliving their assets, individual participants may purchase annuities from insurance companies. In order to address the higher cost of purchasing annuities individually, plan sponsors can contract with insurance companies to provide annuities at institutional prices. These annuity options can be outside the DC plan, part of the plan as a benefit payment election at retirement, or part of the plan as an investment choice that adds to the annuity as assets are accumulated during employment.

Although plan sponsors have been changing plan designs from DB to DC, it is believed that DB plans are more efficient for providing a sufficient level of retirement income to participants. Some reasons include the longer investment horizon and greater investment expertise of institutions sponsoring pension plans compared to the individual participants. Another reason is that pension plans cover a large number of participants, so gains and losses from the idiosyncratic longevity risks of the individual participants can balance out. One estimate of the cost reduction due to longevity pooling in a pension plan is 15 percent (Almeida and Fornia 2008).

New plan designs will likely emerge in the future, melding traditional DB plans where the sponsor bears all of the risks with DC plans where participants bear the majority of the risks. A discussion on potential methods to share the risks between sponsors and participants is taking place in the United Kingdom (Department for Work and Pensions 2008), and at least one plan sponsor in the United Kingdom has successfully implemented a plan change that shared the longevity risk between the sponsor and participants in the DB plan. Effective starting in 2006, BAE Systems introduced a Longevity Adjustment Factor, which reduces a portion of the pension benefits as life expectancies rise (BAE Systems 2006). Another method being discussed to share the longevity risk is to increase the retirement age as life expectancies increase. New design innovations could be driven by UK risk-sharing consultancies spurred by plan sponsor interest in managing risks without completely shifting them to the participants.

Transfer risk to insurance companies

The traditional method of eliminating all of the risks of sponsoring a DB plan (including longevity) is plan termination. In a standard termination, the plan has enough assets to pay all of the accrued benefits and the plan either purchases annuities from an insurance company or pays benefits as a lump sum. After a typical standard termination, all of the sponsors' obligations and responsibilities associated with the plan are eliminated (except for any misrepresentations in the annuity contract). Although many plans terminate each year, that vast majority are very small plans. More than 1,200 plans went through a standard termination in 2007 in the United States, but 75 percent of the plans had fewer than 25 participants. These terminations represented payments of $3.1 billion, with $1.9 billion of lump-sum payments and $1.2 billion of group annuity premiums (Pension Benefit Guaranty Corporation 2008).

Purchasing a group annuity contract from an insurance company to terminate a plan (sometimes referred to as a buyout) is often perceived as being expensive. When pricing terminal annuities, insurance companies use assumptions between best estimates and a worst-case scenario, which often end up being more conservative than the assumptions used to calculate liabilities for ongoing funding and accounting purposes. In particular, the mortality assumption used by insurers includes projections for future mortality improvements. Now that the PPA requires some sort of projected improvements to be factored into liability calculations for funding purposes, these improvements will likely be adopted for accounting purposes as well. This will reduce the gap between the cost of annuities and the ongoing liabilities.

Another change in the PPA that could make standard terminations less costly for those offering lump-sum payment options is a change in the applicable interest rate. Regulators have required changing the rate used to compute lump sums from Treasury yields to corporate bond yields, to be fully phased in for plan years starting in 2012. Nevertheless, while the difference between the liabilities calculated for funding or accounting purposes and annuity purchases is decreasing, plan terminations will still be viewed as costly in most cases. Most plans are significantly underfunded on an accounting basis as of the end of 2008 and will need to fund this shortfall in order to purchase annuities.

There are also alternatives referred to as partial buyouts where certain risks can be transferred to an insurance company. Partial buyouts can be structured to cover only a portion of the liabilities; they can also transfer the risks for only a portion of the participants (e.g., retirees in payment status only) or for only a portion of the benefits (e.g., up to $1,000 per month per participant). Partial buyouts of the retirees only can be a cost-effective way to reduce liabilities and risk, since the cost of purchasing annuities for retirees is typically closer to the ongoing accounting liability than for active employees or those terminated but not yet in payments status. It is important to monitor whether a partial termination would occur when considering a partial buyout, since this could require full vesting of all participants. Another alternative to a buyout is a buy-in. In a buy-in, an annuity contract is purchased from an insurance company but, rather than transferring the liabilities to the insurance company, the annuity contract is held as an investment in the asset portfolio. Buy-ins do not reduce the liabilities but can reduce the risk similar to buyouts. Since buy-ins can be viewed as purchasing an investment rather than eliminating a liability, some of the rules governing buyouts, like partial terminations, should not be of concern. Buy-ins are more common when covering only a portion of the participants.

There has been much effort over the past few years to develop innovative alternatives to plan terminations involving group annuity contracts from an insurance company. A number of companies have been established in the United Kingdom to challenge the two dominant insurance companies in this market. Many of the newer companies in the United Kingdom are also set up as insurance companies. This market saw around £8 billion in transactions in 2008, with most of the transaction volume being buy-ins for retirees (LCP 2009*b*).

In the United States, several large investment banks announced their presence in the buyout market also with a few startup companies backed by private equity firms. In contrast to the majority of new entrants in the United Kingdom, most new US entrants were not set up as insurance companies. The intended structure of these noninsurance buyouts was to maintain the pension plan but transfer all of the responsibilities for sponsoring the plan to a new company. Yet before this market had a chance to take off, the US Treasury Department and IRS issued a ruling banning these transactions (Internal Revenue Service 2008). In conjunction with the ruling, the Treasury released a framework for future legislation consisting of conditions under which a noninsurance buyout could be allowed (United States Treasury Department 2008). It is interesting to note that the ruling covers transactions where the sponsorship of an entire plan is transferred to another company. There appears to be room for innovations where an insurance-based buyout is the first step toward sharing the risk with a noninsurance company or even noninsurance-based buy-ins. However, since many of the companies that had been pursuing new solutions in this market are currently capital-constrained and most pension plans now have a low funded status, new ideas in this area may not develop rapidly.

Hedging longevity risk

In recent years, products are being developed to hedge, rather than completely eliminate, longevity risk. Some target the longevity risk only, leaving it up to the plan sponsor's investment committee to decide whether to combine this with any risk management strategy addressing financial market risks. Several investment banks have introduced indices to help trade longevity products in the United States. Other companies in the United States are evaluating this area and there are even more companies in the United Kingdom actively pursuing this market.

One instrument that can be used to hedge longevity risk is a longevity swap. A longevity swap is similar in concept to an interest rate swap. A pension plan executing a longevity swap would agree to make fixed payments over the term of the contract based on future mortality expectations in return for receiving floating payments based on the actual mortality experience of the underlying population. For a swap meant to cover a group of retirees currently receiving payments that do not increase with inflation, the fixed payments would be a series of amounts that decrease over time as the participants die and benefit payments cease. If longevity improvements are greater than anticipated, more participants will be receiving benefits than expected, and the pension plan will receive more in floating payments than the fixed amounts it pays. This gain on the longevity swap in the asset portfolio would help to offset the mortality loss experienced on the liabilities. It is important to note that these contracts will have an expiry date much shorter than the length of time over which a typical pension plan is expected to pay benefits. However, it is possible to combine swaps having various maturities in different amounts to try to match the sensitivity of the liability to changes in mortality experience and longevity expectations. The mortality assumptions used to calculate the pension plan's liabilities should be examined in light of any longevity hedge transaction to make sure they are updated frequently to avoid any mismatch where changes in the value of the hedge are not recognized similarly in the liability calculations.

Credit Suisse, JPMorgan, and Goldman Sachs have released longevity indices in the United States with the intention of trading derivative or other financial contracts linked to the indices (Credit Suisse 2009; Goldman Sachs 2009; JPMorgan 2009). The indices include either the future expected lifetimes, mortality rates, or impact of mortality on a group of lives. Some of the index data is split into subindices, divided by age and gender. The Credit Suisse and JPMorgan indices are based on national population data and are updated annually, but with a time lag. The Goldman Sachs indices are based on an insured population of senior citizens and are updated monthly. One of the key considerations when evaluating hedging the longevity risk of a pension plan with a product based on the mortality experience of a different population is the basis risk. It is possible to minimize this basis risk if the true underlying mortality of both populations is known. However, since only a range for the true mortality of the pension plan will be known, the ability to reduce the basis risk is limited. For example, if the hedge is calibrated assuming the true underlying mortality of the pension population was 105 percent of the RP-2000 rates but the actual mortality experienced is 75 percent of the RP-2000 rates, the hedge would not be as effective as anticipated. Instruments based on longevity indices can be quite effective at hedging the longevity trends but not as effective for the basis risk. A few of the significant benefits of a bank trading many contracts based on the same populations are potentially increased liquidity of the product and potentially reduced cost.

The market for longevity derivatives in the US appears to be in its infancy. As was the case with other types of pension risk management strategies and trends, it can be helpful to look at the market in the United Kingdom as a potential guide for what may develop in the United States. There have been longevity-only trades in the United Kingdom but, until recently, these have been with insurance or reinsurance companies managing their annuity books containing pension annuities. The first longevity transaction structured as a derivative took place at the beginning of 2008 between pension buyout company Lucida and JPMorgan. The first longevity swap directly with a pension fund took place in June 2009 between Babcock International and Credit Suisse. In July 2009, the Royal & Sun Alliance pension scheme entered into a deal with Goldman Sachs and its insurance company subsidiary Rothesay Life that included interest rate and longevity risks. These deals should add credence to recent consultant predictions that the longevity swap market will grow rapidly in the next year. Further evidence of the market growth is displayed by over £30 billion of quotations on pension liabilities issued by longevity hedge providers in the last 12 months (LCP 2009a).

Hedging or transferring longevity risk has received much attention in the United Kingdom and the United States. It seems only a matter of time before transactions with pension plans become more common. There are various developments, not all related to product innovations, which can help spur the growth of the market for hedging longevity risk. As noted earlier, increased adoption of LDI programs to manage the financial risks will draw more attention to the longevity risk as it becomes a relatively larger portion of the total plan risk. UK pension plans are further ahead of those in the United States in this respect, since LDI is more prevalent and the longevity risk is more significant due to postretirement benefits being indexed to inflation.

Understanding the true best estimate mortality assumptions and their impact on the pension liabilities is another factor that will benefit the longevity hedging market. Again, pensions in the United Kingdom are ahead of those in the United States in this respect. The cost of implementing a longevity hedge is a critical factor for the potential growth of this market. Pricing in the United Kingdom has recently become more competitive but this has not yet spread to the United States. Another key element in longevity market growth is the ability to understand and handle the basis risk between the hedge and the pension liability. While hedging products based on broad population indices could ultimately be more cost-effective than bespoke solutions, index-based products suffer from a larger basis risk. Finally, examples of plans successfully implementing longevity hedges are also important for market growth. This has just started in the United Kingdom but we have not seen visible signs of an imminent transaction in the United States. Although the United States seems to be behind the United Kingdom in all of these respects, the United States can observe how the market evolves overseas and then apply similar ideas there. This can ultimately allow for more rapid market growth, once it begins.

Additional discussions on pension risk transfer developments involving longevity in the United Kingdom appear in Hymans Robertson (2009), Lucida (2009), and Punter Southall (2009). A discussion of how some risk transfer strategies may evolve in the United States in light of developments in the United Kingdom appears in Monk (2009).

Conclusion

Despite the controversy over whether historic mortality improvements will continue at the same pace as they have in the past, there is little debate that longevity assumptions and experience have a significant impact on pension plans. The attention being paid to the impact of mortality on pension plans is set to increase as the PPA requires more realistic and frequently updated assumptions. Furthermore, as more plans adopt LDI strategies, the portion of total funded status risk due to mortality should increase.

There are a variety of ways pension plans can reduce their mortality risk. These vary from plan design changes that impact only the liabilities to buyouts that transfer all of the risks (and generally all of the assets) to a third party. New solutions are being developed to hedge the longevity risk without eliminating it. Given the amount of focus in this area and recent market developments in the United Kingdom, it seems a matter of time before additional solutions to the longevity issue become more prevalent.

References

Almeida, Beth, and William B. Fornia (2008). *A Better Bang for the Buck; The Economic Efficiencies of Defined Benefit Plans.* Washington, DC: National Institute on Retirement Security.   http://www.calstrs.com/Newsroom/What's%20New/BangForTheBuck Rpt.pdf

BAE Systems (2006). *Longevity Adjustment Factor.* Hampshire, UK: BAE Systems. http://www.baesystemspensions.com//menuId=460

Cairns, Andrew J.G., David Blake, Kevid Dowd, Guy D. Coughlan, David Epstein, Alen Ong, and Igor Balevich (2007). 'A Quantitative Comparison of Stochastic Mortality Models Using Data from England & Wales and the United States,' Pensions Institute Discussion Paper PI-0701. London: The Pension Institute.

Carnes, Bruce A., S. Jay Olshansky, and Douglas Grahn (2003). 'Biological Evidence for Limits to the Duration of Life,' *Biogerontology*, 4(1): 31–45.

Credit Suisse (2009). *Longevity Index.* Zurich, Switzerland: Credit Suisse.http://www. credit-suisse.com/ib/en/fixed_income/longevity_index.html

de Grey, Aubrey and Michael Rae (2007). *Ending Aging: The Rejuvenation Break-throughs That Could Reverse Human Aging in Our Lifetime.* New York: St. Martin's Press.

Department for Work and Pensions (2008). *Risk Sharing Consultation.* London: Department for Work and Pensions. http://www.dwp.gov.uk/docs/pensionrisk-sharing-consultation-june2008.pdf

Goldman Sachs (2009). *QxX Index.* New York: Goldman Sachs. http://www.qxx-index.com/

Hewitt Associates (2008). *Global Pension Risk Survey 2008.* London, UK: Hewitt Associates.

Human Mortality Database (2008). *The United States of America, Life Expectancy at Birth (Period).* Berkley, CA: Human Mortality Database. http://www.mortality.org/hmd/USA/STATS/E0per.txt

Hymans Robertson (2009). *Buy-out Buy-in Longevity Swap Update.* London, UK, April 11. http://www.hymans.co.uk/media/pressreleases/Pages/Buy-outBuy-inlongevityswapupdate.aspx

Internal Revenue Service (2008). *Revenue Ruling 2008–45.* Washington, DC: Internal Revenue Service. http://www.irs.gov/irb/2008-34_IRB/ar07.html

Investment Company Institute (2009). *The U.S. Retirement Market, 2008.* Washington, DC: Investment Company Institute. http://www.ici.org/pdf/fm-v18n5.pdf

JPMorgan (2009). *LifeMetrics.* New York: JPMorgan. http://www.jpmorgan.com/pages/jpmorgan/investbk/solutions/lifemetrics

Lane Clark & Peacock (LCP) (2009a). *Longevity Hedging: 10 Things You Should Know.* London: Lane Clark & Peacock. http://www.lcp.uk.com/docs/Longevity%20hedging%2010%20things%20you%20should%20know.pdf

—— (2009b). *Pension Buyouts 2009.* London: Lane Clark & Peacock. http://www.lcp.uk.com/information/bulletin.asp?ID=477

Lucida (2009). *The Pensions Pulse Survey, October 2009.* London: Lucida. http://www.lucidaplc.com/knowledge-centre/pensions-pulse-report-2009

Milliman (2009a). *Milliman 100 Pension Funding Index January 2009.* Seattle, WA: Milliman. http://www.milliman.com/expertise/employee-benefits/products-tools/pension-funding-study/pdfs/pension-funding-study-Dec08-01-15-09.pdf

—— (2009b). *Milliman 100 Pension Funding Index July 2009.* Seattle, WA: Milliman. http://www.milliman.com/expertise/employee-benefits/products-tools/pension-funding-study/pdfs/milliman-100-pension-funding-07-01-09.pdf

Monk, Ashby H. B. (2009). 'Pension Buyouts: What Can We Learn from the UK Experience?' Working Paper No. 2009-19. Chestnut Hill, MA: Center for Retirement Research at Boston College.

Oeppen, Jim and James W. Vaupel (2002). 'Broken Limits to Life Expectancy,' *Science,* 296: 1029–31.

Olshansky, S. Jay (1988). 'On Forecasting Mortality,' *The Milbank Quarterly,* 66(3): 482–530.

——Douglas J. Passaro, Ronald C. Hershow, Jennifer Layden, Bruce A. Carnes, Jacob Brody, Leonard Hayflick, Robert N. Butler, David B. Allison, and David S. Ludwig (2005). 'A Potential Decline in Life Expectancy in the United States in the 21st Century,' *The New England Journal of Medicine,* 352: 1138–45.

Pension Benefit Guaranty Corporation (2008). *Pension Insurance Data Book 2007.* Washington, DC: Pension Benefit Guaranty Corporation. http://www.pbgc.gov/docs/2007databook.pdf

Punter Southall (2009). *The False Dawn–Key Findings, September 2009.* London, UK: Punter   Southall.   http://www.puntersouthall.com/files/documents/PSTS% 20buyout_key%20findings.pdf

Society of Actuaries (2000). *The RP-2000 Mortality Tables.* Chicago, IL: Society of Actuaries. http://www.soa.org/files/pdf/rp00_mortalitytables.pdf

——(2002). *Table Manager.* Chicago, IL: Society of Actuaries. http://www.soa.org/ professional-interests/technology/tech-table-manager.aspx

Silverblatt, Howard and Dave Guarino (2009). *S&P 500 2008: Pensions and Other Post Employment Benefits.* New York: Standard & Poor's. http://www2.standardand-poors.com/spf/pdf/index/20090602_500_PENSIONS_OPEB.pdf

United States Treasury Department (2008). *Treasury, IRS Issue Ruling Preventing Certain Pension Transfers.* Washington, DC, August 6. https://treas.gov/press/re-leases/hp1110.htm

Chapter 11

Comparing Spending Approaches in Retirement

John Ameriks, Michael Hess, and Liqian Ren

The retirement income challenge – the question of how to optimally generate a sustainable and reliable stream of income in retirement – is one of the biggest unresolved issues facing investors and financial services organizations around the world. The continued confusion, consternation, and debate about the optimal solution for retirement is perhaps surprising, given that solving multi-period consumption and portfolio choice problems under uncertainty is not new to the economics literature. Formal solutions to such problems have been a part of that literature since at least the late 1960s. Yet in both the academic literature and in practice, there is wide variation in solution techniques – both products and methods – used by investors and recommended by advisors and experts. In the academic literature, differences in solutions tend to be driven by differences in assumptions about investor preferences, constraints, costs, and the degree and nature of modeled uncertainty. In practice, solutions may differ for all of the above reasons, plus a host of others, including social conventions, force of habit, or other behavioral or institutional factors.

In this chapter, we take an agnostic, practical look at simulated financial outcomes resulting from the use of different common 'product' or 'draw-down strategy' choices in retirement. Unlike much of the academic literature aimed at comparing retirement income strategies, we do not impose a specific functional form on investor preferences and solve a formal optimization problem; rather we focus on the simulated impact of the chosen strategy on several summary statistics describing various aspects of investment outcomes that real-world retirees seem to care about. There are many merits to formal optimization, but many retirees and practitioners have little notion of the implications of various functional forms for retirement decision-making. In addition, they may have difficulty interpreting or determining whether a summary measure such as a utility metric is, in fact, a good representation of their clients or constituents preferences over various outcomes.

Simulations reveal that these alternative retirement income strategies can produce widely different outcomes in terms of each of the statistics that we measure. Each of these strategies is currently advocated and employed by some group striving to serve the needs of retirees. We interpret this evidence to suggest that future research would benefit by a better understanding and more complete specification of retirees' various needs and objectives. In our view, very productive insights can be derived by building more robust models of retiree preferences that explicitly incorporate the various motivations that appear relevant.

We begin by reviewing some of the previous studies on this topic. We then describe the strategies/products on which we focus and detail the evaluation methodology. Finally, we present and discuss results.

A brief review of prior studies on retirement payouts

Discussion of optimal spend-down in retirement often begins with a focus on payout life annuities. In a standard economic model of risk-averse savers who value only their own lifetime consumption, immediate life annuities can have significant insurance value (Yaari 1965). Economists have subsequently shown that at least partial annuitization may add value even when many restrictive assumptions of the simplified modeling framework are relaxed (Davidoff, Brown, and Diamond 2005; Horneff et al. 2010); even when full annuitization is not indicated, partial annuitization is still generally a part of the optimal spending strategy.

Yet, in practice, investors have been reluctant to adopt annuities and researchers continue to struggle to explain this so-called annuity puzzle. One reason may be that investors typically lose control of annuitized assets, as for all practical purposes, annuitization is irreversible. Such lack of liquidity can be important, if unexpected expenditure shocks such as uninsured medical expenses occur (Sinclair and Smetters 2004; Turra and Mitchell 2008; Ameriks et al. 2009). In addition, in the current environment, many financial services organizations have been forced to turn to taxpayers for financial support, so it is also possible that individuals view as unacceptably high the potential costs of a default by their annuity provider. Another reason, noted by Dushi and Webb (2004) and Mitchell et al. (1999) is the existence of other annuitized resources such as Social Security or employer-sponsored pensions, which could explain why investors may be reluctant to voluntarily annuitize. A further headwind for annuitization is retirees' bequest motives. In the United States, for instance, over half of the elderly plan say they intend to leave a bequest of more than $10,000 (Bernheim 1991; Hurd and Smith 1999). On the other hand, Brown (2001) finds that the bequest motive is not significant in the annuitization decision.

Yet another reason investors may avoid annuitization is that purchasing a traditional fixed annuity with a significant sum of assets precludes investing those assets in equity markets with their historically risk premium over other investments. Of course, variable immediate life annuities (sold in the United States by many insurers) do offer investors the ability to participate in equity market returns while still offering the advantages of higher expected returns via pooled mortality risk as well as the hedge for risk-averse investors who worry about exhausting their assets. Blake, Cairns, and Dowd (2003) show that equity-linked variable annuities should appeal to many investors compared to either a phased withdrawal plan or a fixed payout annuity. Brown and Poterba (2000) demonstrate that equity-linked variable annuities can generate greater utility than fixed annuities for a broad range of risk aversion parameters. While both of these studies take an all-or-nothing approach, Horneff et al. (2010) show that variable annuities can (modestly) enhance an investor's portfolio, particularly if variable annuities can be purchased gradually in retirement allowing both annuities and financial wealth to be held simultaneously. It is perhaps an additional annuity puzzle that immediate variable annuity sales are far below those of standard fixed annuities.

Thus, despite the theory, many real-world investors avoid annuities in favor of holding and managing a portfolio of unannuitized investments. Then their task is to determine a level of 'sustainable' withdrawals during the retirement period (cf. Bengen 1994; Pye 2000).[1] This literature offers a wide range of results, though most propose a broadly diversified investment portfolio of stocks and bonds, together with a 'drawdown rule' amounting to constant inflation-adjusted withdrawals equal to 4–5 percent of the investor's account balance at retirement (taken annually until death or the exhaustion of the retirement portfolio). Such withdrawal strategies may offer some benefits to an investor versus an annuity product, but they also expose the retiree to the risk of running out of money or having to cut consumption substantially.

Another thread in the payouts literature highlights the importance of so-called default arrangements for individual investors (Beshears et al. 2008). Two types of defaults are especially relevant. One type has to do with what is defined as the 'normal' or typical form of benefits provided in defined benefit (DB) plans. It is interesting that these seem to have relatively little effect. Thus, when plan participants in two large pension plans were given choice between an annuity benefit or a lump-sum benefit, very large majorities elected to receive their benefits in the form of a lump sum – despite the fact that the annuity was the normal form or default choice for those benefits (Mottola and Utkus 2007). A second type pertains to the government's rule specifying required minimum distributions (RMDs) that older investors must take from their traditional individual retirement accounts (IRAs) and 401(k)/403(b) retirement plans in order to avoid tax penalties. It appears, based on one large retirement plan provider, that distributions taken according to RMD rules are a large and fast-growing distribution choice of recent retirees (Ameriks 2004). In addition, these rules are cited as the most common reason that retirees offer for withdrawing assets from their IRAs (Holden 2009). In other words, default options may play a role in shaping retirement withdrawal patterns, but more remains to be explored on the topic.

Spending/income models examined

In the last 5 years, deferred variable annuity contracts have become increasingly popular, particularly those that provide so-called living benefits. These usually include a complex combination of guarantees that can incorporate elements of put options on investment returns and deferred life annuities. In this section, we focus on eight spending/income-generating methods we will model and evaluate, including plans that incorporate a specific type of guarantee, namely guaranteed lifetime withdrawal benefits (GLWB). These refer to an annuity that some industry observers argue has the potential to become the 'product of choice' for retirees (see Ibbotson Associates 2007).[2] The eight methods we evaluate include payout funds (endowment-style funds and time-horizon-style funds), balanced mutual fund with fixed real withdrawals, fixed real (inflation-adjusted) immediate annuities, immediate variable annuities (IVA), variable deferred annuities with GLWB, RMDs, half fixed real annuity/half RMD, and half variable immediate annuity /half RMD. We describe each of these methods in detail next.

Payout funds

In the broadest terms, payout funds are pooled investment funds (typically mutual funds) coupled with a specific mechanism for the provision of periodic payments to fund investors. Payout funds are currently offered as daily-valuation mutual funds and can therefore provide investors the same type of daily liquidity as any mutual fund. A net asset value (NAV) for the shares of these funds is struck every trading day, and investors can elect to purchase or sell shares of these funds at that price on that day. Payout funds do not guarantee either a level of payments or returns, but provide either targeted or formulaically determined periodic distributions of fund assets to fund shareholders in combination with a professionally managed investment portfolio. A brief but fairly accurate description of payout funds is that they amount to a prepackaged combination of a specific systematic withdrawal strategy with a mutual fund investment. In fact, a common criticism of the funds is that they 'don't do anything that a motivated investor couldn't do for himself.' This description is also fairly accurate – but of course the key question is whether investors view a prepackaged combination as being a cost-effective or value-added means of implementing a distribution strategy relative to doing so themselves.

In some cases, the payout mechanism bundled with the payout fund is literally implemented as a systematic withdrawal program that a fund investor must proactively enroll in to receive distributions from the 'payout fund.' This design would appear to enable payout rules to differ for different investors in the same fund. But at the time of this writing, no payout funds are implementing distribution schedules rules that rely upon investor-specific data. In other designs, the payouts are made through the fund accounting process of the payout fund itself, and are made to shareholders as periodic distributions per fund share (requiring all shares to be treated equally, and hence all shareholders holding the same number of shares to be treated equally). In this design, distributions are declared and delivered to shareholders in a manner similar to that used to declare and deliver periodic distributions of income, dividends, and capital gains to shareholders. An important aspect of payout funds with this design is that to meet the targeted or formulaically determined distribution amounts, some of the periodic fund distributions may be a return of capital to the investor, and hence *not* interest income, dividends, or realized gains.

The investment management strategies and asset allocation employed in these funds vary across providers, with different providers using different asset allocations, and emphasizing active management, passive management, or the use of alternatives as a part of the underlying investment strategy for the funds. Some providers use only 'traditional' asset classes (long-only stocks, bonds, and cash-like investments), while others are including or at least envisioning the use of alternatives such as long–short strategies, commodities, futures, and other types of investments.

Payout mutual funds first became available to investors beginning in 2006, and as of this writing there were at least six financial services organizations offering some type of payout fund (Baron Funds, Charles Schwab & Co., Fidelity Investments, John Hancock, Russell Investment Company, and Vanguard).[3] The specific design and objectives of payout funds are not uniform across providers. While designs continue to evolve, two basic designs or flavors of these funds appear to have emerged (described later), and we will focus on these two basic outlines in what follows.[4]

ENDOWMENT-STYLE PAYOUT FUNDS

Endowment-style payout funds are designed to provide periodic distributions/payments to fund shareholders on an ongoing basis, and are not tied to a specific investor's age or life expectancy. As with all payout funds, there are no guarantees, and the size of periodic payments can vary as a consequence of investment returns, formulaic adjustments to the periodic payments, the impact of fund expenses, or the provider altering the specified distribution policy. The payout rules or strategies adopted by these funds are nevertheless designed with the goal of providing some payments to shareholders indefinitely.

As mentioned, specific payout mechanisms and the levels of payout available in payout funds vary among providers. In this analysis, we focus on a hypothetical payout fund that distributes payments to shareholders on a quarterly basis. In the simulations to follow, these quarterly payments are set once a year equal to 5 percent of the 12-quarter trailing historical average of the net value of the investment in the fund. There is at least one provider that in practice uses a distribution rule very close to this.

TIME-HORIZON PAYOUTS FUNDS

Instead of being managed to produce payments in perpetuity, time-horizon funds are designed to provide a sequence of formulaically determined payouts over a set period (e.g., 10, 20, or 30 years), fully exhausting invested amounts at the end of that period. There are no investment or payment guarantees; periodic payments may vary due to investment returns, payment adjustments, fund expenses, or to the provider altering the specified distribution policy.

In what follows, we model a time-horizon fund with a 30-year distribution period. The initial target payout rate will be approximately 5 percent, and payments will be distributed on a quarterly basis. Each year, the target payout rate changes (according to the schedule shown in Table 11A.1), and the quarterly distribution amounts are recalculated.

Systematic distributions from a balanced mutual fund

In addition to the payout funds, we also examine a strategy based on fixed inflation-adjusted withdrawals from a typical balanced mutual fund. Despite the popularity of this kind of drawdown rule in financial planning circles and in the popular press (cf. Updegrave 2007), we are not aware of any fund company that currently offers a service that will automatically compute and implement inflation-adjusted annual withdrawals as a distribution option on a standard mutual fund. Most companies will allow a shareholder to specify a dollar or percentage amount to distribute from the fund on a periodic basis, but the fund investor must then compute the required inflation adjustment to the payments each year and then submit those revised instructions to the fund provider.

In our modeling, we assume the shareholder withdraws an amount equal to 5 percent of initial wealth at the time of investment, with distributions paid on a quarterly basis. Each year, these payments will be adjusted to reflect the previous year's change in inflation.

Fixed lifetime income annuity

Income annuities are a form of insurance intended to address the uncertainty investors face when planning for income for the rest of their lives. In exchange for permanently surrendering access to a portion of their assets, annuitants receive a stream of income as long as they live. Fixed income annuities are different from the first three approaches discussed, in that the annuity provider guarantees that the investors will receive a specific level of income as long as they live. This guarantee removes the uncertainty of longevity risk and the possibility of exhausting assets later in life, but it also introduces some additional costs and risks. The costs include potentially high insurance fees; risks include the loss of liquidity, the possibility of leaving a diminished estate, and the possible failure of the guarantee provider.[5]

In what follows, we model a fixed single-life annuity that adjusts annually for inflation. We assume the investor is a 65-year-old male, and the initial payout amount is based upon an actual January 30, 2009 insurance quote from Vanguard.com. Annuity payments are assumed to be made quarterly, and adjustments to the payout amount be conducted annually based on the change in the consumer price index.

Variable immediate annuity

Similar to fixed income annuities, variable annuities deliver guaranteed income for life, but the income amount is not fixed, instead being subject to the investment performance of the underlying funds relative to the assumed interest rate (AIR). The guarantee of variable income for life introduces many of the same costs and risks as those associated with fixed annuities, plus the additional risk that investment returns will be poor and diminish the value of ongoing payments. When investing in a variable annuity, investors have the opportunity to choose the structure of the underlying investments, and, as mentioned, the distribution amount for a variable annuity is subject to the performance of the underlying funds in relation to the AIR (which the investor also chooses). This gives investors the ability to benefit (via increased payouts) from market returns when times are good, but when market returns are poor, decreased payout amounts are a possibility. In other words, the payout stream will rise if the underlying fund performance is higher than the AIR, and it will fall if the underlying fund performance is lower than the AIR.

In our analysis, we focus on a 65-year-old male investor who purchases a variable annuity with an AIR of 3.5 percent. The initial payout amount is based upon a January 30, 2009, quote from Vanguard.com, and distributions are made on a quarterly basis. Payments are adjusted on a quarterly basis and calculated based on the underlying fund performance relative to the AIR.

Variable annuities with GLWB

A relatively new innovation in variable annuity products is the GLWB rider that can be added to a deferred variable annuity contract.

Two features of a variable annuity with GLWB set it apart from traditional variable annuities. First, the GLWB rider gives investors the ability to protect their retirement income from market declines while still having the opportunity to profit when the market increases. This is a form of a 'put option,' at least with regard to the level of income that can be generated from the investment in the contract. Mechanically, the insurer establishes a 'guaranteed income base' for the contract that is equal to the initial deposit (premium) on the contract. This guaranteed income base cannot decrease as long as withdrawals from the contract are no more than the guaranteed minimum amount. The guaranteed income base can 'step up' on the rider anniversary date should the markets perform well and the remaining investment value in the contract exceed the amount of the initial deposit. The guaranteed income base cannot decline as a result of investment performance. The guaranteed minimum level of withdrawals are expressed as a set fraction of this guaranteed withdrawal base, which the provider guarantees will not decrease (but could increase) over the life of the contract.

A second feature of the GLWB rider is that any remaining *investment value* in the contract (the initial investment, plus returns and any subsequent investments, minus costs and any guaranteed or other withdrawals) can be withdrawn at any time or bequeathed at death, cancelling the contract at that point. Withdrawals in excess of the guaranteed minimum amount can also be taken at any time but reduce the guaranteed income base in the same proportion as such withdrawals reduce the remaining investment value in the contract (potentially to zero if 100 percent of the investment value is withdrawn).

When we consider the 65-year-old male investor, we assume the GLWB rider offers this investor the ability to withdraw 5 percent of the guaranteed income base each year, with distributions being made on a quarterly basis. Each year on the rider anniversary date, the guaranteed income base will be reevaluated based on the net performance of the underlying funds, after the withdrawals and annual rider fees have been deducted. If the investment value in the contract at that point exceeds the guaranteed income base, it will be 'stepped up' from that point forward. We also assume that the investor holds a fixed portfolio allocation throughout retirement, although there has been some evidence that the options embedded in this type of variable annuity structure may impact portfolio allocation (Milevsky and Kyrychenko 2008).

RMD withdrawal plan

We also simulate the results that an investor would achieve by taking distributions from their retirement assets in accordance with the RMD rules published by the Internal Revenue Service (IRS). These rules establish an amount of income that must be distributed (in order to avoid tax penalties) to investors each year, beginning the year after the account owner turns age 70.5. Distribution amounts are a specified proportion of the account that varies with investor age according to IRS tables (listed in Table 11A.1). We also simulate and evaluate two strategies that are a combination of the RMDs rules with the use of fixed real and variable immediate annuities.

Summary of assumptions

Our goal is to focus on the real-world difference in simulated outcomes for retirees pursuing each of these different drawdown strategies. To do so, several additional assumptions are needed regarding investment allocations and fee levels for the strategies described, summarized in Table 11.1. While these are subjective, we believe they are a reasonable reflection of 'standard,' 'typical,' or 'average' investment allocations and fee levels for the products and strategies of interest.

In all cases, to generate asset returns, we use 10,000 simulations of 30-year sequences of assets returns and inflation rates, using a proprietary capital markets simulation engine created and used at Vanguard to simulate asset returns. This model is based on the estimation and simulation of a vector auto-regression model of monthly asset returns, inflation, interest rates, and other economic factors based on data from 1960 through 2008. Additional details on the model can be found in Davis, Wallick, and Aliaga-Diaz (2009); summary statics describing the simulation output and the asset classes we focus on are shown in Table 11.2.

TABLE 11.1 Descriptive statistics for empirical data analysis

Strategy	Asset allocation (%)					Fees (Basis points)
	US equities	International equities	Nominal fixed	Commodities	Market neutral	
Endowment-style payout funds	35	25	15	10	15	60
Time-horizon payout funds[a]	50	12	38	0	0	67
Balanced mutual fund	48	12	40	0	0	20
Variable annuity with 3.5% assumed interest rate (AIR)	48	12	40	0	0	79
Variable annuity with guaranteed life withdrawal benefit (GLWB)	48	12	40	0	0	100
Required minimum distribution (RMD)	48	12	40	0	0	20
50% in real fixed annuity/50% in RMD[b]	48	12	40	0	0	20
50% in variable annuity with 3.5% AIR/50% in RMD	48	12	40	0	0	50

[a] Asset allocation in first year of payout. See Appendix 11A for detailed glide path.

[b] Asset allocation represents the portion that is RMD portfolio.

Note: Real fixed annuity is not included in the table due to no underlying asset allocation or implicit fees.

Source: Authors' calculations; see text.

TABLE 11.2 Summary of asset simulations over 30-year horizon

	Median annualized return (%)	Median standard deviation (%)
US equity	9.3	19.1
International equity	10.6	21.8
Nominal fixed income	5.0	6.7
Commodities	6.1	14.6
Market neutral	3.7	6.4

Notes: US equities represented by the MSCI US Broad Market Index; international equities by the MSCI EAFE + EM Index; the broad taxable bond market by Barclays Capital US Aggregate Bond Index; commodity futures by the Dow Jones-AIG Commodity Index; and the market-neutral by the Citigroup 3-Month Treasury Bill Index.

Source: Authors' calculations; see text.

Results and discussion

We display results in three ways, reporting statistics related to the levels of periodic cash flows provided by the strategies, statistics related to the evolution of remaining wealth over the lifetime of the retiree, and data on the internal rates of return (IRRs) of the simulated strategies at different horizons.

Cash flows generated by the strategies

Table 11.3 illustrates the average level and a volatility metric for real cash flows from each of these strategies, for investment horizons of 5, 20, and 30 years after retirement (the volatility metric is a ratio of the mean level of income to the lower semi-variance of income across all simulations; higher is better). The eight different drawdown options are organized in descending order of the median level of simulated cash flow at the 20-year horizon. Results show that, in terms of providing stable real cash flow measured by the ratio of mean cash flow to lower semi-variance, the real annuity and the constant inflation-adjusted withdrawals from a balanced mutual fund appear significantly more attractive than other options.

Figures 11.1 and 11.2 present some summary statistics on volatility in cash flows over the entire 30-year horizon. Figure 11.1 shows the fraction of quarters in which the *nominal* distributions from the strategy are more than 5 percent lower than in a year earlier. The columns are sorted in decreasing order, from highest (most volatile) to lowest, illustrating the relative downside volatility of the IVA, RMDs, time-horizon payout funds, and the IVA/RMD

TABLE 11.3 Total real cash flow excluding ending balance

Strategy	5 years		20 years		30 years	
	Median ($)	Mean/ volatility[a]	Median ($)	Mean/ volatility[a]	Median ($)	Mean/ volatility[a]
Real fixed annuity	0.34	234.1	1.35	183.8	2.03	207.6
Balanced mutual fund	0.25	234.1	0.98	15.0	1.47	4.3
50% in real fixed annuity/50% in RMD	0.17	234.1	1.15	8.2	1.96	5.7
Variable annuity with GLWB	0.25	18.0	0.97	5.8	1.40	4.4
Time-horizon payout funds	0.26	10.7	1.11	4.5	1.77	3.7
Variable annuity with 3.5% AIR	0.37	9.9	1.58	4.4	2.47	3.5
50% in variable annuity with 3.5% AIR/50% in RMD	0.19	9.9	1.26	4.0	2.18	3.2
Required minimum distribution	0.00	0.0	0.94	3.5	1.89	2.9
Endowment-style payout funds	0.24	13.7	0.95	4.2	1.42	3.3

[a]Measured as mean total real cash flow across all simulations divided by the lower semi-variance of the mean total real cash flow across all simulations; higher is better.

Note: See Table 11.1 for definitions.

Source: Authors' calculations; see text.

combination. The GLWB is at the opposite extreme with no nominal downside volatility, with other strategies in the middle range. Figure 11.2 presents data on median *real* annualized growth rates of the distributions of income from each of the strategies, again in decreasing order, showing at the median, RMDs/annuity combinations produce the highest growth in payments, while balanced funds, real annuities, endowment-style payout funds, and the variable annuities with GLWB produce the least average/typical growth.

Table 11.4 shows data on the median balances remaining at three different points in the horizon for investors, and the level of cross-sectional volatility. Here, the time-horizon payout funds have a slightly higher mean-to-semi-variance, with several other strategies following close behind. Yet the relative performance of the various strategies varies widely by time

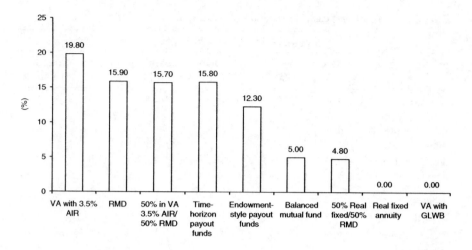

Figure 11.1 Percentage of quarters with 5 percent or more loss in year-over-year cash flow over 30-year horizon (nominal), by type of holding. *Note*: See Table 11.1 for definitions. *Source*: Authors' calculations; see text.

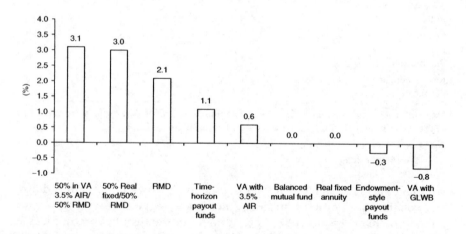

Figure 11.2 Median annualized growth of cash flow over 30-year horizon (real), by type of holding. *Note*: See Table 11.1 for definitions. *Source*: Authors' calculations; see text.

horizon, with perhaps the exception of the endowment-style payout funds that have a median residual balance that is similar at all horizons.

Figure 11.3 presents data on the typical volatility (measured as standard deviation) of the remaining asset balance available to the retiree. The greatest volatility in balance is generated by the time-horizon payout

TABLE 11.4 Median ending portfolio balance (real)

Strategy	5 years		20 years		30 years	
	Median ($)	Mean/ volatility[a]	Median ($)	Mean/ volatility[a]	Median ($)	Mean/ volatility[a]
Time-horizon payout funds	0.95	5.1	0.56	2.7	0.00	0.0
Required minimum distribution	1.26	5.3	1.25	2.5	0.84	2.1
50% in variable annuity with 3.5% AIR/50% in RMD	0.63	5.3	0.62	2.5	0.42	2.1
50% in real fixed annuity/50% in RMD	0.63	5.3	0.62	2.5	0.42	2.1
Endowment-style payout funds	1.00	4.3	0.96	2.2	0.94	1.9
Variable annuity with GLWB	0.94	4.9	0.71	2.0	0.52	1.5
Balanced mutual fund	0.98	4.7	0.89	1.7	0.77	1.3
Variable annuity with 3.5% AIR	0.00	0.0	0.00	0.0	0.00	0.0
Real fixed annuity	0.00	0.0	0.00	0.0	0.00	0.0

[a] Measured as mean total real cash flow across all simulations divided by the lower semi-variance of the mean total real cash flow across all simulations; higher is better.

Note: See Table 11.1 for definitions.

Source: Authors' calculations; see text.

funds. All of the investment-related solutions have very similar volatility levels, while the annuity solutions (trivially) have no volatility, as there is no remaining balance.

Finally, Table 11.5 presents summary data on the real IRRs at different horizons for each of the strategies. The data show that as investor horizons lengthen or shorten, the implications for differences in relative IRRs across the strategies can change quite dramatically. Of course, the starkest examples are the immediate annuities, which produce the worst relative results at short horizons, but the best results at the long horizons. Most of the investment-related strategies produce similar IRRs across the different implementations and product designs, largely a result of the fact that the investment allocations are quite similar across the various products.

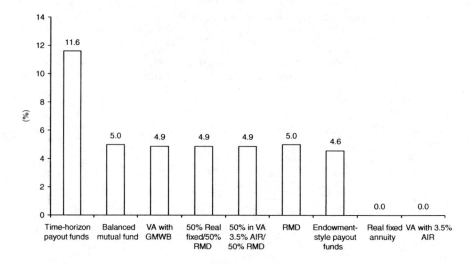

Figure 11.3 Median standard deviation of quarter-over-quarter change of balance over 30-year horizon, by type of holding. *Note*: See Table 11.1 for definitions. *Source*: Authors' calculations; see text.

Conclusion

This simulation exercise shows that different commonly advocated retirement income strategies produce a wide variety of possible outcomes. Some of the largest differences in outcomes are related to the impact of the various drawdown strategies and products on the residual/bequeathable wealth levels. Annuity options obviously provide relative stability of income flows but have strong negative impacts on residual wealth early in retirement. Drawdown strategies lack the pooling of mortality risk provided by the annuity so are less effective at providing stable income over very long horizons, but they tend to offer enhanced residual value of retirement assets upon death at shorter horizons. Insurance guarantees such as the GLWB rider can introduce very limited levels of annuitization that can have some value in the worst states, combining some of the features of drawdown with annuitization.

All of the approaches analyzed are useful to some degree in achieving the objective of providing a source of periodic payments. In addition, it is clear from the simulation analysis that none of the proposed strategies is dominated by any of the others if one admits the possibility that residual wealth levels are of great importance to retirees. The reluctance of retirees to voluntarily annuitize assets is strong evidence that maintaining full control over and possession of their assets is of significant value to many retirees.

TABLE 11.5 Median annual internal rates of return (real) for various holding periods

Strategy	5 years		20 years		30 years	
	Median (%)	Mean/ volatility[a]	Median (%)	Mean/ volatility[a]	Median (%)	Mean/ volatility[a]
Real fixed annuity	−30.4	−286.0	3.2	55.0	5.5	134.3
50% in real fixed annuity/50% in RMD	−4.9	−1.4	4.3	2.6	5.1	4.1
50% in variable annuity with 3.5% AIR/50% in RMD	−4.5	−1.1	4.9	1.8	5.8	2.4
Required minimum distribution	4.7	1.1	4.8	1.8	4.9	2.1
Variable annuity with 3.5% AIR	−28.2	−9.5	4.9	1.7	7.1	2.8
Time-horizon payout funds	4.2	1.0	4.1	1.7	4.0	1.8
Balanced mutual fund	4.6	1.1	4.6	1.6	4.6	1.6
Endowment-style payout funds	4.9	0.9	4.8	1.6	4.8	1.9
Variable annuity with GLWB	3.8	0.9	4.0	1.5	4.0	1.8

[a] Measured as mean IRR across all simulations divided by the lower semi-variance of the mean IRR across all simulations; higher is better.

Note: See Table 11.1 for definitions.

Source: Authors' calculations; see text.

All of these approaches are currently in use in the retirement market-place. A follow-up question that arises is what specifications of retiree preferences or desires might help explain why individuals appear to embrace investment strategies and solutions that emphasize continued growth of residual assets.

Acknowledgments

Opinions expressed herein are those of the authors alone and do not necessarily reflect the views of The Vanguard Group, Inc., its affiliates, management, or trustees. The authors are solely responsible for any errors.

Appendix 11A Glide Path for Asset Allocation

TABLE 11A.1 Payout rates and asset allocation patterns by age

Age	Year	Required minimum distribution (RMD) payout rate (%)	Time-horizon fund payout rate (%)	Time-horizon fund asset allocation		
				US equities (%)	International equities (%)	Bonds (%)
65	1	0.0	5.09	50.3	12.2	37.5
66	2	0.0	5.18	49.5	11.9	38.7
67	3	0.0	5.27	48.6	11.6	39.8
68	4	0.0	5.38	48.0	11.1	41.0
69	5	0.0	5.50	47.3	10.6	42.1
70	6	3.6	5.63	46.8	10.1	43.2
71	7	3.8	5.77	46.2	9.6	44.2
72	8	3.9	5.93	45.9	9.3	44.9
73	9	4.0	6.10	45.5	8.9	45.6
74	10	4.2	6.30	45.2	8.5	46.4
75	11	4.4	6.50	44.8	8.0	47.2
76	12	4.5	6.75	44.4	7.7	48.0
77	13	4.7	7.01	43.9	7.3	48.8
78	14	4.9	7.31	43.2	7.0	49.9
79	15	5.1	7.65	42.5	6.6	50.9
80	16	5.3	8.03	41.8	6.2	52.0
81	17	5.6	8.47	41.1	5.8	53.1
82	18	5.8	8.98	40.2	5.4	54.4
83	19	6.1	9.58	39.3	5.0	55.7
84	20	6.5	10.29	37.7	4.6	57.8
85	21	6.8	11.15	36.0	4.1	59.9
86	22	7.1	12.20	33.7	3.7	62.7
87	23	7.5	13.52	31.3	3.2	65.5
88	24	7.9	15.23	27.4	2.9	69.7
89	25	8.3	17.53	23.5	2.6	73.9
90	26	8.8	20.74	19.6	2.3	78.1
91	27	9.3	25.59	15.7	1.9	82.4
92	28	9.8	33.79	11.8	1.6	86.6
93	29	10.4	50.35	7.9	1.3	90.8
94	30	11.0	100.00	4.0	1.0	95.0

Note: See Table 11.1 for definitions.

Source: Authors' calculations; see text.

Notes

[1] The drawdown methods that these studies recommend are at odds with most rules that arise from standard economic models of consumption and portfolio choice; see in particular Sharpe, Scott, and Watson (2008).

[2] Recent events in the financial markets coupled with the apparent failure or inadequacy of the hedging programs employed by some insurers to back these promises have raised some questions about the viability of these types of products going forward. Providers are already increasing prices for some of these guarantees.

[3] Based on information in the Retirement Income Data Bank maintained by Ernst & Young.

[4] Another type of payout fund appears similar to more common 'income-oriented' mutual funds, differing only in that the income target for the funds is quantified and explicitly targeted. Despite the announced target, the level of income and the periodic payments that the funds will make to shareholders will vary with the amount of income actually earned by the portfolio, just like a typical mutual fund.

[5] Tax considerations may also be important for after-tax investors. Ameriks and Ren (2008) review these issues and provide some additional simulation analysis illustrating the impact of taxes.

References

Ameriks, J. (2004). 'How Do Retirees Go from Stock to Flow?,' in O.S. Mitchell and S. Utkus, eds., *Pension Design and Structure: New Lessons from Behavioral Finance.* Oxford, UK: Oxford University Press, pp. 237–58.

——and L. Ren (2008). *Generating Guaranteed Income: Understanding Income Annuities.* Malvern, PA: Vanguard Investment Counseling & Research.

——A. Caplin, S. Laufer, and S. Van Nieuwerburgh (2009). 'The Joy of Giving or Assisted Living? Using Strategic Surveys to Separate Bequest and Precautionary Motives,' SSRN Working Paper No. 982674. Rochester, NY: Social Science Research Network.

Bengen, W.P. (1994). 'Determining Withdrawal Rates Using Historical Data,' *Journal of Financial Planning*, 7(4): 171–80.

Bernheim, B.D. (1991). 'How Strong Are Bequest Motives? Evidence Based on Estimates of the Demand for Life Insurance and Annuities,' *Journal of Political Economy*, 99(5): 899–927.

Beshears, J., J. Choi, D. Laibson, and B. Madrian (2008). 'The Importance of Default Options for Retirement Saving Outcomes: Evidence from the United States,' in Stephen J. Kay and Tapen Sinha, eds., *Lessons from Pension Reform in the Americas.* Oxford, UK: Oxford University Press, pp. 59–87.

Blake D., A. Cairns, and K. Dowd (2003). 'Stochastic Pension Plan Design During the Distribution Phase,' *Insurance: Mathematics and Economics*, 33(1): 29–47.

Brown, J.R. (2001). 'Private Pensions, Mortality Risk, and the Decision to Annuitize,' *Journal of Public Economics*, 82: 29–62.

Brown, J.R. and J.M. Poterba (2000). 'Joint Life Annuities and Annuity Demand by Married Couples,' *Journal of Risk and Insurance*, 67(4): 527–53.

Davidoff T., J.R. Brown, and P. Diamond (2005). 'Annuities and Individual Welfare,' *American Economic Review*, 95(5): 1573–90

Davis, J., D. Wallick, and R. Aliaga-Diaz (2009). *Vanguard Capital Markets Model.* Malvern, PA: Vanguard Investment Counseling & Research.

Dushi, I. and A. Webb (2004). 'Household Annuitization Decisions: Simulations and Empirical Analyses,' *Journal of Pension Economics and Finance*, 3(2): 109–43.

Holden, Sarah (2009). 'The Role of IRAs in U.S. Households' Saving for Retirement, 2008,' *ICI Research Fundamentals*, 18(1): 1–20.

Horneff, Wolfram, Raimond Maurer, Olivia S. Mitchell, and Michael Stamos (2010). 'Variable Payout Annuities and Dynamic Portfolio Choice in Retirement,' *Journal of Pension Economics and Finance*, 9: 163–83.

Hurd, M.D. and J.P. Smith (1999). 'Anticipated and Actual Bequests,' NBER Working Paper No. 7380. Cambridge, MA: National Bureau of Economic Research.

Ibbotson Associates (2007). *Retirement Portfolio and Variable Annuity with Guaranteed Minimum Withdrawal Benefit (VA+GMWB).* Chicago, IL: Ibbotson Associates. http://corporate.morningstar.com/ib/documents/MethodologyDocuments/ IBBAssociates/VA_GMWB.pdf

Milevsky, Moshe and Vladyslav Kyrychenko (2008). 'Asset Allocation Within Variable Annuities: The Impact of Guarantees,' in J. Ameriks and O.S. Mitchell, eds., *Recalibrating Retirement Spending and Saving.* Oxford, UK: Oxford University Press, pp. 276–94.

Mitchell, O.S., J.M. Poterba, M.J. Warshawsky, and J.R. Brown (1999). 'New Evidence on the Money's Worth of Individual Annuities,' *American Economic Review*, 89(5): 1299–318.

Mottola, G.R. and S.P. Utkus (2007). *Lump Sum or Annuity? An Analysis of Choice in DB Pension Payouts.* Malvern, PA: Vanguard Investment Counseling & Research.

Pye, G.B. (2000). 'Sustainable Investment Withdrawals,' *Journal of Portfolio Management*, 26(4): 73–83.

Sharpe, W.F., J.S. Scott, and J.G. Watson (2008). 'Efficient Retirement Financial Strategies,' in J. Ameriks and O.S. Mitchell, eds., *Recalibrating Retirement Spending and Saving.* Oxford, UK: Oxford University Press, pp. 209–26.

Sinclair, S.H. and K.A. Smetters (2004). 'Health Shocks and the Demand for Annuities,' CBO Technical Paper 2004-9. Washington, DC: Congressional Budget Office.

Turra, C.M. and O.S. Mitchell (2008). 'The Impact of Health Status and Out-of-Pocket Medical Expenditures on Annuity Valuation,' in J. Ameriks and O.S. Mitchell, eds., *Recalibrating Retirement Spending and Saving.* Oxford, UK: Oxford University Press, pp. 227–50.

Updegrave, Walter (2007). *Retirement: The 4 Percent Solution.* New York: *Money Magazine.* http://money.cnn.com/2007/08/13/pf/expert/expert.moneymag/index.htm

Yaari, M. (1965). 'Uncertain Lifetime, Life Insurance, and the Theory of the Consumer,' *Review of Economic Studies*, 32: 137–50.

Chapter 12

Risk Budgeting for the Canadian Pension Plan Investment Board

Sterling Gunn and Tracy Livingstone

The Canada Pension Plan Investment Board (CPPIB) was created in 1999 to manage the surplus contributions of the Canada Pension Plan (CPP). In its early days, CPPIB fund management was outsourced to external managers who passively managed to market indexes. By 2005, the group had built internal active management capabilities and was moving away from the outsourcing business model. While management was already operating under a total portfolio approach, the methodology was refined to explicitly consider trade-offs between risk and return at the fund level, with the development of the Risk–Return–Accountability Framework. In turn, this prompted the design and implementation of a risk-budgeting framework. This chapter explains why risk budgeting is necessary to help public fund managers handle contributions not needed to pay current benefits. In what follows, we first discuss the origins of the CPP and the CPPIB. Next, we take up the implementation of risk budgeting as an integral part of business planning.

Origins of the CPP[1]

During the 1960s, Canada was 'fully engaged in building a welfare state that would render the ravages of the Great Depression in the 1930s a thing of the past' (Little 2008: 2). In 1963, a minority government was elected on a party platform that included a national pension plan and national health insurance. Discussions and negotiations between the Federal government and the nine of the 10 provinces continued until an agreement was reached in 1966 to initiate the CPP. The province of Quebec administers its own pension plan, parallel to the CPP, known as the Quebec Pension Plan (QPP).

Although it is a defined benefit (DB) plan, the CPP was never meant to provide full or near-full support for a beneficiary; rather it was intended to be part of the answer to senior poverty. The CPP is a component of

Canada's three-tier national pension system. The first tier consists of two government support programs paid out of general revenues. Old Age Security (OAS) was put in place in 1952, and it provides a low level of income primarily to senior citizens who never worked for a wage. The Guaranteed Income Supplement (put in place in 1967) is means-tested, and it offers further support to seniors who depend almost entirely on the OAS for their income. The second tier includes the CPP and workplace pensions. These pensions may be DB or defined contribution (DC); beneficiaries and often their employers contribute to these plans, enabling the funds to grow in a tax-deferred environment. The third tier consists of personal saving, whether in a tax-deferred Registered Retirement Savings Plan or in some other saving vehicle.

The design of the CPP was a triumph of compromise. Federal and provincial jurisdiction in Canada separates accountability and authority in ways that are not always intuitive. For instance, the Federal government has exclusive jurisdiction over criminal law, but the provinces have jurisdiction over the administration of justice. The health-care system is administered by the provinces, but substantial funding is provided by the Federal government. In fact, the provinces had full jurisdiction for pensions until the constitutional amendment that instituted OAS in 1952. 'Nonaged benefits' such as disability and survivor benefits remained part of provincial jurisdiction until a subsequent constitutional amendment in 1965 allowed the Federal government to provide these benefits as well. The end result was shared accountability for pensions and a national solution that included pension benefits, disability payments, and survivor benefits. An additional compromise was the change process inserted in the Act. Changes to the CPP require agreement from two-thirds of the provinces with two-thirds of the population, a higher threshold than required for amending the Canadian constitution.[2] From the outset of the negotiations, Quebec chose not to participate in the CPP, and formed its own provincial plan, the QPP. However, agreement was reached between the Federal government and Quebec such that the legislation supporting the CPP and the QPP are identical. The contributions and benefits are the same, and the plan is portable between Quebec and the other provinces.

As originally structured, the CPP did not focus on intergenerational fairness and equity. The generation of Canadians that had lived through the Great Depression and World War II had little opportunity to put aside savings, and faced a poor retirement. The CPP was designed to ensure some support would be available for them, regardless of the length of their participation. Full benefits were to be phased in after the first 10 years of contributions. 'At the extreme, it would be possible for some people to contribute for only ten years and then retire with full CPP benefits for the rest of their lives' (Little 2008: 36). As illustrated in Table 12.1, the return

TABLE 12.1 Internal rates of return on contributions: Canadian Pension Plan (CPP) (1910–2000)

Birth year	Nominal (%)	Real (%)
1910	33.6	25.3
1920	21.9	14.2
1930	15.6	9.6
1940	10.4	6.2
1950	7.2	4.1
1960	5.6	3.0
1970	4.9	2.4
1980	4.8	2.2
1990	4.7	2.2
2000	4.7	2.2

Sources: TOCA (2009) for birth years 1910–30; TOCA (2006) for birth years 1940–2000.

on contributions was substantial for the first beneficiaries, born in 1911, who retired with full benefits in 1976. The return for later beneficiaries would be significantly lower. In any case, the CPP continues to provide a fully portable, fully indexed, and effectively risk-free pension promise. 'Given plausible inflation-indexed bond returns the CPP would need to charge significantly higher sustainable contribution rates in the 11 to 12½ percent range if it faced the total costs of private annuity providers' (Arnold et al. 2009: 15). On a risk-adjusted basis, the CPP was a great deal for the earlier participants, and it remains a good deal for later participants.

The Evolution of the CPP

The CPP was changed several times over the next 20 years. The retirement age was reduced from 69 in 1966 to 65 in 1970. Both the CPP and the QPP enhanced benefits during the 1970s and added full indexing to inflation in 1974. Survivor benefits were extended to widowers as well as widows. In 1984, the QPP brought in a provision for early retirement with a reduction in benefits paid; the CPP followed suit in 1987. For the first 20 years, alterations to the CPP involved increases or enhancements to benefits; little attention was devoted to long-term funding considerations.

The original contribution rate was 3.6 percent of salary, shared equally between employees and employers, though it was recognized that

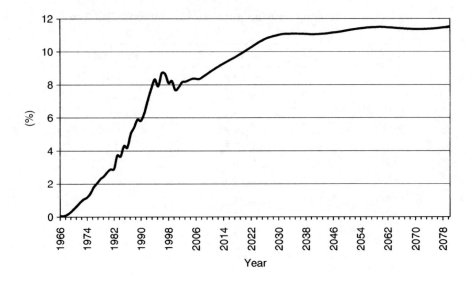

Figure 12.1 Projected pay-as-you-go rates for the Canada Pension Plan (CPP). *Sources*: Authors' calculations derived from TOCA (2006) and CPPIB (various years).

3.6 percent would not be sufficient over the long term. CPP retirement benefits were capped at 25 percent of Yearly Maximum Pensionable Earnings (related to average earnings), and benefits were inflation-adjusted (initially capped at 2 percent per year). The system was mainly pay-as-you-go, after accumulating 2 years of benefit payments in a buffer fund. Other than a small amount of cash retained for liquidity, the monies collected were used to purchase nonmarketable provincial bonds (i.e., the funds were loaned to the provinces at an interest rate equal to Government of Canada 20-year bonds). Until 1999 when the first cash transfers from the Federal government were provided to CPPIB, the basic financing structure remained the same.

Full benefits were first paid to participants in the CPP in 1976. In its first 10 years, the CPP was collecting money at the full 3.6 percent contribution rate, far in excess of what was needed to pay benefits. As illustrated in Figure 12.1, by 1975, while the contribution rate was still fixed at 3.6 percent, the pay-as-you-go rate was only 1.5 percent though it was climbing steadily.

It was known that there would come a time when the pay-as-you-go rate would reach and surpass the fixed contribution rate. The Chief Actuary of the CPP projected that this would occur in 1985 but it came earlier. By

1983, the cost of the CPP had reached 3.7 percent but contributions remained at 3.6 percent. The Stewards of the CPP, the Ministers of Finance for the Federal government, and the nine participating provincial governments responded with a 5-year schedule of increases of 0.2 percent, starting in 1987, and thereafter raising them 0.15 percent each year for the following 20 years. The problem was thus alleviated in the short term but not solved in the longer term.

The contribution rate versus the pay-as-you-go rate was not the entire source of system financing, since the CPP received additional revenue from interest earned on the surpluses loaned to the provinces. Thus, total system revenues were contributions plus interest received on the provincial loans. In 1987, the Chief Actuary forecast that total revenues would be sufficient to pay benefits for another 10 years, until sometime between 1995 and 2000. This day of reckoning again came early: in 1993, the CPP began to use its capital to pay benefits.

The new fiscal responsibility

Thirty years after the launch of the CPP, the issue of financing the plan for future generations finally hit the front page: Canadians had lost confidence that the CPP would provide them with retirement income. An Angus Reid public opinion survey in 1993 found that only 17 percent of Canadians believed CPP benefits would remain the same in their retirement (HRSDC 1995: 7). Another 50 percent believed that the CPP would be providing significantly reduced benefits and 31 percent believed the plan would no longer exist.

The Chief Actuary's 15th review of the CPP in 1995 confirmed that this lack of confidence in the CPP was warranted. With the demographic and economic assumptions in the 15th review, the Office of the Chief Actuary (OCA) forecasted the plan was going to run out of money by 2015, meaning that, as structured, the plan was unsustainable with the current contribution rate structure. In fact, in 1995, the OCA forecasted that a pay-as-you-go contribution rate would be 14.2 percent by 2030 to sustain the CPP. Stakeholders were concerned that such a high contribution level would create intergenerational inequities, inhibit economic growth, and stifle job creation.

A new government was elected in 1993 on a platform of reducing Canada's dependence on deficit financing. The first budget in 1994 ran a deficit, although it was reduced from the previous year. The next year, Paul Martin, the Minister of Finance at the time, put a new budget in place that turned federal finances around, and in 1997–8, led to the first in a series of 11 budget surpluses. These surpluses caused Canada's federal debt as a percentage of GDP to drop from a peak of 68.4 percent in 1997–8 to 29.8 percent in 2007–8. Although some of Canada's fiscal house was being put in order, the long-term status of the CPP remained a serious challenge. Nevertheless, one of the compromises put into place in 1966 meant the Federal government could not fix the CPP unilaterally: two-thirds of the provinces with two-thirds of the population would need to agree on any proposed changes.

The day of reckoning

In February 1996, the Federal and provincial governments of Canada issued a joint document entitled 'Information Paper for Consultations on the Canada Pension Plan.' This document 'provide(d) Canadians with an opportunity to assess the challenges facing the CPP, form their own opinions, and make their views known during upcoming consultations' (TFPTGC 1996: 7). It laid out the choices the governments were considering and the potential outcomes of those choices. More significantly, the document asked questions of the participants in the CPP and looked for answers: 'How high can the rates go before they become unaffordable? ... What is the appropriate balance between contribution rate increases and changes to benefits? ... If a fuller funding approach to the financing of the CPP were adopted, a much larger CPP fund would build up. ... Should CPP funds be invested so as to earn maximum returns? How could this be done?' (TFPTGC 1996: 47).

These questions made it clear what the governments were asking the stakeholders of the CPP to consider: increased contribution rates, reduced benefits, and a much larger reserve fund. And in a series of meetings held across the country in 1996, the CPP's stakeholders responded with a clear message: the CPP should be maintained. The balancing act between increased contributions and reduced benefits was fundamental to the discussion, but the issue of a bigger fund, and what to do with the money, was also key.

The necessity of increased contributions was recognized. There was general mistrust of the government's ability to manage a large fund, and concern about the impact such a fund would have on the Canadian capital markets. However, it was clear that depending on a portfolio of nonmarketable government bonds invested at below market rates was not a viable investment policy to sustain the system for future generations of Canadians. Instead the preferred outcome was to be a professional investment organization, managing the resulting fund at arm's length from government, specifically exempt from government interference, and 'maximizing return without undue risk of loss' (CPPIB Act 1997).

The 1997 agreement

Several changes intended to improve CPP sustainability were proposed in 1997 by the finance ministers of the Federal and provincial governments. Legislation was enacted that put in place a series of contribution rate increases and modestly reduced the growth of future benefits. In addition, the legislation introduced a default mechanism for adjusting the contribution rate should the Chief Actuary ever deem the contribution rate to be insufficient. Agreement was reached to raise contribution rates to 9.9 percent by 2003, a level viewed as sufficient to sustain the CPP as a partially funded plan. As illustrated in Figure 12.2, the pay-as-you-go rate exceeded the contribution rate in the late 1980s and early 1990s. However, the steady increases in the contribution rate surpassed the pay-as-you-go rate by 2000. Even though the pay-as-you-go rate after 2020 was projected to exceed the contribution rate, the investment income from the Fund is forecasted to be sufficient to sustain the CPP.

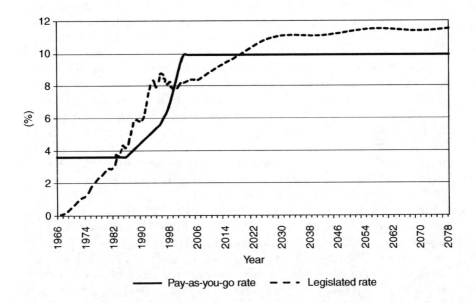

Figure 12.2 Projected pay-as-you-go rates versus legislated rates for the Canada Pension Plan (CPP). *Sources:* Authors' calculations derived from TOCA (2006) and CPPIB (various years).

Early days of the CPPIB

This 1997 legislation also created the CPPIB, a federal crown corporation that operates as an independent professional investment organization. While most Canadian crown corporations are run by the government with a specific mandate administered by the appropriate Minister of the Canadian Parliament, CPPIB is specifically exempt from Divisions I through IV of Part X of the Financial Administration Act that would have made it ultimately accountable to the Minister of Finance. The founding Board of Directors of CPPIB was assembled in 1998, chosen from the provinces and territories to provide a diversity of views and carefully selected to ensure the Board is composed of professionals with relevant experiences and skill. The independence of CPPIB and its Board of Directors from the Federal and provincial governments is central to the firm's governance: Federal and provincial government involvement in the management of CPPIB, defined in the Canada Pension Plan Investment Board Act, is limited to the appointment of the members of the Board of Directors. Apart from appointing the members of the Board, the government remains at arm's length from CPPIB operations. A stringent code of conduct stipulates that any attempt by any level of government to influence investment decisions, hiring practices, or procurement must be appropriately escalated within the organization in order to determine what appropriate action should be taken.

The first transfer of funds from the Federal government to CPPIB occurred in March 1999, and by the end of the month – also the end of the fiscal year – CPPIB had $12 million in investment assets (CPPIB 1999) as reported in the first annual report. That first report also contained projections from the Federal government that the Fund would grow to $88 billion by 2008. The size of the CPP Fund increased rapidly over the next 5 years. Growth came from excess contributions flowing in from contributors and positive investment returns. By June 30, 2005, the Fund had reached $87 billion, almost 3 years ahead of the forecast. By March 31, 2008, the Fund had reached $122.8 billion.

For the first year, the Canadian equity in the CPP Fund was managed passively, as per the legislation. In 2000, the CPPIB Act was revised to allow 50 percent of the Canadian equity in the CPP Fund to be managed actively. And then in 2001, the Act was revised again to allow 100 percent active management. Foreign investments were restricted until the Foreign Property Rule was repealed, effective June 2005. And, even though there were no restrictions on active management after 2001, for the most part, the Fund was still passively managed (Raymond 2009). The risk of the Fund was measured, but investment decisions were motivated by passively managing to a set of benchmarks rather than the risk a particular investment might create.

Initial Risk and Performance Concepts at CPPIB

During its early years, CPPIB performance was compared to a set of benchmarks including a real rate of return calculated by the OCA. By 2004, CPPIB had also adopted the risk-adjusted net value-added (RANVA) performance measure developed by Keith Ambachtsheer (1996). RANVA, defined as the gross return on assets less the return on a risk-free asset (R_{assets}), costs (C), and a charge on risk capital ($\lambda \times$ Risk), is similar to many of the risk-adjusted performance measures used by banks and other financial institutions:

$$\text{RANVA} = R_{assets} - (R_{risk-free} + C + \lambda \times \text{Risk})$$

Ambachtsheer defined the risk-free rate as 'that economic return which would be certain to keep a fully funded plan fully funded' and he further stated 'the best estimate of such a return is the return on a portfolio of default-free bonds with the same duration and inflation indexation as those implicit in the accrued pension liabilities' (Ambachtsheer 1996). He acknowledged there was no single right way to measure either the risks taken by a pension fund or assess the risk charge needed to calculate RANVA, but he argued that RANVA was for people 'who would rather measure the right things imperfectly than either measure the wrong things perfectly, or measure nothing of consequence at all' (Ambachtsheer 1996).

The CPPIB RANVA implementation adopted Canadian government real return bonds (RRBs) as the 'minimum-risk' portfolio (a substitute for the risk-free asset called for in the RANVA model). These bonds were thought to be a reasonable proxy for the CPP net liabilities. Risk capital was estimated using a 90th percentile value-at-risk (VaR) measure of the asset–liability mismatch. Yet the CPPIB implementation diverged from the RANVA specification in several ways. First, the CPP was a partially funded plan and was always intended to be only partially funded with surpluses intended as a buffer. This was very different from other pension plans and from the fully funded plan Ambachtsheer had envisioned. Second, the CPPIB RANVA implementation modeled the plan's net cash flows rather than just the liabilities. The cash flows (annual contributions less benefits paid) from the CPP plan are forecast to be positive until roughly 2020, at which point benefits paid are projected to exceed contributions collected and some proportion of investment income would be used to pay benefits (see Figure 12.3).[3]

Third, Ambachtsheer's approach had assumed the CPP net liabilities could be represented by a portfolio of RRBs. In fact, however, CPP net liabilities differ significantly from the liabilities of a typical, fully funded

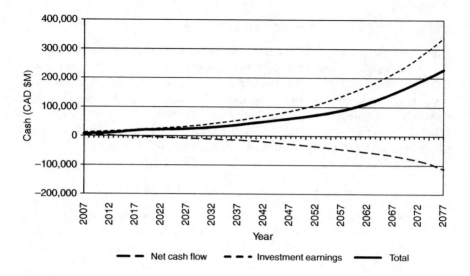

Figure 12.3 Forecast of net liabilities and investment earnings for the Canada Pension Plan (CPP). *Sources:* Authors' calculations derived from TOCA (2006) and CPPIB (various years).

plan or that of a bond portfolio. As a result, CPPIB moved away from the RANVA construct and developed a more sophisticated approach that modeled the net liabilities directly rather than through proxies (James 2007; Ross 2007). In addition, Ambachtsheer's risk-free asset was assumed to have returns sufficient to maintain the sustainability of the plan, but CPPIB's chosen proxy, RRBs, did not. In fact, given the Stewards' policy decision to cap contributions at 9.9 percent, the Chief Actuary's forecast indicated CPPIB needed to generate long-term real returns exceeding 4 percent, well beyond any reasonable long-term return expectation for a portfolio of RRBs. As a result, investing solely in RRBs would have almost certainly threatened the financial stability of the plan, leading to an increase in contribution rates and/or reduction in benefits. Accordingly, equity investments were deemed necessary to finance the liabilities over the long term. The RANVA model looked at total fund performance, adjusted for relatively short-term risk. Although attractive in its simplicity, RANVA was not appropriate to the circumstances of the CPPIB, where total fund performance was considered over long horizons and management was accountable solely for adding value. Plan performance was also sensitive to other factors affecting cash flows, including policy choices,

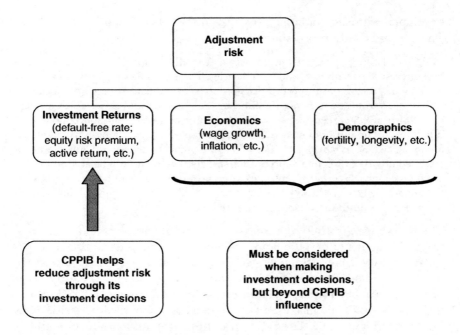

Figure 12.4 Factors affecting financial stability of the Canada Pension Plan (CPP). *Source*: Authors' calculations; see text.

demographic risks, economic risks, and financial risks as illustrated in Figure 12.4. Many of these were beyond the control of the CPPIB.

The year 2005 proved to be a watershed for the CPPIB. While the Fund was not the largest in Canada, it was recognized that its position in the Canadian marketplace was becoming more significant, and the management of the Fund had to evolve in response. David Denison (who became the second president of the CPPIB in 2005), John Ilkiw (vice president of Risk and Research) and Don Raymond (vice president of Public Market Investments, PMI) developed a Risk–Return–Accountability Framework to continue the Fund's evolution. Their goal was to take Ambachtsheer's guidance to heart and begin to measure the right things, though perhaps imperfectly.

The Risk–Return–Accountability Framework

The two control mechanisms that constitute the Risk–Return–Accountability Framework, the CPP Reference Portfolio and the Active Risk Limit, were developed with the guidance provided in the 1997 Stewards' Agreement. The Stewards had proposed:

CPP funds [will] be prudently invested in a diversified portfolio of securities in the best interest of contributors and beneficiaries. This new policy is consistent with the investment policies of most other pension plans in Canada and the QPP. Prudent assumptions indicate investing the fund in the market could generate an average real return of 3.8 percent per year – i.e., a return of 3.8 percent above the rate of inflation.... The fund will be managed professionally at arm's length from governments by an investment board. The CPP Investment Board will be governed by a qualified board of directors of up to 12 members. The Board will be accountable to the public as well as governments and will report its investment results regularly to Canadians.... The Board will be subject to broadly the same investment rules as other pension funds in Canada. (HRDC 1997: 13)

The Reference Portfolio represents the Board of Directors' long-term passive investment strategy, the point of comparison for determining management's value-adding strategies. It is a viable, low-cost, and investable portfolio embodying the Stewards' long-term risk tolerances and return preferences. CPPIB's management discretion to pursue value-adding strategies is controlled by an active risk limit that constrains tactical decisions, as outlined in Figure 12.5. The CPPIB uses historical simulation VaR methodology to estimate active risk, incorporating at least 10 years of historical data, at 90 percent confidence, over a 1-year time horizon. The methodology produces results that are repeatable and verifiable, with underlying assumptions that are transparent and not subject to management interpretation. The 10-year history ensures that the scenario set incorporates enough information to dampen business cycle effects. The 1-year investment horizon was chosen to provide a longer-term view of potential losses than is common in institutions with a shorter-term view of the market.

The CPP Risk–Return–Accountability Framework clarifies stakeholder accountabilities. The Board of Directors, acting on behalf of the Stewards, is held accountable for policy decisions exposing the Fund to the many factors affecting the Fund stability, including the desire to passively harvest long-term capital market returns. Management is held accountable for adding value relative to the Board of Directors' long-term risk and return expectations, as embodied by the Reference Portfolio. Unlike a typical policy portfolio, the Reference Portfolio does not bind management to a set of asset allocations. Rather, investment discretion is governed by an active risk limit, not by bands around a target allocation. Numerous authors have noted that policy portfolios tend to generate most of the returns and risks (Brooks et al. 2001; Brinson, Hood, and Beebower 1986). Thus, the choice of Reference Portfolio is the most important investment decision made by the Board of Directors of the CPPIB.

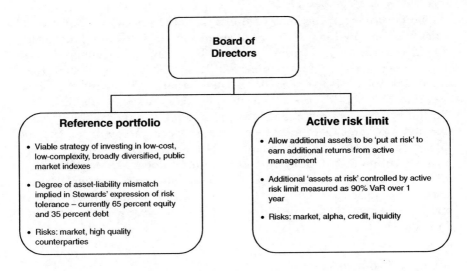

Figure 12.5 Two levers governing strategic risk-taking at the Canada Pension Plan Investment Board (CPPIB). *Source*: Authors' calculations; see text.

Designing the first Reference Portfolio

The first Reference Portfolio was designed in late 2005, reflecting the Board's risk preferences while still having a reasonable expectation of delivering the actuarially required rate of return needed to fund the plan. It was clear that a portfolio of RRBs would not provide sufficient returns to sustain the Fund:

We then considered the risk factors driving CPP liabilities and the risk mitigating characteristics of easy-to-implement, low cost exposures to broad market and publicly priced asset classes: foreign equities, Canadian equities, Canadian real returns bonds and Canadian nominal bonds. After considering their expected return patterns and risk-mitigating behavior, and the legacy portfolio of Federal-provincial non-marketable bonds, we settled on sub-asset class exposures that would be optimal under reasonable capital market and liability behavior assumptions. (Ilkiw and Raymond 2005)

The original CPP Reference Portfolio contained 65 percent equity (40 percent unhedged foreign equity and 25 percent Canadian equity) and 35 percent Canadian fixed income (25 percent Canadian nominal bonds and 10 percent Canadian RRBs). This portfolio mix was reasonably expected to provide the level of return necessary to sustain the Fund over the long term,[4] and it represented the systematic risk deemed acceptable by the Board.

The governance provisions of the Risk–Return–Accountability Framework are contained in a suite of documents, both public and proprietary. CPPIB's constitution document is the 'Statement of Investment Objectives, Policies, Return Expectations and Risk Management for the Investment Portfolio of the Canada Pension Plan' (CPPIB 2008), which describes the CPPIB's investment objectives, and describes the Reference Portfolio, the associated Board Active Risk Limit, and the factors affecting the ability of the CPP to meet its objectives. A companion document, the 'Policy for the Measurement, Management, and Reporting of CPP Investment Portfolio Risk' is a proprietary nonpublic document describing risk management practices, defining the methodology for measuring VaR, and specifying the active risk limit. These two documents, with other supporting proprietary documents, describe the Risk–Return–Accountability Framework.

Total portfolio management

CPPIB believes it can best meet its objectives by managing the risk and return characteristics of the total portfolio, rather than allocating capital in a disjointed fashion to individual investment departments. As a result, the Reference Portfolio design is not an exercise in traditional asset allocation, but instead is designed to meet the long-term risk and return expectations of the Board. The outcome of both exercises – asset allocation or total portfolio design – is superficially the same. But the thought process, the focus, and the governance models at CPPIB are risk-based – quite different from a traditional asset allocation.

It should be noted that pension funds and other investors often hold investment managers accountable for policy decisions and risk factors beyond their control. The use of non-investable performance measures (such as inflation plus benchmarks) is likely to lead to management explaining discrepancies from target to the stakeholders, or fund managers being given credit unfairly for positive results. Neither circumstance is under the fund manager's control nor achieves the objective of holding fund managers accountable for their investment decisions. The CPP Risk–Return–Accountability Framework clarifies management's accountabilities. The Active Risk Limit, incorporating market and credit risk measured relative to the Reference Portfolio, differs from the limit structures in place at many other pension funds. Within the Active Risk Limit, CPPIB management has the discretion to improve overall portfolio performance by investing in non-Reference Portfolio asset classes and by pursuing alpha-type strategies. These strategies can add value through excess returns and/or improved total portfolio diversification.

As noted earlier, CPPIB expects to receive significant positive net contributions over the next 10 years, causing assets to grow extraordinarily. Therefore, the CPPIB is willing to take on opportunistic investments that might appear disproportionate in the current portfolio, knowing its portfolio will grow into such position over time. As a result, CPPIB pursues opportunistic strategies not explicitly limited by allocations. Each such opportunistic investment is analyzed in terms of its potential impact on the risk and return profile of the total portfolio. Sizable real estate and infrastructure investment opportunities, for example, arise infrequently. So during the initial growth of the Fund, CPPIB management has not governed these investment strategies by setting allocations. Instead, management reviews these opportunities as they arise and makes decisions based on contributions such proposed investments would make to long-term total portfolio risks and returns.

Risk budgeting

In order to enable the investment process to be truly risk-based, firm-wide, and transparent, risk budgeting was the next iteration in the development of the Risk–Return–Accountability Framework. Yet the concept of risk budgeting means different things to different investors. For instance, Pearson (2002: 7) stated: 'Narrowly defined, *risk budgeting* is a process of measuring and decomposing risk, using the measures in asset-allocation decisions, assigning portfolio managers *risk budgets* defined in terms of these measures, and using these risk budgets in monitoring the asset allocations and portfolio managers.' By contrast, de Bever et al. (2000) argued that a portfolio's risk budget

is a measure of risk tolerance, defined as the loss one rarely expects to exceed over a specific time horizon. The portfolio's estimated 'risk capital usage' must fall within this risk budget. The appropriate time horizon and the definition of 'rarely' depend on the organization. Ontario Teachers' Pension Plan ('Teachers') has a long-term focus on managing surplus (assets-liabilities) and surplus risk, so we express our 'surplus risk' budget as the annual surplus loss we are prepared to absorb in the 1 in 100 worst-case outcome.

And still a third approach was offered by Brooks et al. (2001) who stated that risk budgeting refers 'to the process of establishing a) how much investment risk should be taken; and b) where it is most efficient to take it in order to maximize returns.'

The distinguishing feature of these definitions is not their similarity but rather the linkage each makes to investment objectives. In an investment

environment where managers are working to achieve a target asset allocation, assigning a fixed risk budget is simple in concept. By contrast, in an
environment where growth is rapid and the horizons of investment strategies differ greatly, greater flexibility is required.

Risk budgeting at CPPIB

CPPIB management has been refining its forecasting of active risk since
the approval of the first Reference Portfolio in 2006. By the end of fiscal
2007, an informal risk budget for fiscal 2008 was negotiated between the
PMI department and the president. Over the course of fiscal 2008, the
PMI risk budget was measured and monitored as part of the regular risk
reports. In April 2008, a formal project was initiated, engaging an outside
consultant to determine the shape of risk budgeting at CPPIB. This
project was completed in August 2008, and its recommendations formed
the basis of the risk budgets put in place for fiscal 2010, starting in April
2009.

   To develop risk budgeting at CPPIB, it was first necessary to clarify its
purpose. CPPIB embarked on a series of internal interviews to gather
viewpoints of different investment and finance groups. Many questions
arose regarding risk 'philosophy' including: Are risk budgets limits or
targets? And if a risk budget effectively represents a limit, is it a hard limit
or a soft limit? How granular does the analysis of results have to be? What
measures will be used to negotiate risk budgets and to track results? Could
investment departments allocate risk within their risk budgets to the
groups within their respective departments? What are potential outcome
scenarios, and what kind of discussions should result? How often are results
monitored and reported? And then, who takes responsibility for risk budgeting? In practice, there was widespread agreement on the value of risk
budgeting: when risk is a scarce resource, it is a clear advantage to the firm
to have a risk-budgeting framework in place and operating effectively. And
a main benefit of risk budgeting is the enhanced transparency it brings to
the process of making investment decisions.

   Since the development of the Risk–Return–Accountability Framework
and the expansion of CPPIB's active investment programs, there has been
a conscious consideration of the risk an investment adds to the Fund,
particularly in the case of large lumpy investments like real estate and
infrastructure. Risk budgeting enhances that consideration by first
providing a formal mechanism with a defined methodology for measuring
the risk return trade-off, and second, by reinforcing that risk is a scarce
resource which must be used in an efficient and cost-effective manner. In

order for risk budgeting to be effective, the investment decision process becomes a collaborative effort between the investment departments, Portfolio Design and Investment Research (PDIR), and Investment Risk Management.

Budgets versus expectations

PMI was accustomed to a conscious consideration of the trade-offs between risk and return, using an information ratio to measure the success of internal and external managers. And since PMI had been operating under an informal risk-budgeting regime for fiscal 2008, the implementation of a formal risk budget was almost a nonevent. Discussions with the real estate investments (REI) and private investments (PI) groups were more challenging. As discussed earlier, the CPPIB business model treats alternative investments as opportunistic, without specific allocations, yet strict risk budgeting would require explicit allocations to real estate, private equity, and infrastructure. Accordingly, management developed a fundamental definition of risk budgeting that was more appropriate to the opportunistic aspects of CPPIB's investment strategy. The 'Risk-Budgeting Operating Framework' is therefore 'judgment-based, supported by analytics' (Gunn, Livingstone, and Wyman 2008). A graphical overview of the process appears in Figure 12.6.

Accountability for risk budgeting

The collective viewpoint of management at CPPIB is conveyed through the Investment Planning Committee (IPC), chaired by the president, with its membership comprised of the Investment SVPs, the COO, the CFO, and the SVP of PDIR. PDIR is the working arm of the IPC, and as its name suggests, is accountable for the research and analysis that motivate the design of the Reference Portfolio and the Active Risk Limit, as well as the active investments in the Fund. The risk tolerance of the firm as expressed through risk budgeting is an integral part of portfolio design. PDIR has the accountability for negotiating risk budgets with the investment departments on behalf of the IPC, and bringing them to the committee for approval. Investment Risk Management is responsible for measuring outcomes versus approved risk budgets and reporting the results to the investment departments and to management. Midyear adjustments, due to unforeseen market events or responses to opportunistic investments, are within PDIR's accountability as well.

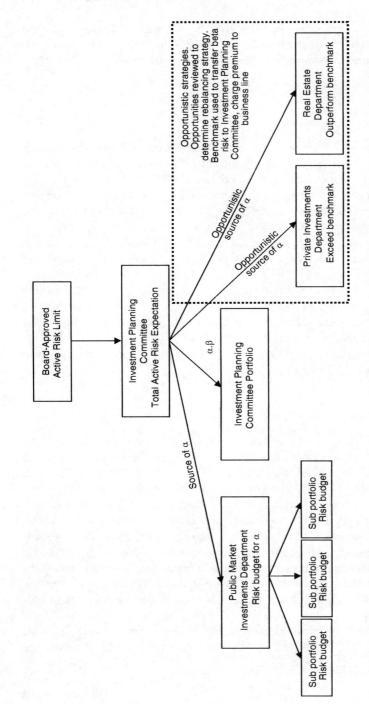

Figure 12.6 The risk-budgeting framework of the Canada Pension Plan Investment Board (CPPIB). *Source*: Authors' calculations; see text.

Measurement of risk-budgeting outcomes

CPPIB uses VaR to measure risk relative to the CPP Reference Portfolio. It was recognized that the investment departments do not manage their investment activities using VaR. However, during the course of the risk-budgeting design project, it was determined that it was better to be consistent with the firm-wide risk measure than to design a different measure that would then have to be reconciled to the firm-wide risk measure. A VaR measure relative to the Reference Portfolio is used at the investment department level to set the risk budgets in the performance agreements and to monitor against them.

Investment department group risk budgets

In order to motivate the groups within the investment departments to maximize their opportunities within the department risk budgets, the SVPs may choose to disaggregate their risk budgets and assign group risk budgets. These intradepartmental risk budgets may be in terms of risk measures more appropriate for managing the activities of the various groups. For example, groups within PMI have typically managed to a dollar-based volatility target expressed as a standard deviation. The transformation of a risk-budgeting target expressed in terms of VaR to another volatility measure is usually straightforward, and then an allocation within the department can be accomplished.

Benefits to the CPPIB of risk budgeting

As a management tool, risk budgeting will strengthen accountability and transparency. Improved accountability for risk-adjusted returns is provided through Investment Department performance agreements that define departmental accountability for risk and return, and in aggregate, align with commitments to the Board for value added and risk. Transparency is improved through dialogue and disclosure around risk and return expectations, initially as performance agreements are negotiated, and subsequently as results are monitored, reported and discussed, and decisions are made based on the outcomes. The decision framework reveals the trade-offs between the opportunities within a department and between departments, and the marginal risk and return impacts on the total portfolio.

As an investment tool, risk budgeting will enhance efficiency and prioritization. The ratio of risk vs. return highlights explicitly the cost of return – that is, how much risk is expended to achieve a measured level of return – revealing the efficiency of portfolio decisions. Risk, return and efficiency ratios provide an objective and transparent method of choosing one investment opportunity over another. (Gunn, Livingstone, and Wyman 2008)

PDIR, the department responsible for recommending the Reference Portfolio design and risk budgets, gained final approval for the risk-budgeting process at the August 2008 meeting of the IPC. Risk budgets are now part of investment department Performance Agreements, which specify the level of returns necessary to meet performance targets and are an integral part of the business planning process.

PDIR kicked off fiscal 2010 risk budgeting in September 2008, 6 months in advance of the start of fiscal 2010. Preliminary meetings were scheduled with each of the investment department heads to discuss business plans for the coming year. It was expected that these discussions would establish the baseline for the fiscal 2010 risk budgets. But CPPIB found itself developing its risk budgets in the midst of a financial perfect storm.

Risk budgeting to a moving target

Capital markets were crumbling, levered investors were selling into a falling market, and regulators were struggling to address systemic issues that threatened to swamp the global financial system. A flight to quality was crushing the equity and credit markets. By the end of September 2008, the S&P 500 had dropped to 1166.36, from its peak of 1565.15 as at October 8, 2007. CPPIB investment returns were −8.5 percent for the quarter ending September 30, 2008.

CPPIB's total portfolio approach meant risk budgeting required forecasts for a number of moving parts. But risk estimates were sensitive to the value of assets held in the portfolio, the volatility of the asset prices, and to the interdependencies between the asset prices. And all of these variables were changing dramatically during the market upheaval. And when correlations between assets increase dramatically during a crisis, diversification benefits disappear.

Private and public equity, for example, were considered a single asset class over the long term and were treated as such when rebalancing the portfolio. But in such volatile markets, how much equity would CPPIB have at the beginning of the coming fiscal year? Public equity was revalued continually, and forecasts readily available, but private equity was revalued infrequently and forecasts were difficult to develop. Public markets, represented by the S&P 500, had dropped a further 22.56 percent between September and December. Would private equity valuations follow? Estimating the starting value of these assets for the coming fiscal year had become challenging.

The markets continued to drop. CPPIB reported third quarter returns as of December 31, 2008 of −6.7 percent – and assets under management were now $108.9B CAD, down from $122.8B CAD at March 31, 2008. Elsewhere, public reports and market intelligence indicated many other funds, in efforts to raise cash, were being forced to sell and realize significant losses. CPPIB management was monitoring the effects of the market downturn on its own balance sheet, as part of an effort to 'keep its powder dry.' Because of its balance sheet flexibility, a luxury lost to many other fund managers, CPPIB management felt well positioned to take advantage of market opportunities in the coming year.

Performance agreements

PMI

The performance agreement for active strategies within PMI included a fixed-dollar risk budget. Consistent with being a purely active manager, PMI was allocated risk, not assets, and so no initial asset value was required to set the fiscal 2010 performance agreement. The level of risk was a stretch target for PMI, intended to encourage PMI to find value-adding opportunities. The return hurdles were set to reward PMI for achieving high quantile realized information ratios (the ratio of excess return relative to risk taken), so that PMI was incentivized to take on only those transactions that were expected to pay for the risks taken.

REI

The REI department was pursuing an opportunistic investment strategy in private real estate, with long-term multiyear objectives. There were a number of phases in the development of the REI performance agreement. Changes in the REI portfolio could arise from changes in the value of existing assets, and from the acquisition of new assets. So PDIR and REI reviewed the real estate deal pipeline, developing a sense of the potential to originate new real estate assets in fiscal 2010. The result was a set of low, mid, and high net new real estate asset origination projects. PDIR and REI then worked to estimate the value of the real estate portfolio at the beginning of fiscal 2010. These two factors, the initial starting value plus the value of net new real estate assets, were used to estimate the low, mid, and high values of the real estate portfolio. PDIR also reviewed the balance sheet implications of these scenarios, including the funding strategies.

PI

The PI group is responsible for private equity, infrastructure, and private debt. PDIR worked with PI to estimate low, mid, and high scenarios for the dollars invested of the private equity, infrastructure, and private debt portfolios. Again, PDIR also reviewed the balance sheet implications of these scenarios, including funding strategies. Once these individual scenarios were developed, PDIR then estimated a number of risk measures associated with these strategies.

Total fund risk budget

PDIR estimated the stand-alone risk measure for each department. These numbers were somewhat comparable to the risk budget allocated to PMI. PDIR then combined the low, mid, and high scenarios of the departments, and then for each resulting scenario measured the risk contribution each department made to the active portfolio and to the total Fund. This analysis provides a sense of the range of risk contributions each department might make. These contribution measures also provide insights into the strategies diversification benefits for the total and active portfolios.

IPC approval

By December, having performed a number of risk-budget iterations in response to the volatile capital markets, CPPIB management had become proficient at updating and revising its risk budget forecasts. In January 2009, the IPC accepted the recommended risk budgets, which anticipated the market would present a number of opportunities as other investors were forced to sell. Board approval was gained in February 2009.

Conclusion

The mission of CPPIB is to safeguard the CPP for 16 million participants by establishing a clear link between investment objectives and outcomes, and between actions and accountability. This chapter has reviewed the CPP and CPPIB's history, and the risk-budgeting design process to illustrate why risk budgeting was seen as an appropriate course of action, as well as why the strict risk-budgeting framework was reworked to fit within the opportunistic business model for illiquid assets in place at CPPIB. Risk budgeting is a familiar construct in the capital market sector, and the PMI group has always worked within a 'risk budget,' looking at the quantitative measures of volatility and risk in the context of investment decisions. The PI and REI

groups have considered the implications of risk in their investment decisions, but on a more qualitative basis. Changing the business model to fit
within a risk-budgeting framework was never considered; rather risk budgeting was changed to fit the business model.

In an environment where risk is a scarce resource, prioritization of scant
resources and increased efficiency in the use of risk can only have positive
implications. While formal risk budgeting has only been in place for a short
time at the CPPIB, it is expected that it will provide real and measurable
benefits. As a management tool, the risk-budgeting process allows CPPIB to
define accountabilities clearly and increase transparency into the trade-offs
implicit in investment decisions.

Notes

[1] This section draws on Little (2008).
[2] Amendments to the Canadian constitution require approval by the Canadian
House of Commons, the Canadian Senate, and two-thirds majority of the provincial legislatures representing at least 50 percent of the population.
[3] The OCA forecasts that no more than approximately 34 percent of investment
earnings will be needed to pay benefits. Real growth is expected to slow, but a sale
of assets is not anticipated.
[4] Although the Stewards' Agreement in 1997 specified a return of 3.8 percent, the
Chief Actuary later determined that a real return of 4.2 percent was necessary.

References

Ambachtsheer, Keith (1996). 'How All Pension Funds Should Be Measured.' *Ambachtsheer Newsletter 130–131*. Toronto, CA: K.P.A Advisory Services.

Arnold, Jennifer, John Ilkiw, Steven James, and James Pesando (2009). 'The Fair
Value of the Canada Pension Plan: The Role of Risk and Cost Structure.' Rotman
Institute Working Paper. Toronto, CA: Rotman School of Management at the
University of Toronto.

Brinson, Gary P., L. Randolph Hood, and Gilbert L. Beebower (1986). 'Determinants of Portfolio Performance,' *Financial Analysts Journal*, 42(4): 45–51.

Brooks, Mike, David Bowie, Martin Cumberworth, Allistari Haig, and Bernie Nelson
(2001). *The Practicalities of Budgeting, Managing and Monitoring Investment Risk for
Pension Funds*. Guernsey, UK: Faculty and Institute of Actuaries, Finance and
Investment Conference. http://www.actuaries.org.uk/__data/assets/pdf_file/
0019/26308/brooks.pdf

Canada Pension Plan Investment Board (CPPIB) (1999). *Annual Report*, Toronto,
CA: CPPIB.

Canada Pension Plan Investment Board (CPPIB) (2008). *Investment Statement,* Toronto, CA: CPPIB.

Canada Pension Plan Investment Board Act (CPPIB Act) (1997). *The Canada Pension Plan Investment Board Act, 1997, c. 40.* Ontario, CA: CPPIB.

de Bever, Leo, Wayne Kozun, Valter Viola, and Barbara Zvan (2000). 'Pension Risk Budgeting: Something Old, Something New, Something Borrowed . . . ,' *Journal of Performance Measurement,* 4(4): n.p.

Gunn, Sterling, Tracy Livingstone, and Oliver Wyman (2008). *Risk Budgeting Governance and Measurement Principles.* Toronto, CA: CPPIB.

Human Resources and Skills Development Canada (HRSDC) (1995). *Phase I of the Evaluation of the Canada Pension Plan (CPP) – July 1995.* Ontario, CA: HRSDC. http://www.hrsdc.gc.ca/eng/cs/sp/sdc/evaluation/sp-ah008e/page07.shtml#fn85

Human Resources Development Canada (HRDC) (1997). *Securing the Canada Pension Plan: Agreement on Proposed Changes to the CPP.* Ontario, CA: HRDC.

Ilkiw, John and Donald Raymond (2005). *Derivation of CPP Reference Portfolio.* Toronto, CA: CPPIB.

James, Steven, (2007). *CPPIB Internal Memo.* Toronto, CA: CPPIB.

Little, Bruce (2008). *Fixing the Future: How Canada's Usually Fractious Governments Worked Together to Rescue the Canada Pension Plan.* Toronto, CA: Rotman/University of Toronto Press.

Pearson, Neil D. (2002). *Risk Budgeting: Portfolio Problem Solving with Value-at-Risk.* New York: John Wiley & Sons.

Raymond, Donald (2009). 'Integrating Goals, Structure, and Decision-Making at the Canada Pension Plan Investment Board,' *Rotman International Journal of Pension Management,* (2)1: 22–9.

Ross, Raymond (2007). *CPPIB Internal Memo.* Toronto, CA: CPPIB.

The Federal, Provincial and Territorial Governments of Canada (TFPTGC) (1996). *An Information Paper for Consultations on the Canada Pension Plan,* Ontario, CA: TFPTGC.

The Office of the Chief Actuary (TOCA) (2006). *Actuarial Report on the Canada Pension Plan as at 31 December 2006.* Ontario, CA: TOCA.

——(2009). *Internal Rates of Return on Contributions: Canadian Pension Plan 1910–1930.* Ontario, CA: TOCA.

Chapter 13

Can VEBAs Alleviate Retiree Health-Care Problems?

Aaron Bernstein

Recent negotiations between the United Auto Workers (UAW) and Detroit automakers have focused attention on a potentially innovative response to the costly problem of retiree health insurance. To alleviate the companies' chronic losses, the union agreed to establish Voluntary Employees' Beneficiary Associations (VEBAs) at General Motors (GM) Corporation, Ford Motor Corporation, and Chrysler Corporation. These nonprofit trusts, which are run by an independent board of trustees, were set up to assume responsibility for UAW retirees' medical care starting in 2010, allowing the three companies to remove a total of more than $100 billion in long-term liability from their books (Maynard and Chapman 2007). When the trusts are up and running, the UAW and its retired members will shoulder the risk of ensuring that the funds are sufficient to cover the cost of future medical inflation. As medical inflation increases the cost of retiree health care, workers increasingly face the issue of how they can pay for it and whether they should try to put aside funds for this purpose along with other post-employment saving.

A Detroit-style employee VEBA poses a complex challenge for labor in both the private and public sectors. Union members in VEBAs funded at least partially by employers enjoy tax breaks denied to nonunion employees. As a result, such trusts can be a tax-efficient way for organized workers to save for post-employment health coverage. However, for unionized employees covered by an employer-paid plan, it may be a second-best option to go along with a GM-style defeasance VEBA, so-called because it allows employers to sever their debt obligations for health-care legacy costs. The first portion of this chapter describes the general history of VEBAs and why they have surfaced as an issue at unionized companies. Next, we examine the advent of stand-alone employee VEBA like those under construction in the auto industry. We then focus on the bargaining trade-offs made by GM and the UAW as they negotiated the new employee VEBA, and how the agreement they reached in 2007 stood up when GM went through a bankruptcy reorganization in 2009. Finally, we look at VEBAs in the larger context of declining retiree health coverage in the United States and discuss ways in which the idea could address the issue for both union and nonunion employees. We also examine how employee VEBAs may apply in the public sector, where many employers face legacy costs as burdensome as those in the auto and steel industries.

Why VEBAs came to the fore

A VEBA is a tax-exempt trust as defined under Section 501(c) (9) of the Internal Revenue Code. Its purpose is to give employers and/or employees a tax-advantaged method for funding not just medical care, but virtually any qualified employee benefit, such as dental care, prescription drugs, life and accident insurance, or vision care. VEBAs even can be used to pay for things like vacations, child care, training, education, legal expenses, or supplemental unemployment benefits (Richardson and Salemi 2007). They can do so not just for employees but also for their spouses and dependents.

Federal law sets low limits on how much money employers and employees can put into a VEBA for nonunion workers, which restricts their usefulness for most of the US workforce. But for those who qualify, they offer one of the best tax breaks available. If set up properly, contributions by employers and employees alike are not taxed going in, any earnings the trust makes over the years are not taxed, and the money withdrawn to cover a retiree's medical care is not taxed either (Richardson and Salemi 2007). This surpasses the tax benefits available through conventional retirement plans such as a pension or 401(k), whose distributions in retirement are fully taxable.

VEBAs also are remarkably flexible. They can be set up as individual accounts akin to a 401(k), in which contributions are made by the employer, the employee, or both. Or they can be a 'commingled trust' that functions more like a traditional defined benefit (DB) pension and pays a fixed dollar amount to cover qualified benefits. Companies also can use a hybrid approach, in which the trust is funded by a defined contribution (DC) such as a lump sum, yet pays the premiums of a traditional health plan. Employers can decide whether to fund a VEBA themselves or require employees to pay part or all of the contribution. Some VEBAs in the public sector even use sick days or other compensable time off as a funding source. The employer contributes the value of the time off, either annually or on a onetime basis when the employee retires (Richardson and Salemi 2007).

Most of the 11,996 VEBAs in existence as of 2008 were set up by employers as tax-advantaged funding schemes (IRS 2008). A VEBA board selects professional investment managers and investment vehicles and decides on distribution options and levels (NCPERS 2006). The new VEBAs at the auto companies will be run independently of the companies. Although called stand-alone or employee VEBAs to emphasize the point that employees bear all the risk that the employer has severed, these trusts are legal entities separate from both the employer and the union.

VEBAs first appeared in the early twentieth century as a way for workers to fund insurance for life, health, and accident, as well as other benefits that employers typically did not cover at the time. After several courts decided that they should be taxed, Congress granted them tax-exempt status in 1928 (McGuinness 2007). The tax rules changed several times in subsequent decades, most drastically in 1984. That year, Congress imposed low limits on how much employers could contribute to a VEBA and required companies to pay unrelated business income tax on any annual gains earned on funds exceeding the limits. The purpose was to crack down on companies abusing VEBAs as tax shelters (Schultz and Francis 2007).

Nevertheless, VEBAs at unionized employers remained exempt from the restrictions, so workers there can make tax-free contributions and receive tax-free benefits from the VEBA (Employee Benefit Research Institute 2005). As a result, these have remained popular at companies with large unionized workforces in both the public and private sectors. The trusts have been especially prevalent in industries such as utilities, where the annual employer contributions can be built into the rate base, and in defense, where companies can build them into cost-plus federal contracts (Schultz and Francis 2007). Typically, employers use them to pre-fund their long-term retiree health obligations. VEBAs also are used for this purpose by multiemployer health and welfare plans, which usually involve a union that has set up a plan covering members at multiple companies.

VEBAs are attractive to companies for another reason as well. Just like a corporate pension fund, any extra returns earned by the company-sponsored plan are included in a company's bottom line (assuming the plan is a traditional one and not the newer stand-alone variety such as in the auto industry). For example, Procter & Gamble Company's VEBA added more than $600 million to the company's earnings in 2005 and 2006 (Schultz and Francis 2007). Indeed, despite the 1984 limitations, the number of VEBAs in the United States more than doubled in the 1970s and 1980s, reaching a peak of 15,048 in 1993 (Figure 13.1).

While few employer surveys shed light on the reasons for this growth, it likely stemmed, in part, from companies' desires to save funds to defray the mounting costs of an aging workforce, especially in mature unionized industries. Retirees also were living longer, further ratcheting up a long-term obligation that employers could use VEBAs to fund. It was this

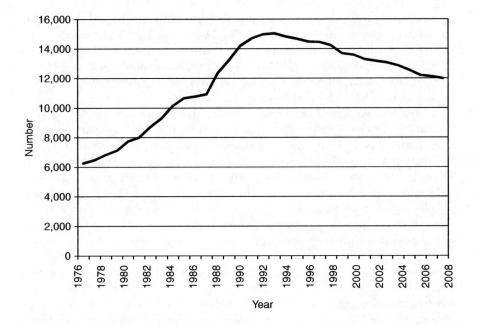

Figure 13.1 Number of Voluntary Employees' Beneficiary Associations (VEBAs) in the United States, 1976–2008. *Source*: Author's calculations using IRS (various years).

swelling long-term liability that eventually led employers to the idea of using VEBAs to transfer retiree health responsibility to union members.

This notion stems back to a 1990 regulatory action that for the first time required employers to record retiree health obligations as a corporate obligation. Until then, most employers simply paid the annual cost of retiree health premiums out of their general budgets, an approach often called 'pay-as-you-go' financing. But that year, the Financial Accounting Standards Board, which provides guidelines for the financial reports of public corporations, issued Financial Accounting Statement (FAS) No. 106 (Fronstin 2005). Starting in late 1992, FAS 106 required companies to use what is called an 'actuarial accounting method,' which requires them to record a liability on their books for the total cost of all unfunded retiree medical obligation. Put another way, companies had to state the present value of what they would need to pay in the future for all retiree health coverage, both for retirees and active workers.

Even before FAS 106 focused attention on the issue, concerns over swelling legacy costs had begun to degrade the credit ratings and stock values of employers with large ratios of retirees to active workers. But the

FAS move had a profound impact on employer-paid retiree health benefit offerings. As a result, many corporations had decided that the expense was simply too large and had begun abolishing retiree health insurance. Much of the retrenchment came among large employers which had always been more likely to offer retiree coverage than smaller ones (Fronstin 2005).

FAS 106 heightened the concern by requiring employers to post a liability on their balance sheet that for many large corporations ran into the millions or even billions. Some companies responded by taking a onetime charge against their earnings. Other chose to stretch out the cost over many years (Employee Benefit Research Institute 2005); a few were even forced into bankruptcy (Richardson and Salemi 2007). Some experts believe this helped to accelerate the decline in retiree coverage. Employer-paid insurance for early retirees, who need it the most before Medicare kicks in, was offered by 46 percent of companies with 500 or more employees in 1993 but only 28 percent in 2004 (Fronstin 2005). Since then, the number of VEBAs has drifted downward as well, to 11,996 in 2008 (IRS 2008).

Some private firms that elected to continue paying for retiree health benefits decided to use VEBAs to pre-fund the obligations, as did some public-sector employers (Employee Benefit Research Institute 2005). GM itself had set up an internal VEBA years ago, long before it asked the UAW to take over responsibility for retiree coverage. By the time the 2007 round of bargaining began, GM had put away $16 billion into this preexisting VEBA (GM Corporation 2007*b*).

Stand-alone employee VEBAs

The new employee VEBAs used by the three auto companies to shed legacy costs have taken a different form from the traditional VEBA. These new ones are DC trusts, into which the company puts a specified set of assets to be used to cover all future benefits. Unlike a traditional pension or a DB VEBA, a stand-alone VEBA carries no guarantee by the employer of a certain level of benefits, leaving employees to bear the risk that the assets will not keep pace with future medical inflation.

A tax lawyer's phrase for what the auto companies have sought to do is 'defeasance,' which means setting aside assets to void a debt obligation. Management-side labor lawyers dislike the term, since many companies have asserted that retiree health is not a legal obligation at all. From management's perspective, the cost being shifted is one that many companies voluntarily took upon themselves and therefore represents a decision they are free to reverse at any time.

Employers' legal right to stop paying for retiree health has long been a point of contention between labor and management. Companies face fewer legal hurdles for doing so than they do with pensions, since welfare benefits such as retiree health do not vest under the Employee Retirement Income Security Act of 1974 (ERISA). As a result, the question of whether a company has incurred a legal obligation by offering retiree health coverage over the years depends on the specific facts of what it told employees over the years (Macey and O'Donnell 2003). The issue has been litigated at many companies, with labor prevailing in some instances and management in others. The outcome usually depends on whether employer statements and other actions can be construed as an explicit or implied promise to continue health coverage throughout employees' retirement (Macey and O'Donnell 2003).

While this legal uncertainty can make it difficult for employers to shed retiree health coverage for unionized workers, it is far easier to do so when a company enters bankruptcy. Seeking court protection from debtors allows companies to reduce or eliminate almost all debts, which can obviate the issue of whether retiree health is a legal obligation or not. After dozens of steelmakers failed starting in the late 1990s, more than 200,000 United Steelworker (USW) retirees and their dependents lost coverage as their companies either restructured their debts or simply went out of business (USW 2003).

As a result, most defeasance VEBAs have been set up at companies that have either entered bankruptcy or faced the prospect of doing so (Ghilarducci 2008). The UAW was involved in one of the earliest examples of this, which was a VEBA set up in 1992 during the bankruptcy of International Harvester Company (now called Navistar International Corporation). The company put $500 million into the trust, enough to cover about half of the projected liabilities, and it promised to pay more in subsequent years. This trust continues to cover retirees, whose benefits have increased although co-pays have risen somewhat (Welch and Byrnes 2007). Other experiences have not fared as well, such as a VEBA the UAW agreed to at Detroit Diesel Corporation that has already run out of cash (O'Conner 2007).

One of the most innovative uses of a VEBA involved an effort by the USW union to salvage medical coverage lost following bankruptcies in the steel industry. The effort, which started with the former LTV Corporation and eventually came to involve three other bankrupt steel companies, illustrates how VEBAs like those in the auto industry are typically part of a larger set of bargaining trade-offs unions and employers make to balance the interests of the employer as well as active and retired workers. In 2001, LTV went into bankruptcy and began selling its assets; most of its workforce was laid off, and retirees lost their health insurance.

To save what it could, the USW began negotiating with investor Wilbur L. Ross who sought to buy some of the company's nearly shuttered steel mills. In exchange for supporting his purchase the following year, the union agreed to weaker work rules that allowed Ross's newly formed International Steel Group (ISG) Incorporated to reopen the mills with fewer workers, higher productivity, and lower labor costs. The union also agreed that ISG could buy LTV's physical assets, leaving the $2.3 billion in retiree pension and health obligations that had been a factor in the former company's demise to a shell company with insufficient assets to cover them. The agreement left 70,000 retirees and dependents with no recourse except to apply to the Pension Benefit Guaranty Corporation (PBGC), which guarantees a portion of employee pension payments in case of bankruptcies. They had no similar recourse for health coverage, which is not protected by the PBGC (Arndt 2003; Byrnes 2003). In return, Ross agreed to rehire laid-off LTV workers as the company recovered and to negotiate a new labor pact with the USW. The deal eventually came to cover Bethelem Steel Corporation, Acme Metals Incorporated, and Georgetown Steel (Ross sold ISG and the company name was changed to ArcelorMittal USA).

Although the union's priority was to save as many jobs as possible, it also negotiated an unusual VEBA with Ross that, as of 2009, provided limited health coverage for the four companies' retirees. Because ISG, as it was know then, had no profits and an uncertain future when the USW reached the agreement in 2002, the two sides decided the company could not afford to make any hard commitments to retiree health benefits. Instead, it set up a VEBA that is funded by a percentage of operating cash flow per ton of steel shipped (USW 2002). The arrangement paid nothing until 2005, when the trust had accumulated enough money to start modest benefit coverage. Initially retirees got prescription drug coverage for a co-pay of $10 a month (USW 2006). The following year, as the company continued to earn profits, the VEBA's assets swelled to $469 million, enough to allow it to pick up the tab for part of retirees' Medicare Part B premium (Mittal Steel USA 2006). The trust earned enough to repeat the benefit in 2007 (USW 2007a).

While such benefits are better than nothing, they are a far cry from full coverage. The trust has not been able to build up a fund like those being established in Detroit and at Goodyear, which will be able to guarantee at least some level of benefits for many years. Instead, coverage for Arcelor-Mittal retirees will fluctuate with the company's fortunes (USW 2007b).

How GM and the UAW split cost and risk

While the USW's experience at ArcelorMittal exemplifies how the innovative use of a VEBA can aid retirees who would have otherwise lost all coverage, GM's defeasance VEBA offers more lessons likely to be of use to a broad cross-section of unions and employers. The primary obstacle faced by employers that hope to shed a retiree health burden, in addition to prevailing upon their unions to agree, is to find enough assets to fund the trust at a level that would be likely to cover future medical inflation. For unions, the key issue is ensuring that the trust will be funded as fully as possible. During the 2007 negotiations, GM and the UAW devised a package of creative financing options that allowed them to reach a middle ground on this central question.

This carefully crafted arrangement came undone in 2009 after the global economic crisis led GM and Chrysler (although not Ford) to seek assistance from the US government (Bunkley 2009). As part of that process, the government asked the companies to substitute company stock for up to half of the cash contributions the firms had agreed to make to the VEBAs set up in 2007 (GM Corporation 2009*a*, 2009*b*). Subsequently, both GM and Chrysler declared bankruptcy. Chrysler emerged in June through a complex deal that split ownership in the new company in three ways. First, the US government received an 8 percent stake in exchange for its $9 billion in loans; second, Fiat got a 20 percent share for providing Chrysler with small-car designs and engines it can build and sell in the United States; and third, the VEBA received 55 percent (Linebaugh 2009). Despite the VEBA's majority share, the UAW agreed that Fiat and the government could name all of Chrysler's new board of directors except one, which the union chose itself. The following month GM also emerged from bankruptcy via a similar restructuring deal. The new company's ownership was split four ways, with the US government getting 60.8 percent, the VEBA receiving 17.5 percent, the Canadian and Ontario governments, which contributed bailout funds, getting 11.7 percent, and the old GM keeping 10 percent (GM Corporation 2009*a*).

The substitution of stock for cash contributions from the companies drastically altered the 2007 contract regarding the VEBAs, placing substantially more risk onto UAW members and retirees. Still, the existence of the VEBA gave the union a much stronger hand to play when GM and Chrysler declared bankruptcy. The companies had entered into legal obligations with the VEBA trusts that were more difficult for them to abrogate than might have been the case if they had only had the prior disputed obligations to cover retiree health costs. As tangible legal entities, the VEBAs gave the union a powerful bargaining tool that allowed them to extract equity on an equal footing with the US and Canadian governments and Fiat, ahead of GM and Chrysler bondholders. Without this privileged position, it is possible that UAW retirees could have lost more or even all of the retiree health benefits they had fought for over the years.

The intricate compromises the companies and the union reached when they agreed to the VEBAs in 2007 shed light on the relatively powerful bargaining position the UAW enjoyed when bankruptcy hit. The middle ground they found then also covered a range of sensitive issues that others would face in a similar process, including how much of the funding expense would be borne by the company, by active workers, and by retires. An examination of how these compromises allowed the parties to structure and fund the new VEBA offers insights applicable to other industries. Its flexibility in the face of the auto industry's near-collapse a year later is instructive as well. Not every union or employer would want or be able to emulate every tactic, but any that pursue a defeasance VEBA would be well served to learn from the UAW's experience at GM.

The GM VEBA created in 2007 came about in very different circumstances from those at ArcelorMittal. It represents the culmination of a long struggle by GM to shed its legacy costs. Successive CEOs at the company had argued that ballooning UAW pension and health-care payments had crippled the company's ability to compete. In many ways, this argument confuses cause and effect. After all, the company's market share slid from 40 percent of the US market 20 years ago to just 25.5 percent in 2007 largely because of its inability to design vehicles that were more appealing than those offered by Japanese rivals (Sixth Circuit Court of Appeals 2007). The market share loss prompted the company to shed hundreds of thousands of workers, which in turn lifted the ratio of retirees to active workers to unsustainable levels.

Whatever the cause, GM, Ford, and Chrysler all still bore the burden of the enormous sums they expend on legacy costs. GM has frequently pointed out in recent years that it is the single largest purchaser of health care in the United States, providing coverage to 1,100,000 active and retired workers and their dependents. The $5.4 billion GM spent on health care in 2005, more than two-thirds for retirees, added $1,045 to the average cost of a GM vehicle. By contrast, its Japanese rivals paid just $450 per vehicle on all health-care benefits, for active workers and retirees alike (Sixth Circuit Court of Appeals 2007).

GM first prevailed on the UAW to reduce retiree health cost in 2005. In an unusual mid-contract concession, the union agreed to changes including higher co-pays and deductibles that cut $17 billion off the company's $67.6 billion retiree health-care obligation (Sixth Circuit Court of Appeals 2007). As part of that deal, it agreed to give up $5.6 billion worth of negotiated future wage hikes and cost-of-living adjustments (COLAs). In return, the company offset a portion of the cutbacks by setting up a DC VEBA funded with three $1 billion payments through 2011, plus at least $30 million a year in profit-sharing payments and additional payments based on increases in GM's stock price (GM Corporation 2007a). This trust was called a 'mitigation VEBA' because it severed only a portion of the company's retiree health obligation, not all of it as the 2007 defeasance VEBA was designed to do. During these negotiations, GM retained responsibility for UAW retiree health coverage, which it will not once the 2007 stand-alone VEBA takes effect in 2010.

An analysis of why the UAW agreed to this extraordinary move sheds light on its subsequent acceptance of the 2007 VEBA. The threats that prompted the UAW to make both concessions were largely the same. In 2005, GM was struggling with deepening financial and competitive woes. Its stock had fallen by more than half, from $53 in 2003 to $19 at the beginning of 2005, and its credit rating had been slashed to junk status (Sixth Circuit Court of Appeals 2007). To address the problem, management closed or idled factories, laid off 37,000 employees, and cut executive salaries and dividends to shareholders. It also demanded that the UAW agree to steep reductions in retiree health benefits. When the union refused, GM threatened to impose them unilaterally, leaving the union with a difficult decision. It could agree to bargain over the mid-contract cuts in the hope of minimizing them, or it could refuse outright and sue if GM cut them on its own. The downside to the latter strategy was that if GM prevailed in court, management could emerge with the unilateral right to eliminate retiree health benefits altogether.

A second threat the UAW faced was that a victory in court could turn out to be a Pyrrhic one. In light of Wall Street's negative view of GM's future, bankruptcy was a distinct possibility should the UAW prevail in a legal battle over legacy costs. If that happened, as the Sixth Circuit Court of Appeals pithily pointed out in a ruling on the legality of the 2005 cuts: '. . . it is well to remember that the Federal Government's Pension Benefit Guaranty Corporation, which provides *pension* guarantees for the employees and retirees of financially distressed companies, has no sister agency that provides the same guarantees for retiree *healthcare* benefits' (Sixth Circuit Court of Appeals 2007). In other words, if GM declared bankruptcy, retirees could lose more than the $17 billion cutbacks the company demanded in 2005, perhaps even all their health coverage. In light of these twin threats, the UAW decided that saving some benefits was better than the risk involved in giving no ground at all.

The UAW made largely the same calculation during the 2007 contract talks. However, this time, the two sides were discussing a full-scale defeasance VEBA that would take the entire remaining retiree health obligation off GM's books. The UAW insisted that in exchange for workers assuming the responsibility for future coverage, the company had to fully fund the trust. The arrangement the two sides eventually agreed on was based on an intricate series of compromises. It allocated some of the funding cost to the company and some to active workers (retirees were spared any further

immediate cuts on top of the ones they suffered after the 2005 concessions). It also split the risks the VEBA would entail for retirees between GM
and union members. Overall, the agreement allowed the UAW to assure its
members that they had wrested enough funding out of GM to ensure full
coverage for retirees (although only for what remained after the $17 billion
reduction in 2005). Yet it did so in a fashion that GM thought at the time
that it could afford, even its distressed circumstances.

The middle ground the parties reached in 2007 came on two levels: the
amount of the funding to be split between GM and union members, and
the key financial assumptions to be employed in the funding calculations.
The latter entailed an assessment of the costs the VEBA would incur, as well
as the returns its assets could be expected to realize to pay for future retiree
coverage. To arrive at a cost figure, the two sides had to decide what rate of
medical inflation to use. Since standard actuarial projections for retiree
health obligations range over 80 years, even a percentage point can have a
huge effect on the size of the total cost. Eventually, the two sides settled on
5 percent as a long-term average for US health-care cost increases (GM
Corporation 2007a).

At first blush, this seems wildly optimistic given the double-digit increases
of recent years. Yet many experts use something in that ballpark for long-
term projections, on the assumption that the current pace is simply unsustainable over many decades.[1] Still, by agreeing to what today seems like a
relatively low assumption, the UAW made the sum to be funded more
affordable to GM. In doing so, it also may have heightened the risk that
the VEBA will face shortfalls, especially in the short to medium term, for
which retirees and the union will be responsible. Those risks will heighten
drastically if GM follows Ford's lead in 2009 and substitutes stock for half of
the funding it had agreed to in 2007.

The 5 percent medical inflation assumption resulted in a present-value
estimate of GM's long-term retiree health obligation that totaled roughly
$47 billion in 2007 (GM Corporation 2007a). This figure represented the
cost as of that time of covering all current retirees and their dependents, as
well as all currently active UAW members at GM and their dependents. It
excluded any new hires GM might make in the future, who will not be part
of the new VEBA. Union members hired after September 2007 will receive
$1 per compensated hour that will go toward covering their retiree health-
care costs, a significant reduction in benefits compared to existing UAW
members (GM Corporation 2007a).

The UAW also agreed to a relatively generous figure for the second
critical financial assumption, about projected returns. Just as the 5 percent
medical inflation assumption made the long-term cost more manageable
for GM, a high assumed rate of return allowed the two sides to put up less
money to meet that cost. Ultimately, the two sides settled on 9 percent,

TABLE 13.1 Funding for the General Motors (GM) 2007 Voluntary Employee Benefit Association (VEBA)

Source	Amount ($ billions)
Panel 1: From GM	
Transfer from existing VEBA	16.0
Cost of paying retiree health until VEBA starts in 2010	5.4
Convertible note	4.37
Backstop payments	1.74
Excess pension funds	1.7
2005 payment due in 2011	1.0
Subtotal	30.21
Panel 2: From the United Auto Workers	
Diverted 2005 wage hikes and cost of living adjustments	5.6
Diverted 2007 wage hikes and cost of living adjustments	2.5
Subtotal	8.1
Total	38.31

Source: Author's calculations derived from General Motors Corporation (2007*a*, 2007*b*).

even though GM said it would employ a much more pessimistic 6 percent on its own books.[2] The higher figure meant that GM only needed to come up with about $38 billion, instead of $47 billion, for the VEBA to be considered fully funded.[3]

This 9 percent rate of return was probably a reasonable assumption for both sides (perhaps even after the market crash that began in the fall of 2008). While GM's own accounting assumption of 6 percent suggested that it may be optimistic, the rate is actually a bit less than the 10 percent long-term average that stocks have returned over the decades. Since the VEBA trust is designed to last for many decades, it made sense to use a rate matching that time horizon (or it seemed so prior to the 2008 market crash). However, it did mean that the trust lacked a large cushion to buffer the inevitable fluctuations in returns, much less a full-scale collapse such as occurred in 2008. If returns slump for many years, trust officials may be forced to reduce benefits at least temporarily, until the stock markets recover.

The two sides reached another series of intricate compromises in 2007 on the divisive issue of how much each of them would contribute toward the $38 billion in required funding. In some sense, union members paid for the entire sum, since the contributions GM agreed to make were given in exchange for job, wage, and work-rule concessions. Still, GM agreed to put up slightly more than $30 billion of the total directly, while UAW workers agreed to pay for the remaining $8 billion by diverting future pay hikes into the VEBA. Next, we offer more detail on each party's contributions (see also Table 13.1).

Sources of GM's Contribution

GM's financial cost was made easier by the $16 billion already saved in the internal VEBA it had set up years ago. The money served as a convenient base on which to build the new defeasance VEBA. Much of the rest of GM's contribution came from financial moves that also will not require new cash outlays by the financially strapped company. The two sides agreed to count as part of the VEBA funding the $5.4 billion GM will pay to continue the current DB retiree health plan through the end of 2009, until the new VEBA is up and running (the start date was set for January 1, 2010.)

The UAW accepted another $4.3725 billion in the form of a note convertible to GM stock. After the note was issued in January 2008, it will require GM to make semiannual interest payments to the trust. Six months before the note matures in 5 years, the trust will have the right to convert it into about 109 million shares of GM stock, based on a $40 conversion price. It can do so before if GM shares exceed $48. While the note is not a straight stock grant, it is also not as solid as cash and thus introduces more uncertainty into the VEBA's long-term financial outlook. For example, if GM declared bankruptcy, the note would rank as unsecured and unsubordinated debt. As a result, it would stand a lower chance of full recovery relative to more senior debt and might well be all but wiped out, a common occurrence with such debt in bankruptcy.

Similarly, if the trust converts the note into GM shares, their value would fluctuate with the market price. In a bankruptcy, their worth would very likely fall close to zero. In addition, the agreement puts strict limits on the VEBA's ability to convert the note. For example, it cannot be sold or even hedged until 2010 without GM's consent. After that date, the trust only can sell about half of the note or converted stock per year. And it cannot sell more than 2 percent of it to one owner. Another significant restriction requires the trust to vote the stock in the same proportion as all other GM shareholders, which effectively deprives the VEBA (and hence the union, which appoints the trustees) of the ownership power to exercise corporate governance rights over GM.

Of course, the note offers the VEBA a potential upside, just as any stock ownership does. The trust stands to gain more than $1 billion for every $10 increase in GM shares over the $40 conversion price. In addition, such a large ownership stake – 109 million shares will represent about 16 percent of GM's outstanding stock – will link the UAW to GM in a new way. A recent Citigroup report said: 'We view the UAW's willingness to accept a $4.4 billion convertible note...as a positive seeing that both sides' interests should be better aligned going forward. The UAW's desire to hold an equity-linked security in the VEBA may also suggest that the union sees future upside potential in GM shares' (Michaeli, Randow, and Reenock 2007).

To allay UAW concerns that the trust might not earn enough to cover future costs, GM has also agreed to make $1.74 billion in twenty annual contingency payments, with the first $165 million guaranteed to be paid in April 2008. These constitute a backstop to take effect if the VEBA's returns fall below projections. GM further agreed to make a payment in any year in which the trust's cash flow projection shows that it lacks enough money to cover all benefit costs over the ensuing 25 years. Nevertheless, even before the 2008 market crash threw out all of the 2007 cost projections, it was likely that the company would have been required to make most or all of the payments, since they were included in the union's analysis that $38 billion would fully fund current retiree health benefits over the long term (UAW 2007).

Another $1.7 billion came from what appeared to be an innovative maneuver to tap excess cash in GM's pension plan. In 2003, the company injected $13.5 billion into the plan from a bond offering and another $5 billion from selling its stake in Hughes Electronics (Sloan 2005). By 2007, the pension was overfunded by $17 billion (Michaeli, Randow, and Reenock 2007), but under federal pension rules the overfunding was insufficient to allow GM to withdraw money to use for the VEBA. Instead, the union agreed to require retirees to contribute $51.67 a month to the VEBA, and offset the cost by a grant GM will make of a special monthly pension increase of $66.70 (GM Corporation 2007b). The pension pass-through, as it is called, was expected to generate $1.7 billion for the VEBA (in present-value terms) at no cost to retirees.

A last part of the funding from GM came from the final $1 billion payment due in 2011 that GM had promised during the 2005 mid-contract cutbacks, which the parties agreed to count toward the new VEBA.

Sources of UAW's Contributions

Union members' largest sacrifice for the VEBA came from the $5.6 billion in wage hikes and COLAs it had agreed in 2005 to divert to retiree health care, to offset the $17 billion in cuts made that year. The UAW also granted GM the option of spreading out the payments over 13 years.[4] During negotiations over the new VEBA in 2007, the UAW agreed to redirect

additional wage and COLA increases it had negotiated, which added another $2.5 billion.

These complex series of compromises made sense in 2007, before the
global recession hit in 2008. By the time the UAW agreed to accept stock for
up to half of what Ford had agreed to put up for the VEBA it had agreed to
in 2007, GM was essentially bankrupt and on life support from the US
government (Bunkley 2009). At this point, the UAW faced a calculation
similar to the one it made in 2007, although a more drastic one. It could
agree to take more stock to fund the VEBAs at the three companies,
dramatically increasing the likelihood that retirees would face steep benefit
cuts should the companies recover slowly, as seemed probable. Or it could
refuse and risk a bankruptcy filing that would very likely end all retiree
health coverage.

One of the few positive conclusions about the events of 2009 is that they
illustrated the remarkably flexible nature of VEBAs. At all three auto
companies, UAW retirees now face a much greater risk that they would
not receive the health coverage anticipated when the VEBA was agreed on
in 2007. Yet they do still have a trust fund, and if the economy and the
company recover, it is possible that they could enjoy everything agreed on
back then. GM's situation was more dire than Ford's in 2009, as was
Chrysler's, but the VEBA structure gives retirees there at least the possibility
of future coverage. Without it, they almost certainly would be left with
nothing after the companies' near collapse.

Furthermore, it is entirely possible that the companies may not have
freed themselves of their retiree obligations despite the elaborate effort
represented by the defeasance VEBAs. For example, the agreement the
UAW and GM reached in 2007 stated that

The UAW and the Covered Group may not negotiate to increase any of the funding
obligations set out herein. The UAW also agrees not to seek to obligate GM to: (i)
provide any additional contributions to the New VEBA; (ii) make any other payments for the purpose of providing Retiree Medical Benefits to the Covered Group;
or (iii) provide Retiree Medical Benefits through any other means to the covered
Group. (GM Corporation 2007*b*)

Presumably, such explicit language is sufficient to convince the Securities
and Exchange Commission that GM no longer will bear responsibility for
UAW retiree medical coverage and therefore can wipe the billions in FAS
106 debt off its books.

It should also be noted that, directly following the earlier language, was a
second sentence which said: 'Provided, that, to the extent that may be
proposed by the UAW, employees are permitted to make contributions to
the New VEBA of amounts otherwise payable in profit sharing, COLA,
wages and/or signing bonuses'(GM Corporation 2007*b*). This second

clause left open the door to new bargaining over retiree health in the future. If the current contract helps GM to prosper again, as it was designed to do, there appears to be little to stop the UAW from demanding pay or profit-sharing increases large enough to satisfy active workers and still leave some left over for the VEBA.

In fact, from the perspective of GM's legal position, its entire battle for the defeasance VEBA would seem to have changed nothing. The company maintained in court that it never had a legal obligation to pay for retiree health care and could terminate it at any time. In this view, the only reason management kept spending billions every year was to avoid a strike by the union. That is exactly the position GM will be in once the new VEBA is set up: the union will be free to threaten work actions to extract promised payments for retiree care that could easily mount into the billions again. The company's legal theory was never tested by the courts, and it is entirely possible that the union would have prevailed in its view that retiree health benefits were indeed a legal debt GM was obligated to cover. Even so, there would appear to be little to prevent the UAW from demanding more payments from a healthy GM in the future.

VEBAs such as those set up in Detroit present a mixed set of problems for unions. They do offer several advantages over employer-provided insurance, most significantly, they put workers in the driver's seat. The GM model will be a stand-alone entity controlled by a board of five UAW-appointed trustees and six public ones whose sole responsibility will be to the beneficiaries (UAW 2008). The trustees can choose a mix of benefits that best suit workers' needs without input from employers. Such stand-alone VEBAs also can help protect both active and retired union members from cutbacks by employers. In addition, such trusts can offer a fair degree of insulation from employer bankruptcy, depending on how well funded they are and how much employer stock they hold. But the disadvantages could very well outweigh these gains.

The flip side of the control an employee VEBA conveys to workers is the risk it brings. When employers pay for retiree health benefits, they bear the cost of future medical inflation. With a stand-alone VEBA, workers and retirees do. If trust assets fail to earn enough to keep pace, as seemed highly likely with the automakers in early 2009, unions will need to make the painful decisions about how to cope. Employees also must deal with any financial deficiencies or even failures caused by mismanagement of an employee VEBA. Employee VEBAs can lead to an even greater level of risk if they are set up from the beginning with insufficient funds. If a union has the clout to convince employers to set up fully funded VEBAs, the independence they offer conceivably might be worth the extra risk. But even prosperous unionized companies may seek VEBAs that sever their retiree health obligations at a discount.

In sum, however, even less than fully funded defeasance VEBAs may be better than the alternative. Both GM and Goodyear threatened to reduce retiree health coverage or eliminate it altogether if they did not agree to sever the company's retiree health liability. Given the uncertainties that would be involved in litigation over such actions, unions facing them run a very real risk of losing all retiree coverage. Similarly, a VEBA half funded by stock in threatened companies is highly risky, but perhaps better than nothing at all.

Discussion

Experts have long suggested that the VEBA concept could also help other employers and employees better manage the mounting cost of retiree health insurance (Macey and O'Donnell 2003; Richardson and Salemi 2007). For instance, public-sector employers may attempt to use VEBAs to shake off burdensome legacy costs, as some analysts began urging them to do after GM succeeded (Miller 2007). But given the different political dynamics of government employment, defeasance could be even more difficult for them to achieve than it has been for corporations. Public-sector legacy-cost pressure is strikingly similar to that in the private sector, though many public employers have focused on the issue only recently. Some estimates peg the total unfunded public-sector liability for retiree health benefits at close to $1 trillion (Miller 2007). The subject has gained new urgency due to the same kind of mandate to report these unfunded obligations that FAS 106 placed on private companies. Several years ago, the Governmental Accounting Standards Board (GASB), the FASB equivalent for state and local governments, issued new standards called Statements Number 43 and Number 45. For fiscal years beginning after December 2006, these require public employers to report their full retiree health liability to taxpayers just as corporations must do, creating similar pressure on them to deal with the problem (Segal Bulletin 2004). Some have already set up internal VEBAs or other pre-funding schemes to cope with the newly visible liability.[5] For example, of the 41 states that pay for some or all retiree health coverage, 30 use the pay-as-you-go method, while 11 pre-fund (Wisniewski and Wisniewski 2004). All those not pre-funding, including counties, municipalities, and other local entities, now must struggle with how to respond to the new accounting rules.

Though the cost burden on some public employers may be just as crushing as it is on some private ones, the response is different. To begin with, public entities do not pay taxes, so there is no tax advantage to them in setting up a tax-free trust like a VEBA. The political nature of governments also poses potential barriers to defeasance that corporations do not face. The beneficiaries usually are voters, which gives them opportunities to object to such efforts that private-sector workers do not have. In addition, most states and larger counties and cities pay for Medicaid, public hospitals, and other public health programs that service the indigent. So if a public entity did curtail retiree health-care coverage, leaving some retirees unable to cover medical expenses, the public sector could find itself picking up some of the tab anyway. Such concerns could make it difficult to emulate the automakers and remove future hires from a retiree health plan.

Still, public employers do have powerful incentives to pre-fund retiree health through a VEBA or other plan, even if they cannot sever the liability through a defeasance approach. Those that continue the pay-as-you-go approach as large future obligations appear on their books may have to pay more to borrow, if the bond market deems them less creditworthy and requires higher interest rates on future efforts to raise money in the capital markets. Pre-funding also could lead to future cost saving. Although setting up a trust requires higher outlays than continuing to make annual payments, as the trust starts to earn a return, the investment income will cover more of the cost. Eventually, pre-funding even could lead to lower yearly outlays (Wisniewski and Wisniewski 2004).

In addition, pre-funding allows public entities to post a lower liability on their books. It does not alter the actual amount they must pay out to retirees in future years, but GASB's accounting rules require governments using pay-as-you-go accounting to use short-term interest rates to calculate the obligation (Segal Bulletin 2005). By contrast, if they set aside money in a trust like a VEBA, they can use long-term rates, which typically are higher. Doing so cuts the size of the measured obligation, just as GM was able to do by using a 9 percent return assumption with the UAW instead of the 6 percent it used with Wall Street. The rationale is that money not in a trust is not necessarily going to be available for long-term investments that historically earn higher average returns.

These benefits must be weighed against the extra up-front outlays that pre-funding requires. Such investments can be extremely expensive, up to 10 times as much as what is required on a pay-as-you-go basis (Segal Public Sector Letter 2007a). Public entities spend their annual budgets on education, police, or other services. Pre-funding retiree health benefits requires them to divert scarce resources from these other needs, often essential ones, which many may be reluctant to do. Similarly, many governments have other long-term obligations to fund such as bonds floated to build roads or schools, and they may not want to sink resources into retiree health coverage instead. In addition, the funds put in a VEBA trust cannot be tapped should a budget deficit or other fiscal crisis hit in the future.

VEBA pre-funding also raises difficult issues of intergenerational equity among taxpayers. When a city or state uses pay-as-you-go accounting for retiree medical coverage, current taxpayers usually are paying for services enjoyed by prior generations of taxpayers. They are also usually shifting costs for workers serving them today onto tomorrow's taxpayers. No generation necessarily comes out ahead or behind, since the cost each bears depends on medical inflation and the relative level of service provided in each era (Wisniewski and Wisniewski 2004). A VEBA or other pre-funding scheme sets up a system in which each taxpayer generation comes closer to paying for the deferred compensation of the employees whose service they receive. This could be perceived as enhanced intergenerational equity. Of course, even if it is, one or more generations must pay the transition costs required for the initial pre-funding payments. It is also difficult to make accurate predictions about medical inflation and other assumptions, which could place too much cost on a particular generation.

For workers in the private sector, VEBA tax advantages could prove beneficial depending on the circumstances of their employment. Under current law, even organized workers' VEBA contributions are taxable if the trust is funded entirely by employees (although the earnings the trust makes accumulate tax-free just like a retirement account; see Macey and O'Donnell 2003). One way to extend the full tax break to them would be for the employer to contribute, even if the amount were small. Failing that, it is possible that an employer could emulate GM and Goodyear, and divert wage hikes and/or profit-sharing into a VEBA. Although such funds would come out of the pockets of employees, it would be by far the most tax-friendly way for them to save for retiree coverage. However, this model has not been tested, and it is possible that the Internal Revenue Service (IRS) or the Department of Labor would look askance at the idea.

Because federal law denies many of the VEBA tax advantages to non-union workers, independent employee trusts are more difficult to set up for the majority of the workforce that today lacks retiree coverage (Fronstin 2005). While nonunion employers can make contributions to a VEBA if they wish, there are strict limits on the amounts (Macey 2007), and employee contributions are after-tax whether the employer contributes or the entire burden is borne by employees. Because of the latter limitation, the relatively few nonunion employer-pay-all VEBAs tend to have few participants (Macey and O'Donnell 2003). Conceivably, nonunion employers also could use a GM-style wage or profit-sharing diversions to set up an employee-pay-all VEBA that would enjoy all the tax breaks of a union plan. The IRS requires fully deductible VEBA contributions to be mandatory, so that employees cannot choose between cash and the contribution. Typically, this is done through a union, which bargains rules that apply to all members (McGuinness 2007; Richardson and Salemi 2007).

One model in a nonunion setting could be for the employer to set up an automatic VEBA contribution with an opt-out provision, much like the rules that allow employers to set up automatic payroll deductions for 401 (k)s. Such an arrangement could be considered as mandatory as union membership, which is voluntary in most circumstances. However, this strategy has not been tested and the IRS might not consider it mandatory enough to satisfy the requirement of a VEBA.

The most straightforward way to help workers save for retiree health care would be a change in federal tax law. Currently, the only tools available are DB pensions and DC plans like 401(k)s. But the money that workers withdraw in retirement from such plans is taxed, even if spent on health care. There is nothing in federal tax law today like an employer medical plan or a Flexible Savings Account, which retirees can use to purchase health care on a pretax basis. One option would be for Congress to pass a law allowing money spent on health care to be withdrawn on a pretax basis from pensions or 401(k)s. Another would be to allow pretax contributions to employee-pay-all VEBAs, which would serve much the same purpose. Of course, new tax breaks could cost many billions, depending on how extensively they were used. Major new tax burdens would likely prove politically divisive, especially in light of all the worries about Social Security and Medicare under funding.

Conclusion

The larger problem with any VEBA-like remedy for falling retiree health coverage is that it would do little to address the central issue facing both retired and active workers, which is the ever-increasing cost and lack of affordable health-care coverage. Already, many Americans are uninsured or underinsured because they can not afford the premiums, co-pays, and deductibles. Giving them a new tax-free saving plan may be better than nothing, but it would likely not be enough to offset double-digit medical inflation. And since many workers already are struggling with stagnant wages, they might be unable to save enough to fund a significant portion of their retiree health needs. As a result, VEBAs may be little more than a Band-Aid able to help some workers get by until a more comprehensive solution arrives.

Congress and the White House were engaged in serious debates about just such a solution throughout the first year of the new Obama Administration. Prospects for national health-care reform remain uncertain, the passage of such legislation could mean that stand-alone VEBAs would turn out to be a real windfall for UAW members, depending on how the law is written. If a new system provided workers with access to affordable care,

UAW members and others with extra funds saved in a VEBA could be much better off. The stock and other funds contributed by the automakers cannot be removed after they are put in to VEBA trusts, which means that union participants could use them to supplement any new national health system. They also would come out ahead if reforms moderated medical inflation, which would improve the odds that VEBAs would not run out of money. While the UAW did not agree to VEBAs with this goal in mind, the union has been actively backing reform proposals, in which case employee VEBAs could turn out to be an unexpected cushion for its members.

Acknowledgments

The author thanks Larry Beeferman, Richard Freeman, and Elaine Bernard for their support and comments, and Kathryn Backich, Rick Johnson, Dan Sherrick, Roger Kerson, Teresa Ghilarducci, and Ron Bloom for their comments. He acknowledges research support from the Jacob Wertheim Fund.

Notes

[1] For example, Medicare projects national health-care expenditures over a 75-year time horizon. In recent years, they have exceeded the gross domestic product (GDP) of the Unites States by several percentage points a year. However, Medicare's standard assumption is that over the next 75 years, expenditures will gradually decline to a long-term growth rate of 1 percentage point over GDP, which put health-care spending increases in the range of 5 percent a year. 'The theory behind this model is that, should medical technology continue to increase rapidly, and expensively, in the future, then eventually society would be unwilling and unable to devote a steadily increasing share of its income to obtaining better health' (Board of Trustees 2008: 168).

[2] A by-product of this decision was that GM will be able to treat the difference between these two figures as a profit. In 2007, the company estimated that its annual earnings would increase by $2.6 billion to $3.6 billion starting in 2010 as a result of the two different rate-of-return assumptions (although the figure could decline somewhat in subsequent years).

[3] The $38 billion would come close to $47 billion under a 6 percent discount rate, according to the UAW (GM Corporation 2007a, 2007b).

[4] The dollar value of these contributions may change because they are based on hours worked, which will fall below projections as GM continues to downsize.

[5] In addition to VEBAs, public employers also can use Internal Revenue Code Section 401(h) accounts or Section 115 trusts to pre-fund post-employment benefits such as retiree health care. Most that already have pre-funded have

used 115 trusts, although that may change now that Goodyear and the auto-makers brought visibility to VEBAs, which allows them to set up trusts for essential purposes (Segal Public Sector Letter 2007*b*).

References

Arndt, Michael (2003). 'Salvation from the Shop Floor,' *BusinessWeek*, February 3.

Board of Trustees of the Federal Hospital Insurance and Federal Supplementary Medical Insurance Trust (Board of Trustees) (2008). *Annual Report.* Washington, DC: US Department of Health and Human Services. http://www.cms.hhs.gov/ReportsTrustFunds/downloads/tr2008.pdf

Bunkley, Nick (2009). 'U.A.W. Agrees to Concessions at Ford,' *New York Times*, February 24: B3.

Byrnes, Nanette (2003). 'Is Wilbur Ross Crazy,' *BusinessWeek*, December 22.

Employee Benefit Research Institute (2005). 'Retiree Health Benefits,' in *Fundamentals of Employee Benefit Programs.* Washington, DC: Employee Benefits Research Institute.

Fronstin, Paul (2005). 'The Impact of the Erosion of Retiree Health Benefits on Workers and Retirees,' *EBRI Issue Brief 279.* Washington, DC: Employee Benefits Research Institute.

General Motors (GM) Corporation (2007*a*). *GM 2007 GM-UAW Labor Agreement.* Detroit, MI: General Motors Corporation. http://media.corporate-ir.net/media_files/irol/84/84530/2007_GM_UAW_Labor_Agreement_Call.pdf

—— (2007*b*). *Form 8-K Filed with the Securities & Exchange Commission.* Detroit, MI: General Motors Corporation.

—— (2009*a*). *2009–2014 Restructuring Plan.* Detroit, MI: General Motors Corporation. http://www.financialstability.gov/docs/AIFP/GMRestructuringPlan.pdf

—— (2009*b*). *The New General Motors Company Launches Today.* Detroit, MI: General Motors Corporation. http://gm-volt.com/2009/07/10/gm-exits-bankruptcy-today-the-new-gm-starts-now/

Ghilarducci, Teresa (2008). *The New Treaty of Detroit: Are VEBAs Labor's Way Forward or the Remnants of a Glorious Past?* Cambridge, MA. http://www.law.harvard.edu/programs/lwp/PDF_pres/GHIL%20VEBA.pdf

Internal Revenue Service (IRS) (various years). *Internal Revenue Service Data Books.* Washington, DC: Internal Revenue Service.

Linebaugh, Kate (2009). 'Five Chrysler Directors Are Named,' *Wall Street Journal*, July 7: B2.

Macey, Scott J. (2007). Author interview, November 9.

——and George O'Donnell (2003). 'Chapter 8,' in *New York University Review of Employee Benefits and Executive Compensation – 2003.* Albany, NY: Matthew Bender & Co. Inc.

Maynard, Micheline and Mary Chapman (2007). 'G.M. Pact Calls for a Push for Health Care Reform,' *New York Times*, October 6.

McGuinness, Jeffrey C. (2007). 'Recent Prominent Agreements Renew Interest in VEBAs.' *Memorandum 07-119.* Washington, DC: HR Policy Association.

Michaeli, Itay, Will Randow, and Christopher Reenock (2007). 'Company Flash on General Motors Corp,' *Citigroup Global Markets Equity Research.* New York: Citigroup.

Miller, Girard (2007). *A Lesson from Detroit.* Washington, DC: Congressional Quarterly.

Mittal Steel USA (2006). *Summary Annual Report for Mittal Steel USA Inc. Retiree Drug Plan.* London: ArcelorMittal.

National Conference on Public Employee Retirement Systems (NCPERS) (2006). *Creating a Retiree Medical Trust: How Employers & Employees Can Use Pre-Tax Dollars to Fund Their Retiree Medical Costs.* Washington, DC: NCPERS. http://www.ncpers. org/Files/HealthCare/RMTreports_2Ed.pdf

O'Conner, Brian J. (2007). 'Most Call VEBA Good Deal for GM,' *The Detroit News,* September 27.

Richardson, Michael I. and Daniel Salemi (2007). 'Funding Postretirement Health Benefits Through a VEBA,' *Benefits & Compensation Digest,* 44(9): 26–31.

Schultz, Ellen E., and Theo Francis (2007). 'What Might GM Trust Fund Mean for Workers Elsewhere?,' *The Wall Street Journal,* September 27: A14.

Segal Bulletin (2004). *Accounting and Financial Reporting for Postemployment Benefits Other than Pensions: GASB's Final Standards.* New York: The Segal Company. http://www.segalco.com/publications/bulletins/aug04GASB.pdf

—— (2005). *GASB Issues Long-Awaited OPEB Implementation Guide.* New York: The Segal Company. http://www.segalco.com/publications/bulletins/oct05 OPEBguide.pdf

Segal Public Sector Letter (2007*a*). *Retiree Health Care: Implications of OPEB Liabilities.* New York: The Segal Company. http://www.segalco.com/publications/publicsec-torletters/aug2007.pdf

—— (2007*b*). *In Search of OPEB Remedies: Good Medicine Includes Managing Retiree Health Costs.* New York: The Segal Company. http://www.segalco.com/govern-ment/pub-govt.cfm?ID=776

Sixth Circuit Court of Appeals (2007). UAW et al. v. General Motors Corp. et al. Nos. 06-1475/2064. Washington, DC: Sixth Circuit Court of Appeals.

Sloan, Allen (2005). 'Multibillion Gamble Put GM Pension Funds on the Road to Independence,' *Washington Post,* July 5.

United Auto Workers (UAW) (2007). *UAW GM Report: A Message to UAW GM Retirees.* Detroit, MI: United Auto Workers. http://www.uaw.org/contracts/07/gm/gm07. php

—— (2008). *UAW, Union Retirees File Proposed Settlement Establishing VEBA Trust.* Detroit, MI: United Auto Workers. http://www.uaw.org/news/newsarticle.cfm? ArtId=463

United Steelworkers (USW) (2002). *Exhibit A-6, Retiree Benefit Trust, 2002 USW Labor Agreement with ISG Inc.* Pittsburgh, PA: United Steelworkers.

—— (2003). *Restructuring American Steel.* Pittsburgh, PA: United Steelworkers. http://www.usw.org/our_union/workplaces?id=0004

—— (2006). *New Benefit Is Latest Innovation in USW's Continuing Commitment to Retirees' Security.* Pittsburgh, PA: United Steelworkers. http://benefitslink.com/ pr/detail.php?id=39865

—— (2007*a*). *United Steelworker Retirees to Receive Additional Benefits in 2007*. Pittsburgh, PA: United Steelworkers. http://legacy.usw.org/usw/program/content/4039.php

—— (2007*b*). *Questions and Answers About the 2007 Medicare Part B Premium Reimbursement Benefit*. Pittsburgh, PA: United Steelworkers. http://www.usw.org/usw/program/adminlinks/docs//Mittal%20VEBA%20Q%;20and%20A%20Medicare%20Part%20B%20Benefit.pdf

Welch, David and Nanette Byrnes (2007). 'Is GM's Health Plan Contagious?,' *BusinessWeek*, October 10.

Wisniewski, Stan and Lorel Wisniewski (2004). 'State Government Retiree Health Benefits: Current Status and Potential Impact of New Accounting Standards.' Washington, DC: AARP Public Policy Institute. http://assets.aarp.org/rgcenter/health/2004_08_benefits.pdf

End Pages

The Pension Research Council

The Pension Research Council of the Wharton School at the University of Pennsylvania is committed to generating debate on key policy issues affecting pensions and other employee benefits. The Council sponsors interdisciplinary research on private and social retirement security and related benefit plans in the United States and around the world. It seeks to broaden understanding of these complex arrangements through basic research into their economic, social, legal, actuarial, and financial foundations. Members of the Advisory Board of the Council, appointed by the Dean of the Wharton School, are leaders in the employee benefits field, and they recognize the essential role of social security and other public sector income maintenance programs while sharing a desire to strengthen private sector approaches to economic security. For more information, see http://www.pensionresearchcouncil.org.

The Boettner Center for Pensions and Retirement Security

Founded at the Wharton School to support scholarly research, teaching, and outreach on global aging, retirement, and public and private pensions, the Center is named after Joseph E. Boettner. Funding to the University of Pennsylvania was provided through the generosity of the Boettner family whose intent was to spur financial well-being at older ages through work on how aging influences financial security and life satisfaction. The Center disseminates research and evaluation on challenges and opportunities associated with global aging and retirement, how to strengthen retirement income systems, saving and investment behavior of the young and the old, interactions between physical and mental health, and successful retirement. For more information, see http://www.pensionresearchcouncil.org/boettner/

Executive Director

Olivia S. Mitchell, *International Foundation of Employee Benefit Plans Professor*, Department of Insurance and Risk Management, The Wharton School, University of Pennsylvania.

MetLife
Mutual of America Life Insurance Company
Pacific Investment Management Company LLC
Prudential Financial
Pyramis Global Advisors
Social Security Administration
TIAA-CREF Institute
The Vanguard Group
Towers Watson

Institutional Members
AARP Public Policy Institute
Financial Engines, Inc.
International Foundation of Employee Benefit Plans
Loouis, Sayles and Company, LP
Mercer Human Resource Consulting
Ontario Pension Board
Society of Actuaries
Symetra Financial
Texas Municipal Retirement System

Recent Pension Research Council Publications

Fundamentals of Private Pensions. Dan M. McGill, Kyle N. Brown, John J. Haley, Sylvester Schieber, and Mark J. Warshawsky. 9th Edition 2010 (ISBN 0-19-954451-6).

The Future of Public Employees Retirement Systems. Olivia S. Mitchell and Gary Anderson, eds. 2009 (ISBN 0-19-957334-9).

Recalibrating Retirement Spending and Saving. John Ameriks and Olivia S. Mitchell, eds. 2008 (ISBN 0-19-954910-8).

Lessons from Pension Reform in the Americas. Stephen J. Kay and Tapen Sinha, eds. 2008 (ISBN 0-19-922680-6).

Redefining Retirement: How Will Boomers Fare? Brigitte Madrian, Olivia S. Mitchell, and Beth J. Soldo, eds. 2007 (ISBN 0-19-923077-3).

Restructuring Retirement Risks. David Blitzstein, Olivia S. Mitchell, and Steven P. Utkus, eds. 2006 (ISBN 0-19-920465-9).

Reinventing the Retirement Paradigm. Robert L. Clark and Olivia S. Mitchell, eds. 2005 (ISBN 0-19-928460-1).

Pension Design and Structure: New Lessons from Behavioral Finance. Olivia S. Mitchell and Steven P. Utkus, eds. 2004 (ISBN 0-19-927339-1).

The Pension Challenge: Risk Transfers and Retirement Income Security. Olivia S. Mitchell and Kent Smetters, eds. 2003 (ISBN 0-19-926691-3).

A History of Public Sector Pensions in the United States. Robert L. Clark, Lee A. Craig, and Jack W. Wilson, eds. 2003 (ISBN 0-8122-3714-5).

Benefits for the Workplace of the Future. Olivia S. Mitchell, David Blitzstein, Michael Gordon, and Judith Mazo, eds. 2003 (ISBN 0-8122-3708-0).

Innovations in Retirement Financing. Olivia S. Mitchell, Zvi Bodie, P. Brett Hammond, and Stephen Zeldes, eds. 2002 (ISBN 0-8122-3641-6).

To Retire or Not: Retirement Policy and Practice in Higher Education. Robert L. Clark and P. Brett Hammond, eds. 2001 (ISBN 0-8122-3572-X).

Pensions in the Public Sector. Olivia S. Mitchell and Edwin Hustead, eds. 2001 (ISBN 0-8122-3578-9).

The Role of Annuity Markets in Financing Retirement. Jeffrey Brown, Olivia S. Mitchell, James Poterba, and Mark Warshawsky. 2001 (ISBN 0-262-02509-4).

Forecasting Retirement Needs and Retirement Wealth. Olivia S. Mitchell, P. Brett Hammond, and Anna Rappaport, eds. 2000 (ISBN 0-8122-3529-0).

Prospects for Social Security Reform. Olivia S. Mitchell, Robert J. Myers, and Howard Young, eds. 1999 (ISBN 0-8122-3479-0).

Living with Defined Contribution Pensions: Remaking Responsibility for Retirement. Olivia S. Mitchell and Sylvester J. Schieber, eds. 1998 (ISBN 0-8122-3439-1).

Positioning Pensions for the Twenty-First Century. Michael S. Gordon, Olivia S. Mitchell, and Marc M. Twinney, eds. 1997 (ISBN 0-8122-3391-3).

Securing Employer-Based Pensions: An International Perspective. Zvi Bodie, Olivia S. Mitchell, and John A. Turner, eds. 1996 (ISBN 0-8122-3334-4).

Available from the Pension Research Council web site: http://www.pension-researchcouncil.org/

Index

Appendices, figures, notes and tables are indexed in bold.